standard catalog of®

FERRARI
1947-2003

Mike Covello

©2003, Krause Publications

Published by

krause publications
An F&W Publications Company

700 East State Street • Iola, WI 54990-0001
715-445-2214 • 888-457-2873
www.krause.com

Our toll-free number to place an order or obtain a free catalog is 800-258-0929.

Library of Congress Catalog Number: 2003101360

ISBN: 0-87349-497-0

Printed in the United States

Editor: Karen O'Brien
Designer: Jamie Griffin

Front cover:
1961 Ferrari 250 GT SWB. (John Lamm)
1992 Ferrari 512TR. (John Lamm)
Ferrari 550 Maranello. (John Lamm)

Title page:
1985 Ferrari 288 GTO. (DA)

Back Cover:
1969 Ferrari Type 365 GTS/4 Daytona Spyder. (DA)

Dedication

I would like to dedicate this book to three men who helped indoctrinate me into the mysterious ways of Ferrari.

First, I would like to thank Dick Fritz of Amerispec fame. He was the service manager at Luigi Chinetti Motors who was willing to hire a 20 year-old for parts department duty, then to promote him to manager. This gave me the opportunity to learn many lessons in running a business and the joys of Ferrari maintenance. Thanks, Dick.

Secondly, I want to dedicate this book to the memory of Luigi Chinetti Senior. His amazing feats as a racecar driver, team owner and most importantly, Importer to America of all things Ferrari ignited the conflagration that is Ferrari fever here in the United States. It's possible that if Luigi didn't bring Ferrari to the United States, some other businessman may have eventually tried. But no one else could have brought such an amazing legacy and inordinate passion to the task.

Finally, I would like to dedicate this book to Luigi Chinetti Jr. Lou is approaching 60 as this book comes to print. He has had many careers as auto designer, Ferrari salesman, and endurance racer and now he is the guardian of his father's legacy. It is my fondest hope to someday read The Chinetti Story, as told by Luigi Chinetti Jr. I would want to be the one to write it, but if not by me, I hope someone chronicles this legend before it's lost to posterity.

Acknowledgments

One person cannot accomplish a work of this size on their own. In this case, I must give proper credit to James Flamming, the author of the first edition of the *Standard Catalog of Imported Cars 1946-1990*. James supplied much of the data for the 1947-90 Ferrari models. Gerald Rousch of the Ferrari Market Letter (770-381-1993, www.ferrarimarketletter.com) was kind enough to provide a list containing original prices, and the most comprehensive list of Ferrari production cars available.

Werner Pfister of Miller Motor Cars, and Wayne Carini of F40 Motorsports provided valuable details on the minutia of Ferraris. My editors, Karen O'Brien and Don Gulbrandsen of Krause Publications were both great to work with. Clay Miller designed the cover and Jamie Griffin designed the book's interior. Dick Fritz has made a name for himself converting cars to U.S. specifications with his Ameritech Company, but I'd like to thank him for taking a chance on me when he hired me for the job in Luigi Chinetti Motors parts department.

I cannot forget my faithful friends and editors, Bob Larson and Richard Moriarty who assisted me on this and so many other projects. Jeff Ehoodin of Ferrari North America provided information on current models.

But most of all thanks to my family, Mary, Bill, and Elyse for being so wonderful as I jetted around the country to snap photos, and spent hours away from family fun while I wore out another keyboard on my computer.

Mike Covello
May, 2003

Photo Credts

The photos used in this book are from the following sources:

DA = Dennis Adler
DG = David Gooley
EAS = Everett Anton Singer
FSpA = Ferrari S.p.A. Maranello (Modena), Italy
FSpA/WG = Ferrari sales literature image from the Winston Goodfellow archives
MC = Mike Covello
WG = Winston Goodfellow

Contents

On July 19, 1999, Ferrari launched the 400-hp 360 Modena at the Meadowlands horsetrack in New Jersey accompanied by 400 thoroughbred race horses. (MC)

For the small number of cars produced each year, Ferraris have an unbelievable effect on our culture. In a world where millions of cars are manufactured every year, a handful of exotic masterpieces issuing from Maranello continue to delight, excite, and inspire enthusiasts throughout the world. No other manufacturer has set their sights as high as Ferrari. You'll never see an economy Ferrari, any more than you'll ever get stuck behind a Ferrari SUV in traffic. Enzo Ferrari had an enormous passion for the automobile, and he had the drive and determination to turn his dreams into an object that has become synonymous with excellence throughout the world.

When people mention an illustration of a successful Italian, Enzo Ferrari is often the first name that comes to mind. His example of turning his youthful dream into a business reality is inspirational for people of all nationalities. Ferrari was born in Modena, Italy on February 18, 1898. Enzo's father owned a metal shop, and was successful enough that he was able to purchase one of the first automobiles in town. When Enzo was ten years old, they attended a race in nearby Bologna, and it's safe to say that young Enzo's life was forever changed. He learned cars were not just for transportation, they could be used for competition, and to thrill and entertain. He discovered that he had a talent for driving racing cars when he started as test driver and deliveryman for CMN in Milan. In his first race, he placed fourth in the three-liter class at the Parma-Berceto hill climb. More impressively, he showed his potential when he claimed second in the legendary Targa Florio in 1920 during his first drive for Alfa Romeo.

It was his win at Ravenna that had a lifelong influence on Ferrari and all of his faithful followers. The parents of Francesco Barrack, a WWI ace pilot, bestowed on Ferrari their family crest. The Prancing Horse emblem has adorned almost every vehicle bearing the proud name of Ferrari.

Ferrari found himself drawn to the organizational aspects of running Alfa Romeo's racing team. One of his most fortuitous hires was Luigi Bazzi. Not only did Bazzi become Ferrari's closest collaborator, but also he suggested taking on Vittorio

1949 Ferrari Stabilimenti Farina Type 166 convertible. (DA)

Jano. Jano's success at designing racing cars for Fiat was so overwhelming, that he soon found himself with little to do. Jano's superiors considered the racing Fiats from 1922 to be perfection, so they forbade further development. Jano's arrival at Alfa produced the P2 that won its first race, and that was only the beginning. The next important name to enter our story was Gioacchino Colombo, who studied under Jano. The engineering knowledge he gained would later prove to be a godsend for Ferrari's fledgling company.

But first, Enzo established Scuderia Ferrari. Since Alfa wanted to remove themselves from direct competition, yet still maintain a presence in racing, their backing gave Ferrari the opportunity to independently run a racing team. It wasn't

Palm trees and Ferraris go hand-in-hand at the Cavalino Classic in Palm Beach, Fla. (MC)

1951 Ferrari Vignale Type 212 Berlinetta. (DA)

long before circumstances changed, and Enzo was hired back to run the now in-house Alfa team. He left in 1939 over a personality conflict with another employee, Pegaso designer, Wilfredo Ricart.

Although Enzo's contract forbade him racing any cars under his own name until 1943, he was unable to resist the offer to build two cars for the 1940 Mille Miglia. He formed the Auto Avio Costruzioni in Modena and set about building the Vettura 815. This simple, but rugged 2,010-lb., 1904-cc V-12 racer is considered to be the first "Ferrari."

World War II intervened, and racing cars were swept aside as all of Europe geared up for the military endeavor. After peace returned, Enrico Nardi assisted Ferrari in realizing his dream of building sports/racing cars of his own design. Setting up shop on family land just ten miles south of Modena, Enzo assembled a group of remarkable

talent. Ferrari had always been impressed with "the song of a twelve," so he directed Gioacchino Colombo to design a 1500-cc V-12 engine. While the first Ferrari V-12 engine made only 118 hp, it was the spiritual basis for every ensuing powerplant to issue from the shops at Maranello. In 1946 the Tipo (Type) 125C, the first road/racing model was announced. Like all early Ferraris, they were essentially handcrafted. A total of three cars were built in 1947, Ferrari's first year of "production," followed by nine in 1948, and rising to thirty in 1949. The original engine was bored out to 1902-cc displacement to create a Type 159; then it was soon enlarged again to become the 1995-cc Type 166 Sport. The initial cars were labeled Spyder Corsas, and the cycle fenders barely masked their racing origins; they bore serial numbers 002C and 004C. Gabriele Besana and his brother, Count Sovane Besana, are listed as the first customers for Ferrari's fledgling firm. On the

1956 Ferrari Type 410 Superfast. (DA)

1956 Ferrari Type 410 Superamerica. (DA)

race circuit, Ferrari would eventually take eight Mille Miglia victories, starting in 1948, commemorated by an "MM" designation on later models of the original chassis.

Ferrari's practice of supply the engine and chassis while coachbuilders crafted the bodywork began in 1948. He produced a single carburetor version of the Type 166 suitable for street use and called it the Inter. Stabilimenti Farina supplied both coupe and cabriolet bodies. Bertone, Zagato, and Touring were also early suppliers. By 1950, Ghia and Vignale added their designs to the bewildering array of early Ferrari efforts. With so many contributors to the early Ferrari mix is it any wonder many folks find their pedigrees confusing?

Luigi Chinetti achieved Ferrari's first Le Mans victory in 1949 in a most spectacular fashion. The winner of both the 1932 and 1934 Le Mans, he was forced to drive over 23 hours of the 1949 endurance classic when his co-driver fell ill. Despite this rather significant handicap, Chinetti still managed to bring the 166 home ahead of all the competition. This is just one of the early Ferrari early victories that ignited enthusiasts' passions throughout the world.

Progress continued in 1950 with the Type 166 engine receiving a larger 65 mm

bore resulting in a 2341-cc engine installed in the Type 195. Horsepower rose to 130 for the road-going Inter and 180 for the Sport edition. Next up came the Type 212, which had a bore of 68 mm, increasing the size of the engine to 2562 cc. At this time, the terms Sport and Export seemed to be used almost interchangeably. The road going 212 Inter also was known as the 212 Europa. Still another 2 mm bore increase begat the Type 225 Sport (Export) that had a 2712-cc engine that made 210 hp at 7200 rpm.

While Gioacchino Colombo's contribution to Ferrari's early success is inarguable, his student could be said to have had an even longer lasting effect on the Ferrari legacy. Aurelio Lambredi was taken under Colombo's wing in 1947 as his assistant. He soon questioned his instructor's insistence that a 1.5-liter supercharged engine was the path to success in the Grand Prix arena. His assertion that a 4.5-liter naturally-aspirated engine could provide both better fuel economy and more power caused Ferrari to give the gifted young engineer's ideas a try. When these engines proved to be successful, Lampredi was promoted to chief design engineer, and Colombo returned to Alfa Romeo.

The first Lampredi-derived V-12 in a Ferrari was announced late in 1950. The

1958 Ferrari Series 1 Pininfarina 250 GT. (DA)

Type 340 America displaced 4101 cc and produced 220 hp. The car was quite successful, winning the 1951 Mille Miglia in its first attempt. This car had the top speed necessary to compete and win; it was capable of some 137 mph in basic form. Modifications were made to strengthen the engine and chassis of the 340, and it became known as the 340 Mexico and 340 MM when they were raced in the U.S. The 340 Mexicos were said to have produced 280 hp. Following his race-bred tradition of continually improving the breed, Ferrari displayed the 342 America chassis at the

1960-1963 Ferrari GT Spyder California. (EAS)

Brussels Auto Show in January of 1951, followed by a fully functional model at the Turin Show in the spring of 1951.

As the factory's experience grew, so did the displacement of the Ferrari engine. The Type 375 was available as both a 4523-cc V-12, and the 4954-cc version that produced about 344 hp and could hit 60 mph in seven seconds, to say nothing of top speeds beyond 160 mph. Things were going very well for Ferrari's dream of becoming a major force in international racing. By this time, Ferraris had won the 24-Hour Le Mans, Spa, and Turin races, as well as Grand Prix events in

Luxembourg, Switzerland, Belgium, Sweden, Holland, and Britain. Luigi Chinetti, who would become Ferrari's distributor in the U.S., held the one-hour, 200-kilometer and 100-mile records at the Montlhery track.

The 1953 Paris Salon marked the debut of what many consider to be the first "production" Ferrari, the 250 Europa. It used a Lampredi V-12 that displaced 2963 cc and produced either 200 or 220 hp with three Weber 36 DCF carburetors. At a time when 100 mph seemed daringly fast to the average motorist, Ferrari bragged of a 133-mph top speed for the Europa. Ferrari's

1964 Ferrari Type 500 Superfast. (DA)

genius was not only in engineering, but also in marketing. He realized that there were drivers who wanted something even more exclusive, so the 375 America was unveiled. He also was shrewd enough to understand economies of scale; both cars used the same chassis and four-speed syncromesh gearboxes. With its 4522-cc engine producing 300 hp, the America could reportedly push the lucky owner and his car to 153 mph.

A 250 GT Europa soon followed, on a 102-in. wheelbase; and a 94.5-in. version would emerge at the end of the decade. A 410 Superamerica appeared in 1956, with a 4962-cc V-12 beneath its hood. Luigi Chinetti made sure that Enzo was well aware of the importance of the American market. Ferrari introduced a "California" convertible for 1959, based on the 250 chassis. Ferraris were all two-seaters until 1960 when Ferrari acknowledged the need for rear seats (albeit tiny ones) with the 250 GT 2+2. Ferrari made available a 2+2, or four-seater, a part of the model line for most of the next few decades. A 330 GT 2+2 was followed by a 365 GT 2+2 in 1967. In 1960, the company changed its name to Societa per Azioni Esercizo Fabriche Automobili e Corse Ferrari.

Seeing how successful Enzo was in using racing to promote his business, Ford made a bid to take over the Ferrari operation early in the 1960s. It's said that negotiations were very close to being finished when Ferrari pulled out of the deal. The result was some of the most epic battles for the sportscar championship throughout the Sixties ever to take place.

Ferrari continued to offer a higher-performance, more-luxurious model, the 400 Superamerica, through the early 1960s. This inspired the even quicker 500 Superfast at mid-decade. Fulfilling every schoolboy's fantasy, Ferrari had a mid-engine model intended mainly for competition, but also suitable for street driving. The 250 LM was competent enough to capture first place at the 1965 Le Mans classic. At the same time, roadgoing Ferraris were represented by the new 275 GTB coupe and GTS Spyder. Racing technology found its way to the street with a five-speed gearbox cast as a unit with the rear differential (forming a transaxle) and the introduction of all-independent suspension. Also in the mid-1960s, the 275 GTB chassis

1964-1966 Ferrari 275 GTB. (EAS)

1965 Ferrari Type 275 GTB/C. (DA)

and 330 GT 2+2 engine were combined to produce the 330 GTC coupe, while the four-seat 330 series itself evolved into a 365 GT 2+2.

Enzo Ferrari's only legitimate son, Dino, tragically died at the tender age of 24 in 1956. To honor the memory of his offspring,

a succession of models were named for him. The Dino 206 GT was introduced in 1967, followed by the more powerful Dino 246 GT two years later. Early Dinos differed from other Ferraris in two significant ways: Instead of the usual V-12s, mid-mounted V-6 engines powered them, and they lacked any Ferrari identification. Some Ferrari fans

1968 Ferrari Type 275 GTB/4 Berlinetta. (DA)

Ferrari 365 GTS/4 & GTB/4 circa 1971. (MC)

consider the 365 GTB/4, which soon became known as the "Daytona," to be the ultimate road-going Ferrari. The combination of a front-engined four-cam V-12 with classic Pininfarina lines epitomized both Ferrari's grandeur and the exuberance of the all-out muscle car era. *Road & Track* featured the open 365 GTS/4 Spider convertible on the cover to celebrate its birth.

The Dino badge graced the nose of one more Ferrari model in 1973, the 308 GT4. Besides having a Bertone (instead of a Pinnafarinna design) body, it also differed from previous models by boasting a mid-mounted V-8 engine (a first for road

Ferraris) instead of the former V-6. In this time of innovation, Ferrari also showcased a different type of engine in their top-of-the-line model. A horizontally opposed (flat) 12-cylinder powered the 365 GT4 BB "Boxer." These were known as "boxer" engines, because the back-and-forth motion of the pistons was akin to two boxers punching back and forth at one another. Meanwhile, over in Europe, the 365 GT4 2+2 evolved into the four-seat 400i, and by the mid-1980s, the 412i with a still larger V-12 engine. American Ferrari dealers and fans were thrilled when a new 308 GTB arrived in 1975, followed by a Targa-topped 308 GTS two years later. Early 308 models wore

Ferrari 365 GTB4 Daytona. (MC)

1985 Ferrari 288 GTO. (DA)

fiberglass bodies rather than the usual steel, but that experiment was abandoned after 1977. Those models lasted into the late 1980s, turning to four-cam (*Quattrovalvole*) engine configuration and then to a larger 328 version. The 1980s also brought Ferrari's Mondial (world) series, with four-cam V-8 power, on a longer wheelbase than the 308.

Although they were produced long enough to be quite plentiful, the dramatically styled Testarossa (which repeated a name used on Ferrari race cars in the 1950s) didn't debut until 1985, a year after the race-oriented 288 GTO coupe with its four-cam V-8. As if Ferrari's offerings through the years weren't "super" enough, the company announced its startling F40 coupe in 1987. Rival to the Porsche 959

supercar, the F40 was to be produced in limited number, with a top speed that edged past 200 mph and 0-60 mph acceleration well under four seconds. After considerable difficulty, Ferrari managed to certify the F40 for U.S. sale, but only a few hundred wealthy folk would ever be able to sit behind the wheel, after paying a price that soon soared to the half-million-dollar mark and beyond. On a more modest (for Ferrari) level, the 328 evolved into a 348 and the Mondial to a 't' version before the decade ended. Those and the Testarossa remained in production into the 1990s.

The 1990s were a very exciting decade for Ferrari. Production started on the 348 series, which lead to the 355 Coupe, Targa, and Spider. At the turn of the century they launched one of the most sensuous models

Even standing still, Ferrari's F40 looks as if it's racing. (MC)

The 1995 Ferrari F512M is always popular at shows. (MC)

ever, the 360 Modena. All of these V-8 models continue to delight their owners as horsepower rose from 300 to 400, with commensurate increase in braking and cornering prowess. The 1992 456GT signaled the return of the classic 2+2 to the Ferrari lineup. Those folks looking for a modern replacement for their 365 GTB/4 Daytonas must have been thrilled with the 1997 introduction of the classic front-engine V-12 550 Maranello.

For those who missed out on owning a brand new F40, Ferrari made the F50 available. With its body and chassis made from racecar materials and its 513-hp V-12 engine, the F50 was a racing car barely tamed for street duty. As of this writing, the factory has just taken the wraps off the F50's successor, the Enzo Ferrari. All indications point to a new star in the supercar annals.

Ferrari Model Numbering Note: Ferraris were normally called *Tipo* (Type), followed by a numerical designation: sometimes logical, sometimes not. Until recent years, model numbers indicated displacement in cubic centimeters (rounded-off) of each cylinder. Thus, the displacement of each cylinder in the Type 166 was equal to 166.25 cc. After the mid-1950s, the figures generally stood for total number of liters, but

1995 Ferrari 456 GT 2+2. (DA)

1996 Ferrari F355 Spyder. (DA)

there were many exceptions to the rule. Letters in the model number had varied meanings: A 'C' (*Corsa*, or race) suffix went on the first racing cars, but 'C' later stood for *Competizione* on one-seat racers. An 'I' (Inter) designation went on sports/race models. At first, odd numbers in the three-digit designation were used for "road" models, even numbers for competition versions; but that separation soon became ambiguous as dual-purpose models emerged. A 'GT' designation stands for Gran Turismo (Grand Touring). 'GTO' identifies a GT *omologato* (homologated, or sanctioned for racing). The 'GTB' suffix designates a *berlinetta* (coupe), while 'GTS' identifies an open model: either a Targa roof or full convertible (Spider, or Spyder). A '4' suffix indicates a Ferrari with

four-cam engine, while 'i' identifies a fuel-injected engine. The "Superamerica" models were sometimes identifed as "Super America" or "SuperAmerica."

Model Availability and Specification Note: Especially in the early years, Ferraris were basically custom-built, by no means mass-produced. Specifications varied, too, among examples under the same general designation. Therefore, dimensions of a specific car may vary from those shown below, which are typical rather than absolute. Engines also varied considerably, not only in horsepower and torque ratings but also in displacement. Listed in these pages are the best-known sizes and ratings, but a large number of variants also were produced, especially for racing purposes.

1997 Ferrari F50. (DA)

1948 Ferrari 166 Spider Corsa s/n 00101. (WG)

TYPE 166 SPORTS — V-12 — It would be hard to imagine the vast Ferrari empire that would be created if you were to glimpse the humble beginnings of the Ferrari cars. The Type 166 Sport was an evolution of the original Type 125. With its 1500-cc V-12 engine, this was the racing model that started the whole Ferrari myth and mystique. No more than two of the compact notchback coupes were built, powered by a 1995-cc enlargement of the V-12. In its racing debut (as an open model) in April 1948, the car won the Targa Florio road race in Sicily, driven by Clemente Biondetti. A month later, Biondetti won the Mille Miglia in the same car, which then wore an Allemano coupe body.

TYPE 166 INTER — V-12 — Using the 166 Sport model as a basis for their first road car established the company's design theme for the next decade. The 166 Inter couldn't deliver all the performance that its appearance promised. While it was powered by the 1995-cc "Colombo" V-12, horsepower was only rated at 110. Using alternate compression ratios and carburetion, the 60-degree V-12 could be coaxed to make as much as 150 hp. This basic engine design would continue into the

1960s. Each bank used a chain-driven camshaft, actuating inclined valves via rocker arms and finger followers. Each valve was closed with twin hairpin springs. The Inter (and Sport) engine had one twin-choke Weber carburetor, while the more potent 'MM' (Mille Miglia) made use of triple twin-choke Webers. Both block and heads were made of aluminum alloy, with cast-iron cylinder liners and a seven-bearing (six-throw) crankshaft. The 166 MM engine (which won the 1949 Le Mans race) used needle rod bearings. Some examples had compression ratios high enough to require the use of alcohol fuel.

A tubular steel ladder-type chassis built from oval-section main tubes and round-section cross tubes was stretched and compressed into various wheelbases, ranging from 86.6 inches (in the MM barchetta coupe) to 103.1 inches. Up front, the independent suspension used a transverse leaf spring. A "live" (rigid) axle with semi-elliptic leaf springs brought up the rear. Lever-action Houdaille hydraulic shock absorbers were installed (except on the first few examples). Hydraulic brakes had aluminum drums with cast-iron liners. All models were right-hand drive, with worm and peg steering. An unsynchronized five-speed gearbox worked through a single dry-plate clutch. Later 166 MM models had transmissions synchronized in third and fourth gears. Like most Ferraris that would come in subsequent years, Type 166 Inters wore trademark center-lock (knock-off) Borrani wire wheels.

While Ferrari manufactured most every engine component themselves, Vignale, Allemano, Bertone, Ghia, Pinin Farina, Stabilimenti Farina, and other coachbuilders supplied an almost bewildering variety of body styles. This would be generally true of Ferraris through the 1950s. Perhaps the most influential design was the roadster by Carrozzeria Touring. It had a body side crease line that flowed gracefully from the top of the front fender across the top of the rear fender, and then gently curved down at the back. While the Ferrari literature never called it a barchetta (little boat), this name became widely used. After a time, its basic design found its way onto several cars, including the AC Ace and Cobra.

Another body style, the berlinetta coupe by Touring, displayed rear quarter windows, the same type of body side crease, and a crosshatch (eggcrate) grille of rounded rectangular shape. It had small round parking lights alongside the grille, faired-in headlamps set back slightly from the grille, a scoop at the front of the hood, and no bumpers. The final 166 model made no efforts to hide its

1950 Ferrari 166 MM Touring 0034M at a recent Mille Miglia. (DG)

1949 Ferrari 166 Berlinetta Le Mans s/n 02C/020I. (WG)

1949 Ferrari 166 Berlinetta Le Mans s/n 02C/020I. (WG)

racing origins. The Spyder Corsa, a two-seat open racer with cycle fenders, separate headlamps, and a body-colored grille.

TYPE 195 — V-12 — While the 195 (introduced in 1950) was similar to the 166 Inter in style, chassis, and dimensions; the 195's engine displaced 2341 cc, a result of enlarging the bore by 5 millimeters. A single Weber carburetor endowed the Inter (road) version with 130 hp, while triple Webers pushed the competition Sport engine to160 bhp or more. Top speed of the 195 Inter was about 110 mph. A variety of coachbuilt body styles were offered again, as two-seat touring or sports-racer berlinettas (coupes) and convertibles. Pinin Farina or Vignale did the majority. Only some two-dozen were produced during the brief model run.

TYPE 212 —V-12 — The 212 Inter (road) and Export (racing) used an even larger engine, though they were otherwise similar to the 166/195 series. By boring out this version of the V-12 to 68 mm, a displacement of 2562 cc was achieved. Horsepower ratings were no more potent than the smaller 195 engine, but top speed reached as high as 120 mph (140 mph in the Export version). One Weber carburetor produced 130 horsepower or more, while a trio of Webers was good for 150 bhp or better. Remaining in production longer than the 195 (as late as 1953), at least two-dozen Export models were produced, compared to about 80 of the 212 Inters. While the 212 earned more attention than the smaller-engine 195 from American fans, the 340 America (which debuted in 1951) would generate an even bigger buzz.

Model Note: 166/195/212 models came with a wide variety of custom bodies, so specifications varied.

I.D. DATA: Not available.

Model	Body Type & Seating	Engine Type/CID	P.O.E. Price	Weight (lbs.)	Prod. Total
TYPE 166 SPORTS (1947-48)					
166	2-dr Coupe	V12/122	N/A	N/A	2
TYPE 166 (1948-51)					
166 Inter	2-dr Coupe-2P	V12/122	N/A	2140	Note 1
166 Inter	2-dr Conv Cpe-2P	V12/122	N/A	2140	Note 1
166 MM	2-dr Coupe-2P	V12/122	N/A	1740	Note 1
166 MM	2-dr Conv Cpe-2P	V12/122	N/A	1740	Note 1
TYPE 195 (1950-51)					
195 Inter	2-dr Coupe-2P	V12/143	N/A	2100	Note 2
195 Inter	2-dr Conv Cpe-2P	V12/143	N/A	2100	Note 2
195 Sport	2-dr Coupe-2P	V12/143	N/A	1930	Note 2
TYPE 212 (1950-53)					
212 Inter	2-dr Coupe-2P	V12/156	Note 3	2200	Note 4
212 Inter	2-dr Conv Cpe-2P	V12/156	Note 3	2200	Note 4
212 Export	2-dr Coupe-2P	V12/156	Note 3	2140	Note 4

Note 1: A total of 37 Type 166 Inter models were produced from 1949-50; and about 32 Type 166 MM (including 12 coupes).
Note 2: Approximately 26 Type 195 models were produced, in 1950-51.
Note 3: A Type 212 Ferrari sold for approximately $9,500 in the early 1950s.
Note 4: Approximately 80 Type 212 Inters were produced through 1953, plus as many as 26 Type 212 Export models.
Weight Note: Figures shown are the manufacturer's stated weights.
Price Note: Figures shown are approximate (or averages).

ENGINE [Base V-12 (Type 166)]: 60-degree, single-overhead-cam, "vee" type 12-cylinder. Aluminum alloy block and heads (cast-iron cylinder liners). Displacement: 122 cid (1995 cc). Bore & stroke: 2.36 x 2.31 in. (60 x 58.8 mm). Compression ratio: 7.5:1/8.0:1. Brake horsepower: 110 at 6000 rpm (up to 150 bhp depending on compression and carburetion). Seven main bearings. One or three twin-choke Weber 32 DCF carburetors.

Sport/MM Engine Note: The 166 Sport engine, with a single carburetor, produced 90 hp at 5600 rpm. The triple-carbureted 166 MM engine was rated 140/160 bhp at 6600/7200 rpm.

ENGINE [Base V-12 (Type 195)]: 60-degree, single-overhead-cam, "vee" type 12-cylinder. Aluminum alloy block and heads (cast-iron cylinder liners). Displacement: 142.8 cid (2341 cc). Bore & stroke: 2.56 x 2.31 in. (65 x 58.8 mm). Compression ratio: 7.5:1. Brake horsepower: (Inter) 130 at 6000 rpm; (Sport) 160-180 at 6000 rpm. Seven main bearings. One twin-choke Weber carburetor (Inter) or three twin-choke Webers (Sport).

ENGINE [Base V-12 (Type 212)]: 60-degree, single-overhead-cam, "vee" type 12-cylinder. Aluminum alloy block and head (cast-iron cylinder liners). Displacement: 156.3 cid (2562 cc). Bore & stroke: 2.68 x 2.31 in. (68 x 58.8 mm). Compression ratio: 8.0:1. Brake horsepower: (Inter) 130-140 at 6000 rpm; (Export) 150-170 at 6500 rpm. Seven main bearings. One twin-choke Weber carburetor (Inter) or three twin-choke 36 DCF Webers (Export).

CHASSIS: Wheelbase: (166 Inter) 98.4 in. or 103.1 in.; (166 MM Barchetta, 195 Sport) 86.6 in.; (166 MM cpe, 212 Export) 88.6 in.; (166 Sport) 95.3 in.; (195/212 Inter) 98.5 in. Overall Length: (166 Inter) 146-156 in. typical. Height: (166 Inter) 50 in. typical. Width: (166 Inter) 60 in. typical. Front Tread: 49.8 in. Rear Tread: 49.2 in. Wheel Type: Borrani center-lock wire. Standard Tires: (166 Inter) 5.90x15 or 5.50x15.

TECHNICAL: Layout: front-engine, rear-drive. Transmission: five-speed manual (non-synchro on early 166 models). Steering: worm and peg (right-hand drive). Suspension (front): unequal-length A-arms with transverse leaf springs. Suspension (rear): rigid axle with parallel trailing arms and semi-elliptic leaf springs. Brakes: hydraulic, front/rear drum. Body Construction: separate body on tubular steel ladder-type frame.

PERFORMANCE: Top Speed: (166 Inter) 112-120 mph; (195) about 110 mph; (212 Inter) about 120 mph; (212 Export) 140 mph.

PRODUCTION/SALES: Only about three Ferraris were sold in the U.S. during 1950.

Manufacturer: Societa Auto-Avio Costruzioni Ferrari, Maranello (Modena), Italy.

HISTORY: Briggs Cunningham is said to have imported the first Ferrari into the U.S., a 1949 Spider. Ferrari's 340 America debuted at the Paris Salon in October 1950; see next listing for details.

1949 Ferrari Stabilimenti Farina Type166 convertible, the first Ferrari road car. (DA)

1950 Ferrari 166MM Barchetta s/n 0050. (WG)

1951-2 Ferrari 212 barchetta. (DG)

1951-53

TYPE 195/212 — V-12 — Production of the 195/212 Inter models continued into 1951 and 1953, respectively; see previous listing for details. At the Paris Salon in 1952, Ferrari displayed Ghia and Pinin Farina bodies. These were notable for being the first left-hand-drive models. Later Vignale and Farina bodies had a more-modern, curved one-piece windshield, while bodies from Touring Carrozzeria kept their quaint two-piece "vee" windshield.

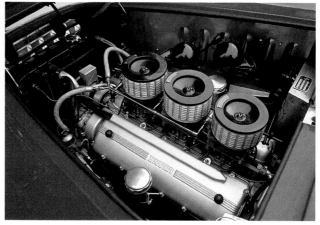

1951 Ferrari 212 Vignale engine. (DG)

TYPE 340 AMERICA — V-12 — The 340 America started a branch of Ferrari evolution that could arguably lead to the F40 and F50. The Lampredi-designed 4101-cc, long-block V-12 engine was originally designed as a racing unit to beat the Alfa Romeo Formula One cars. The engine had first seen competition in 1950, initially displacing 3.3 liters, but later it was enlarged to 4.1 and 4.5 liters. Like the Colombo V-12, it had two inclined valves per cylinders and hairpin-type springs, but its bore centers were spaced farther apart to permit larger displacement. Also, roller cam followers were used instead of the plain finger-type, and intake valve ports were separate rather than "siamesed." Because the block was 42.1 inches long (five more than the Colombo engine), these were known as "long-block" twelves. Output was 220 horsepower in its initial form, using three twin-choke Weber carburetors and a 8.0:1 compression ratio. The all-out racing version was called the 340 Mexico, with a coupe body styled by Michelotti. Its wheelbase was a longer 102.4 inches, and its engine produced 280 bhp. A single-disc clutch sent power to the five-speed gearbox. Custom bodies, especially the berlinetta coupe by Vignale, featured an extremely long hood and short deck, and rode a 95.3-inch wheelbase. In addition to closed coupes, some seven examples wore barchetta bodies by Touring, and several of those went to U.S. buyers. Though small in numbers produced (only 22 in all, from 1951-55) and oriented toward racing, the 340 America led off a succession of evolutionary Ferraris.

TYPE 342 AMERICA — V-12 — Ferrari

debuted the chassis for a grand touring variation of the 340 America at the Brussels show in January 1951. Only six 342 Americas would eventually be built between late 1952 and early 1953. They had the same engine as the 340, but the horsepower was reduced and drove through a more user-friendly, fully-synchronized four-speed transmission instead of the racing-style non-synchro five-speed. Its track dimensions were larger, and the rear-axle heavier in construction. A complete 342 America arrived at the Turin show in spring 1951, sporting left-hand drive. In its minimal production, the

342 replaced the roadgoing 340 after 1952, but both were built concurrently for competition.

TYPE 375 AMERICA — V-12 — Nearly twice

as many 375 Americas left the Ferrari plant as 342 Americas, but the total was still only eleven, starting in 1953. The wheelbase was longer than that of the 340/342, at 110.2 inches (same as the new 250 Europa, introduced for 1954), and the engine was larger. The 4523-cc V-12 produced 300 horsepower in touring trim, and 340 bhp when modified for competition purposes. The 250 was primarily aimed at the European market, where the high cost of gasoline and tight roads favored a smaller, nimble car. The 375 (as its name suggested) was targeted towards Americans, whose wide-open spaces favored bigger powerplants. In addition to the basic model, a 375 Mille Miglia sports-racing version was offered on a 102.3-inch wheelbase. One of the more famous examples was serial #0488 AM constructed for King Leopold of Belgium. Roadster and berlinetta bodies were styled by Pinin Farina.

Model Note: 166/195/212 and 340 models came with a wide variety of custom bodies, so specifications varied. See previous listing for details on the 166 MM, 195 Sport, and 212 Export racing models.

1951 Ferrari 166/212, Gianni Marzotto's "Egg." (DG)

I.D. DATA: Not available.

Model	Body Type & Seating	Engine Type/CID	P.O.E. Price	Weight (lbs.)	Prod. Total
TYPE 195/212					
195 Inter	2-dr Coupe-2P	V12/143	N/A	2100	Note 1
195 Inter	2-dr Conv Cpe-2P	V12/143	N/A	2100	Note 1
212 Inter	2-dr Coupe-2P	V12/156	11000	2200	Note 2
212 Inter	2-dr Conv Cpe-2P	V12/156	N/A	2200	Note 2
TYPE 340/342/375 AMERICA					
340	2-dr Coupe-2P	V12/250	N/A	1980	Note 3
340	2-dr Conv Cpe-2P	V12/250	N/A	1980	Note 3
340 Mexico	2-dr Coupe-2P	V12/250	16000	1980	Note 3
342	2-dr Coupe-2P	V12/250	11500	2650	Note 4
342	2-dr Conv Cpe-2P	V12/250	N/A	2650	Note 4
375	2-dr Coupe-2P	V12/276	N/A	2540	Note 5
375	2-dr Conv Cpe-2P	V12/276	N/A	2540	Note 5

Note 1: Approximately 25 Type 195 models were produced through 1951.
Note 2: Approximately 80 Type 212 Inters were produced through 1953.
Note 3: About 22 Type 340 Americas were produced from 1951-55.
Note 4: About six Type 342 Americas were produced through 1953.
Note 5: At least 12 Type 375 Americas were produced through 1955.
Price Note: Figures shown are approximate (or averages).
Weight Note: Figures shown are the manufacturer's stated weights.

ENGINE [Base V-12 (Type 195)]: Same as 1947-50. 60-degree, single-overhead-cam, "vee" type 12-cylinder. Aluminum alloy block and heads (cast-iron cylinder liners). Displacement: 142.8 cid (2341 cc). Bore & stroke: 2.56 x 2.31 in. (65 x 58.8 mm). Compression ratio: 7.5:1. Brake horsepower: (Inter) 130 at 6000 rpm; (Sport) 160-180 at 6000 rpm. Seven main bearings. One twin-choke Weber carburetor (Inter) or three twin-choke Webers (Sport).

ENGINE [Base V-12 (212)]: Same as 1947-50. 60-degree, single-overhead-cam, "vee" type 12-cylinder. Aluminum alloy block and head (cast-iron cylinder liners). Displacement: 156.3 cid (2562 cc). Bore & stroke: 2.68 x 2.31 in. (68 x 58.8 mm). Compression ratio: 8.0:1. Brake horsepower: (Inter) 130-140 at 6000 rpm; (Export) 150-170 at 6500 rpm. Seven main bearings. One twin-choke Weber carburetor (Inter) or three twin-choke 36 DCF Webers (Export).

ENGINE [Base V-12 (340/342 America)]: 60-degree, single-overhead-cam, "vee" type 12-cylinder (Lampredi). Aluminum alloy block and heads. Displacement: 250 cid (4101 cc). Bore & stroke: 3.15 x 2.68 in. (80 x 68 mm). Compression ratio: 8.0:1. Brake horsepower: (340) 220 at 6600 rpm; (342) 200 at 5000 rpm. Torque: (342) 268 lbs.-ft. at 3000 rpm. Seven main bearings. Three twin-choke Weber carburetors.

Note: Type 340 Mexico engine was rated 280 bhp at 6600 rpm, and 228 lbs.-ft. at 4500 rpm.

ENGINE [Base V-12 (375 America)]: 60-degree, single-overhead-cam, "vee" type 12-cylinder. Aluminum alloy block and heads. Displacement: 276 cid (4523 cc). Bore & stroke: 3.31 x 2.68 in. (84 x 68 mm). Compression ratio: 8.4:1. Brake horsepower: 300 at 6300 rpm (340 at 7000 for competition). Seven main bearings. Three Weber 40 DCZ 3 carburetors.

CHASSIS: Wheelbase: (195/212 Inter) 98.5 or 102.4 in.; (340 America) 95.3 in.; (340 Mexico) 96 or 102.4 in.;

1951 Ferrari Vignale Type 212 Berlinetta. (DA)

1951 Ferrari Vignale Type 212 Berlinetta. (DA)

1951 Ferrari 212 Vignale. (DG)

(342) 104.3 in.; (375) 110.2 in. Overall Length: (195/212) 146-156 in. typical; (340/342) 170 in. average. Height: (195/212) 50-54 in. typical; (342) 56 in. typical; (340 Mexico) 54 in. Width: (195/212) 60 in. typical. Front Tread: (195/212) 49.8-50.0 in.; (340) 50 in.; (342) 52.2 in. Rear Tread: (195/212) 49.2 in.; (340) 49.2 in.; (342) 52 in. Standard Tires: (212 Inter) 6.40x15; (340 Mexico) 6.00x16 front, 6.50x16 rear.

TECHNICAL: Layout: front-engine, rear-drive. Transmission: (342/375) four-speed all-synchro manual; (others) five-speed manual (non-synchro). Steering: worm and peg. Suspension (front): unequal-length A-arms with transverse leaf springs. Suspension (rear): rigid axle with parallel trailing arms and semi-elliptic leaf springs. Brakes: hydraulic, front/rear drum. Body Construction: separate body on tubular steel ladder-type frame.

PERFORMANCE: Top Speed: (195) about 110 mph; (212) 120-124 mph; (340/342/375) 120-149 mph; (340 Mexico) 174 mph claimed. Acceleration (0-60 mph): (340 Mexico) just over 6 sec.

ADDITIONAL MODELS: At least 31 Type 250 MM (for Mille Miglia) coupes and Spiders, serving as racing versions of the forthcoming 250 Europa, were built in 1952-53. Their 2953-cc V-12 engines produced 240 bhp at 7200 rpm, with a 9.0:1 compression ratio. The 250 MM rode a 94.5-inch wheelbase and could hit 158 mph. An all-synchro four-speed gearbox was used. Tests achieved 0-60 mph acceleration times as quick as 5.1 seconds, and a 14.4-second quarter-mile time.

In 1953-54, no more than 18 Type 375 MM racers were built and sold with a 4523-cc V-12 producing 340 bhp at 7000 rpm. Riding a 104-inch wheelbase, the 375 MM could hit 180 mph. Ferrari also built Type 340 MM racecars for the 1953 season, various changes bumped horsepower up to 300 bhp from their 4.1-liter engines.

Manufacturer: Societa Auto-Avio Costruzioni Ferrari, Maranello (Modena), Italy.

Distributor: Luigi Chinetti, New York City; or Ernie McAfee, Hollywood, California.

HISTORY: The 340 America debuted at the Paris Salon in October 1950, with an open Touring body styled like the original 166 barchetta. Other bodies came from Ghia and Vignale, but Pinin Farina was fast becoming Ferrari's favorite. The 340 Mexico adopted that name because it was designed for the Carrera Panamericana race in that country.

The 250 Europa debuted alongside the 375 America at the Paris Salon in October 1953; see next listing for details. Ferrari's 212 scored a long list of race victories. In 1951, Pagnibon and Barraquet won the first Tour de France; Vittorio Marzotto and Piero Taruffi took first and second spots in the Tour of Sicily; and Piero Scotti earned a third at the Mille Miglia. Piero Taruffi and North American importer Luigi Chinetti won the Mexican Carrera Panamericana, where another Ferrari came in second.

1952-3 Ferrari 342 America Cabriolet. (DG)

1952-3 Ferrari 250MM Vignale Spyder. (DG)

Luigi Chinetti: Ferrari Promoter Extraordinaire

It could be argued that without Luigi Chinetti, there would never have been any Ferraris for the street. The legend goes that Enzo Ferrari and Luigi Chinetti met at Enzo's office on a cold Christmas Eve at the end of the 1940s. Ferrari's fortunes were so low at that point that the only heat in the room was from the fireplace. As the flames danced across the faces of these two proud men, Enzo told Luigi of his dreams of continuing to build and race vehicles bearing his name, but despaired of the lack of income such activities generated. The possibility of translating the V-12 technology into streetcars was discussed and Chinetti boldly stated that he would buy the first ten cars that Enzo would build. In recounting the tale Chinetti would remark, *"Can you imagine?* At that time I didn't have the money to buy one car, let alone ten!"

Chinetti was an acknowledged master behind the wheel, especially when it came to endurance racing. Driving for Alfa Romeo, he finished first at the classic 24 Hours of Le Mans in 1932 and 1934. His victory again in 1949 at this historic circuit is particularly significant for two reasons. It not only marked Ferrari's first win at Le Mans, it also saw Chinetti drive an incredible 23 hours and 40 minutes by himself, due to an illness of his co-driver, Lord Snowden. For any individual to complete this marathon is an accomplishment of which to be proud. To have driven so many hours at such a high speed is a remarkable feat, but to have driven well enough to beat the best drivers and cars in the world must be regarded as a towering triumph.

This was just one of the successful chapters in Chinetti's busy life. He went on to establish Luigi Chinetti Motors in New York City in the early 1950s and was the original importer for all the Ferraris sold on the East Coast. Chinetti was a master salesman who never employed high-pressure tactics. Instead, he used his position as purveyor of new Ferraris much as ancient popes once granted indulgences for rich noblemen. Brand new models were sold only to trusted customers, and just because you had the money to pay cash for a new Ferrari didn't mean that you were able to buy one. After the proper courting period you might be allowed out for a test drive. If you passed the driving test without embarrassing yourself, and did nothing to insult him, you might be given the opportunity to purchase one of these rare and beautiful machines.

In matters of service and parts, customers soon learned that speed and availability were on a different plane than American cars of the day. Only a few celebrities and close associates were ever allowed to wait for their cars. Everyone else dropped off their vehicles and were informed in due time when the work was completed. While the factory could be relied on to supply tune-up and body parts for current models, Chinetti's stock of old parts was hoarded as a precious commodity. Woe unto the inexperienced parts man who dared to sell the old parts without checking with Chinetti first!

Besides retailing all of the production models that were U.S. certified, he also commissioned a number of special models. Perhaps the best known, and most desirable, was the 275 GTB4 NART Spyder. While many customers were happy with the 275 GTS production convertible, some longed for a top-down version of the voluptuous 275 GTB4. Chinetti commissioned ten of these powerful Spyders, and today they are among the most sought after Ferraris ever.

In addition to special factory cars, Chinetti also worked with various Italian coachbuilders to create one-off specials. Zigatto and Michelotti were two of his favorites. The 365 GTB4 was perhaps the most customized body. Several special convertibles were made, and even a

Daytona station wagon! Never one to let an opportunity pass him by, Chinetti took a rolled over Daytona Coupe from Herb Chambers in trade on a new Daytona Spyder. Chinetti's son, Luigi Chinetti Jr., designed a long roof for the Daytona with doors that opened to either side, not unlike the back end of a DeTomaso Mangusta.

As well known as he was for his entrepreneurial ways of selling cars, he became even more famous for his North American Racing Team. Chinetti used his connections and skill as a manager to contest many of the legendary endurance races throughout the 1960s and 1970s. The 24 Hours of Le Mans and Daytona, the 12 Hours of Sebring, and the Watkins Glen six-hour endurance were the races on which NART concentrated. The team's most famous victory was the 1965 Le Mans. While the factory Ford and Ferrari teams were running multiple state-of-the art cars, Chinetti's team ran last year's model, the 250 LM. The unlikely pair of Masten Gregory and Jochen Rindt gave themselves little chance of a high place finish, so their plan was to run as hard as possible. They figured that once the car broke, they'd be able to go home early. As one after another of the big cars fell out, the NART entry moved further and further up in the field. It's been said that no one was more surprised than they were when the race ended and they stood atop the victory podium. The 1979 second-place finish at the 24 Hours of Daytona was an equally improbable achievement for the heavy 365 GTB4. This five-year-old racing car came agonizingly close to beating Porsche's latest technological marvel.

Chinetti also possessed an uncanny ability for spotting new talent. The list of drivers who cut their racing teeth with Chinetti reads like a Who's Who of top talent. Mario Andretti, Bob Grossman, Phil Hill, Pedro Rodriguez, and Denise McClugage were just a few of the up and coming drivers that Chinetti put behind the wheel of his prancing horse stable. Very few were paid, and none were well compensated for the privilege of driving Ferraris. But if you possessed sensitivity for keeping your machine going into the wee hours, and your lap times were at least middle of the pack, you stood a chance of having Chinetti offer you a drive.

Luigi lived long enough to sell his business, enjoy retirement, and be the recipient of many accolades from his adoring fans. Few men or women were so successful as a racing driver, automobile importer, and racing team owner. In fact, it's safe to say that no one else has ever possessed the unique combination of talents that distinguished this soft-spoken Italian gentleman.

Partial List of Drivers who have been on the North American Racing Team

World Champions:
Mario Andretti
Phil Hill
Jochen Rindt
Graham Hill
John Surtees

Others:
Sterling Moss
Dan Gurney
Innes Ireland

Peter Revson
Sam Posey
Carroll Shelby
Bob Bondurant
David Piper
Richie Ginther
Roger Penske
Masten Gregory
Bob Bondurant
Jim Hall
Swede Savage

Fireball Roberts
Walt Hansgen
Chuck Parsons
Wilbur Shaw Jr.
Arturo Mezzario
Ronnie Buckman
Jean Pierre Jarier
Luigi Chinetti Jr.
Paul Newman

1953 Ferrari 166 MM. (MC)

Some call it the most beautiful Ferrari to ever perform in a Hollywood film. The sleek lines of the1953 Ferrari Tipo 166 MM/53 epitomizes the notion of automotive beauty when we see the red racer hurtling through the verdant countryside in the 1954 Twentieth Century Fox film, *The Racers*. But this was not some replica made to look good through film slight of hand, this is the genuine article.

It appears that #0272M is one of two 166MMs whose bodies were designed by Ferrari in-house, and constructed by Carrozzeria Autodromo of Modena, Italy. Equipped with a single carburetor and a 7.5:1 compression ratio, the Tipo 166 1,995 cc V12 engine makes 90 hp. Here, in competition trim with 9.5:1 pistons and three Weber 36 IF4c carburetors output jumps to 160 bhp at 7,200 rpms.

On March 21, 1953 Dr. Alberico Cacciari, Pinnazzo di Castelfranco paid 2,750,000 Italian Lire ($1,230) for this fast Ferrari. The sleek Spyder immediately began its racing career, as Enzo intended. Its second race was the classic 1953 Mille Miglia where it finished 56th overall and a very credible third in class. Cacciari's co-driver was R.H. Bill Mason, who today is best known for being the father of Nick Mason of Pink Floyd fame. For the rest of the year, Cacciari entered a string of races with such delicious sounding names as Coppa Braccini, Saline-Volterra, Coppa d'Oro Siricusa, and the Supercortemaggiore sportscar race in Merano Italy.

Apparently, front-end makeovers were popular in Hollywood even back in the Fifties. Such was the fate for #0272M along with a tacked-on external exhaust for its role as a "Spyder Burano" in the movie *The Racers*. Thanks to the optimism of Hollywood writers, this 166MM was portrayed as the winner of the Mille Miglia in 1954. The car was shipped to Hollywood so Kirk Douglas and Cesar Romero could be filmed in the car against a blue screen.

Faithful to the Hollywood love-em and leave-em tradition, after filming Twentieth Century Fox had no use for our star, or any of the other racecars. Tom Carstens of Tacoma, WA purchased the 166MM and the rest of the Burano team cars in order to acquire the HMW single-seater after which he lusted. He arranged for his talented-driving friend, Pete Lovely of Seattle, Washington, to take #0272M off his hands for a mere $2,800.

Lovely campaigned the 166MM in several west coast races, back when cars were driven to the track, competed, and then driven home. When asked for his memories of the car's driving characteristics, Lovely recalls decent brakes, predictable handling, and the need to accelerate carefully. It seems the three Weber four-barrel carburetors were a bit much for the 2.0-liter engine at low rpms; if you jumped on the throttle, the resulting flood of gas would "put out the fires," according to Lovely.

In 1958, Nick Reynolds of the Kingston Trio owned the car. Commuting across the Golden Gate Bridge, Reynolds was frequently stopped by the local constabulary for headlights that were too low. Tired of the harassment, he had the nose altered to bring the offending beams up to regulation height.

Perhaps most interesting about the 166 MM's history are the prices at which it traded. Lovely paid $2,800, and in the spring of 1956 sold it for $4,500. In 1969, Edgar L. Roy paid $3,500, and by 1977 Jon Baumgartner was willing to invest $26,000 in this gracefully aging film star. He sold it in April of 1984 for $65,000, and in February of 1989 it was advertised in the Ferrari Market Letter for $1,350,000. Werner Pfister, of Miller Motor Cars, reports that he brokered the car for a Florida collector in October of 1992 for $500,000. Today, the reclusive starlet enjoys semi-retirement in the Pacific Northwest.

1953 Ferrari 166 MM engine. (MC)

1953 Ferrari 166 MM interior. (MC)

1953 Ferrari 250 MM Vignale s/n 0348. (WG)

1953 Ferrari 250 MM Vignale s/n 0348. (WG)

1954 Ferrari 250 Europa GT. (WG)

1954-55

TYPE 375 AMERICA — V-12 — The "there's no substitute for cubic inches" philosophy continued with the production of this evolution of the 340/342 "America," and went on as late as 1955; see previous listing for details. The beautiful Farina bodies placed on this chassis helped to influence Ferrari in making Pinin Farina the sole supplier of bodies in later years. Added for 1954 was a 375 Plus racing roadster for the factory team, with a 4954-cc engine producing 344 hp at 6500 rpm. Ferrari was well on the way to establishing their racing legend as that car won both the prestigious 1954 Le Mans and the grueling Carrera Panamericana races.

TYPE 250 EUROPA Series 1 & 2— V-12
— There were likely only 20 of the Series 1 Europa produced in 1954. These were the only vehicles that received the smallest (2963-cc) version of the Lampredi V-12 engine. (A quick way to tell the difference between a Lampredi and Colombo engine is to count the number of nuts at the bottom edge of the valve covers. The Lampredi engine has seven, the Colombo engine has six.) Delivering only 200 hp, the Europa could reach speeds up to 135 mph (depending on gearing). But it was not as nimble as some of Ferrari's competition, notably the Mercedes-Benz 300 SLs. In keeping with its luxurious interiors, an easier-to-use all-synchromesh four-speed transmission was fitted. Both the 250 Europa and the 375 America, with the same chassis and wheelbase, were at the 1953 Paris show, ranking as the largest Ferraris of that era—and the company's first serious stab at roadgoing production GT cars. As usual, various Italian coachbuilders supplied custom bodies, but most were a Pinin Farina design: a high-waisted, smooth-lined, semi-fastback 2+2 coupe, of which 22 were built (Europas and Americas). At least one two-seat

cabriolet and four coupes came from Vignale. Nearly all Europas, which rode a 110.2-inch wheelbase, were sold in the U.S.

TYPE 250 GT — V-12 — While the 250 Europa was produced in minimal quantity, the other 250-series model introduced in 1954 was destined to reach far greater numbers. About 2,500 were built. This included 104 of the glamorous California Spider convertibles and 350 of the beautiful Lussos, making this Ferrari's first real production model. All versions rode the familiar large-diameter ladder-type tubular frame with 102.3-inch wheelbase, except for the eventual (short wheelbase) California, GTB, and GTO, which measured only 94.5 inches. This early model became known as the "long-wheelbase" 250 GT, to distinguish it from a shorter version produced from 1959-64, even though it was considerably shorter than the 250 Europa. Ride improved with the use of a front coil spring suspension replacing the previous transverse leaf spring, while a rigid axle was installed at the rear. A new "Colombo" 2953-cc V-12 engine (evolved from the 250 MM race powerplant) was significantly lighter and shorter than the "Lampredi" it replaced. Horsepower started at 220,

but rose as high as 300 in competition form before the series came to a halt in 1962 (the short-wheelbase version would remain into 1964). Ferrari's reluctance to change from drum brakes to discs gave way in 1959, when discs became standard. Initially 250 GTs could be counted on for top speeds around 124-130 mph, but by the end of the series, 155 mph was achievable. Zero-to-sixty acceleration times ran 8 seconds or less.

As was customary, all bodies were designed and built by Italian coachbuilders, mainly Pinin Farina and, to a lesser extent, Vignale. Nearly all were closed coupes, either fastback or semi-fastback. Notable examples included the Pinin Farina coupes built from 1958-60, and the handsome Berlinetta Lusso of 1962-64. The GTO was Ferrari's race/street version, and it achieved notable success both during and after its production run. Some 250 GT competition models also were built, with five-speed gearboxes rather than the usual four-speed.

I.D. DATA: All 250 Europas and 375 Americas had odd serial numbers. "EU" in the serial number indicated an Europa; "AL" was the America Lungo (long wheelbase).

1954 Ferrari 375MM. (DG)

Model	Body Type & Seating	Engine Type/CID	P.O.E. Price	Weight (lbs.)	Prod. Total
TYPE 375 AMERICA					
375	2-dr Coupe-2P	V12/276	N/A	2530	Note 1
375	2-dr Conv Cpe-2P	V12/276	N/A	2530	Note 1
TYPE 250 EUROPA/GT					
250 Europa	2-dr Coupe-2+2P	V12/181	13890	3000	Note 2
250 Europa	2-dr Cabr-2P	V12/181	N/A	3000	Note 2
TYPE 250 GT					
250 GT	2-dr Coupe-2P	V12/180	N/A	N/A	Note 3

Note 1: Approximately 11 Type 375 Americas were produced in 1953-54.
Note 2: Approximately 19 Type 250 Europas were produced in 1953-54.
Note 3: Approximately 2,500 Type 250 GTs were produced over the full model run, through 1962, including 36 Europas.
Body Style Note: Like most early Ferraris, the 250 GT came in a wide variety of body styles, open and closed, from different coachbuilders.
Weight Note: Figures shown are approximate (or averages).

ENGINE [Base V-12 (375 America)]: 60-degree, single-overhead-cam, "vee" type 12-cylinder. Aluminum alloy block and heads. Displacement: 276 cid (4523 cc). Bore & stroke: 3.31 x 2.68 in. (84 x 68 mm). Compression ratio: 8.4:1. Brake horsepower: 300 at 6300 rpm (340 at 7000 for competition). Seven main bearings. Three Weber 40 DCZ 3 carburetors.

ENGINE [Base V-12 (250 Europa)]: 60-degree, single-overhead-cam, "vee" type 12-cylinder (Lampredi). Aluminum alloy block and heads. Displacement: 181 cid (2963 cc). Bore & stroke: 2.68 x 2.68 in. (68 x 68 mm). Compression ratio: 8.0:1. Brake horsepower: 200 at 6000-7000 rpm. Seven main bearings.

ENGINE [Base V-12 (250 GT)]: 60-degree, single-overhead-cam, "vee" type 12-cylinder (Colombo). Aluminum alloy block and heads (cast-iron cylinder liners). Displacement: 180 cid (2953 cc). Bore & stroke: 2.87 x 2.31 in. (73 x 58.8 mm). Compression ratio: 8.0:1-9.0:1. Brake horsepower: 200-220 at 6600-7000 rpm. Seven main bearings. Three Weber 36 DCZ3 carburetors.

CHASSIS: Wheelbase: (375) 110.2 in.; (250 Europa) 104 or 110.2 in.; (250 GT) 102.3 in. Overall Length: (340/342) 170 in. typical; (250 Europa) 170 in. typical, with some examples as short as 144 in.; (250 GT) 175 in. typical. Height: (250 Europa) 48 in. typical. Width: (250 Europa) 60 in. typical. Front Tread: (250 Europa) 50.7 in. Rear Tread: (250 Europa) 51.5 in.

1954/55 Ferrari 500 Mondial. (WG)

1954/55 Ferrari 500 Mondial. (WG)

TECHNICAL: Layout: front-engine, rear-drive. Transmission: four-speed all-synchro manual. Steering: worm and peg. Suspension (front): (375, 250 Europa) unequal-length A-arms with transverse leaf springs; (250 GT) upper/lower A-arms with coil springs. Suspension (rear): rigid axle with parallel trailing arms and semi-elliptic leaf springs. Brakes: hydraulic, front/rear drum. Body Construction: separate body on tubular steel ladder-type frame.

PERFORMANCE: Top Speed: (375 America) 155-161 mph reported; (250 Europa) 115-135 mph; (250 GT) 124-155 mph. Acceleration (0-60 mph): (250 Europa) 7.0 sec.

ADDITIONAL MODELS: Racing Ferraris of this period included the 750 Monza and 121 LM.

Manufacturer: Societa Auto-Avio Costruzioni Ferrari, Maranello (Modena), Italy.

Distributor: Luigi Chinetti, New York City; or Ernie McAfee, Hollywood, California.

HISTORY: Ferrari's replacement for the 375 America, the 410 Superamerica, appeared at the Paris Salon in September 1955; see next listing for details.

1955 Ferrari 375 America s/n 0355 AL. This 1-off was the last 375 America made. (WG)

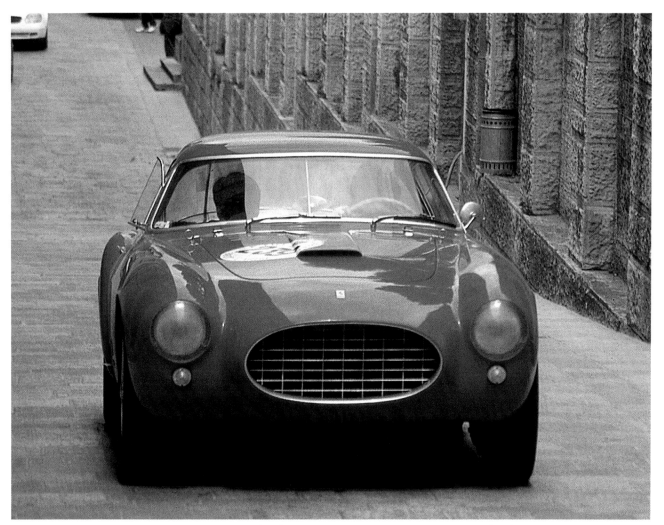

1955 Ferrari 250 GT Speciale at a recent Mille Miglia. (DG)

Ferrari 410 Superamerica. (DG)

TYPE 250 GT — V-12 — Production of the 250 GT, in a variety of body types from separate coachbuilders, continued into the early 1960s; see previous listing for details. One of the most celebrated street/track Ferraris was the short-wheelbase berlinetta (SWB), announced in 1959, for the 1960 model year; see next listing. While early examples had a tiny rear seat, later ones were strictly two-seaters, with a luggage shelf behind the seats.

Many variants of the 250 GT appeared in the mid-1950s, starting with a Farina berlinetta coupe at the Paris Salon in late 1955. Initially it was reported that Farina would supply the coupe bodies, while Boano would build the convertibles. When Ferrari expressed a reluctance to place an order for 500 cars at once, Pinin Farina wound up getting the smaller order for the cabriolets. Then in 1957, body production was taken over by Scaglietti (at Modena). By that time, the berlinetta (which had an aluminum body) was approved as production GT car. Also announced in 1956 was a Pinin Farina-styled notchback coupe, built at Carrozzeria Boano. Later versions had a higher roofline, called "Ellena" or "high-roof" 250 GT coupe. One touring cabriolet by Farina was shown at Geneva in 1957, and went into production that year.

Ferrari 410 Superamerica. Thirty-eight of these beauties were built in three series between 1956 and 1959. (DG)

A Farina-built replacement for the Boana/Ellena, called the "PF coupe," was built through 1960 on the 250 GT chassis. The notchback design had a more angular look. Ferrari buyers were as enamored with open-air motoring as the next sportscar fan: A Series II cabriolet was built by Farina through 1962. This should not be confused with the sportier open roadster called the Spyder California, built by Scaglietti into early 1960. It featured wind-up windows, and a special chassis with extra bracing. In 1959, Ferrari introduced its first fresh-air heating system, courtesy of Pininfarina's close collaboration with General Motors. (It was in 1958 that Pinin Farina officially changed to the one word spelling.) Also, a twin-disc clutch replaced single-disc. At the end of the decade, front disc brakes finally replaced the former drum brakes.

TYPE 410 SUPERAMERICA — V-12 —

Production totals were modest for this aggressively-styled replacement for the 375 America, which was phased out of the lineup. Only 38 were built in all, in three series, from 1956-59. Fast and powerful, built on a new chassis, a 410 was capable of speeds up to 165 mph in peak tune. Brakes were larger than before, torque output greater. Most bodies came from Pinin Farina, in both open and closed form. Coil springs formed the front suspension, as in the 250 GT. Wheelbase was 110.2 inches initially, but shrunk to 102.3 inches by 1958. The

1956 Ferrari Type 410 Superamerica. (DA)

1956 Ferrari Type 410 Superamerica. (DA)

ladder-type frame was made up of oval-section main tubes and round cross-tubes. The Lampredi V-12 was bored out by 4 mm to reach 4962-cc displacement, retaining the former 68-mm stroke. Horsepower was 340 at first, then boosted to 360 bhp and even 400 bhp. Compression was only 8.5:1. A multi-disc clutch sent power to the four-speed gearbox. As many as eight axle ratios were available, ranging from 3.11:1 to 3.66:1.

The 410 Superamerica's appearance was similar to the PF coupe (Boano/Ellena) on the smaller (250 GT) chassis. Ferrari first displayed a highly polished chassis at the 1955 Paris Salon. And, the first complete 410 Superamerica was shown with a Pinin Farina coupe body at the Brussels Salon in January 1956. One of the most distinctive styling features were the side vents located right behind the front wheels. These would be used in many future Ferraris, and could be called a trademark of the Superamericas. Nine Series I coupes similar to that Brussels show car were built, while one wore a finned Ghia body. Also produced were a coupe and cabriolet by Boano. In Series II, eight Farina bodies were built, plus two specials: a chrome-laden, two-tone example by Scaglietti; and a 4.9 Superfast coupe by Farina, known as Superfast II, lacking the Series I's tailfins. Series III appeared at the 1958 Paris show. Under its hood, spark plugs were now outboard of heads, as on the racing 250 Testa Rossa (formerly within the engine's "vee"). Compression was raised to 9.0:1, horsepower to 360.

Drum brake diameter was enlarged, and the gearbox got a conventional H-gate shift pattern. Curved headlamp covers matched restyled front fenderlines, though the final few cars had exposed headlamps. Louvered metal panels were installed where rear quarter windows had been on the prototype.

I.D. DATA: Not available.

Model	Body Type & Seating	Engine Type/CID	P.O.E. Price	Weight (lbs.)	Prod. Total
TYPE 250 GT					
250 GT	2-dr Coupe-2P	V12/180	12500	2650	Note 1
California	2-dr Conv-2P	V12/180	14000	2420	Note 1
TYPE 410 SUPERAMERICA					
410	2-dr Coupe-2P	V12/303	16800	2400	Note 2

Note 1: Approximately 2,500 Type 250 GTs were produced over the full model run; see previous listing for breakdown details.
Note 2: A total of 16 Series I models were built in 1956, six Series II (1957), and 12 Series III (1958-59).
Body Style Note: As usual, Ferraris came in a wide variety of body styles, open and closed, from different coachbuilders.
Price Note: A 250 GT coupe was priced at $12,800 at the 1956 New York Auto Show; the advertised price was down to $12,000 by 1959.
Weight Note: Figures shown are approximate (or averages).

ENGINE [Base V-12 (250 GT)]: 60-degree, single-overhead-cam, "vee" type 12-cylinder (Colombo). Aluminum alloy block and heads (cast-iron cylinder liners). Displacement: 180 cid (2953 cc). Bore & stroke: 2.87 x 2.31 in. (73 x 58.8 mm). Compression ratio: 8.5:1. Brake horsepower: 220-260 at 7000 rpm (240 bhp in

1956 Ferrari Type 410 Superfast. (DA)

1958-59). Torque: 195 lbs.-ft. at 5000 rpm (in 1959). Seven main bearings. Three Weber two-barrel carburetors.

ENGINE [Base V-12 (410 Superamerica)]: 60-degree, single-overhead-cam, "vee" type 12-cylinder (Lambredi). Aluminum alloy block and heads. Displacement: 302.7 cid (4962 cc). Bore & stroke: 3.46 x 2.68 in. (88 x 68 mm). Compression ratio: 8.5:1. Brake horsepower: (Series I) 340 at 6000 rpm; (Series II) 360 at 7000 rpm; (Series III) 400 at 6200/6500 rpm. Torque: (Series I) 311 lbs.-ft. at 5000 rpm; (Series III) 340 lbs.-ft. at 4700 rpm. Seven main bearings. Three or six Weber two-barrel carburetors.

CHASSIS: Wheelbase: (250 GT) 102.3 in.; (410 Series I) 110.2 in.; (410 Series II/III) 102.3 in. Overall Length: (250 GT) 175.5 in. typical; (410 Series II/III) about 185-188 in. Height: (250 GT) 54 in.; (410) 54 in.

Width: (250 GT) 66 in.; (410) 68 in. Front Tread: (250 GT) 53.3 in.; (410) 57.3-57.5 in. Rear Tread: (250 GT) 53.1 in.; (410) 57.1 in. Standard Tires: (250 GT) 6.00x16; (410) 6.50x16.

TECHNICAL: Layout: front-engine, rear-drive. Transmission: four-speed all-synchro manual. Steering: worm and peg. Suspension (front): upper/lower A-arms with coil springs. Suspension (rear): rigid axle with parallel trailing arms and semi-elliptic leaf springs. Brakes: hydraulic, front/rear drum. Body Construction: separate body on tubular steel ladder-type frame.

PERFORMANCE: Top Speed: (250 GT) 126-157 mph depending on gearing; (410) 135-165 mph. Acceleration (0-60 mph): (250 GT) 7.0-8.0 sec. typical (but as little as 5.9 sec. reported). Acceleration (quarter-mile): (250 GT) as little as 16.1 sec. reported. Fuel Mileage (410) about 11 mpg.

PRODUCTION/SALES: Approximately 39 Ferraris were sold in the U.S. during 1958, and 61 in 1959.

ADDITIONAL MODELS: The curvaceous Type 250 Testa Rossa racing model was produced from 1958-61, powered by a 2953-cc V-12 that produced 300 bhp at 7200 rpm, using 9.8:1 compression ratio and six Weber carburetors. Wheelbase was 92.5 inches. A total of 33 were built, capable of 167-mph top speeds. Price at the factory was about $12,900 in 1958.

Superfast I was considered by many to be the hit of the Paris Salon in 1956. Using a shortened 410 SA chassis, the Pinin Farina body featured some of the tallest and most striking fins ever fitted to Ferrari. The greenhouse was quite unique as there were no "A" pillars separating the wraparound windshield from the side windows. This car would prove to be a style-setter for Ferraris over the

1956 Ferrari Type 410 Superfast. (DA)

1957 Ferrari 250GT. (DG)

next few years. A 4962-cc V-12 employed a 9.0:1 compression and three Weber carburetors to produce 380 bhp. Testing by *Sports Cars Illustrated* yielded 0-60 mph acceleration in 5.6 seconds (versus 5.9 for a 250 GT), and a quarter-mile time of 13.9 seconds. A 4.9 Superfast was advertised for sale in the U.S. at $18,500 in 1958.

Manufacturer: Societa Auto-Avio Costruzioni Ferrari, Maranello (Modena), Italy.

Distributor: Luigi Chinetti Motors Inc., New York City; and Ernie McAfee Engineering Co., Los Angeles or Ferrari Representatives, Hollywood, California.

HISTORY: The short-wheelbase 250 GT appeared at the Paris Salon in October 1959; see next listing for details. At the 1956 Paris show, a new one-off "Superfast" fastback displayed a futuristic look with tapered snout, recessed headlamps (behind clear plastic covers), tall tailfins, and the short (102.3-inch)

wheelbase. The 250 GT "California" debuted in the U.S. at the Los Angeles International Auto Show in 1959, described by Pinin Farina as "summing up all the experience of sports." Promotional material noted that it combined "traditional Ferrari elegance and comfort with eminent sports car performance." According to *Classic Sports Cars*, the idea for this open version of the 250 GT came from John von Neumann, Ferrari's agent in Los Angeles.

1957 Ferrari 250GT. (DG)

The 1957 Ferrari Transporter (background) and its trio of passengers attracted crowds of onlookers during the 2001 Pebble Beach Concours d'Elegance, leaving the author a nice shot of this 1965 Ferrari 500 Superfast (foreground) as well. (MC)

If trucks had aspirations, what goal could be higher than to become the world's first purpose-built Ferrari transporter? Picture a Fiat assembly line in 1957 with beefy Tipo 682 R truck chasses rolling along. A representative from custom truck body fabricator Bartoletti points to chassis # 003001 and says, "We'll take that one." While its brethren were destined to become moving vans and garbage trucks, lucky #003001 would go on to lead the life of a hard-working celebrity.

By 1957 Enzo Ferrari had met with enough success that he commissioned Bartollelti to create an exclusive vehicle for hauling the Ferrari Factory Racing Team. From 1957 until 1969 this trusty workhorse delivered three Russo Red Ferraris to Formula One, Formula Two, plus Sport and Prototype racing event throughout Europe. It was also frequently pressed into service to bring cars to the Turin, Paris and Geneva auto shows. Some photos from the Ferrari Factory Yearbooks even depict customers welcoming their new and pre-owned Ferraris in their driveways on this old veteran.

In August of 2001, #003001 caused quite a stir at the 51st Pebble Beach Concours d'Elegance. Tucked away in the furthest corner of the 18th fairway, it towered over its fellow entrants like a longshoreman fraternizing with the jockeys at the Kentucky Derby. While a few of the show cars had occupants in period dress, or motoring accessories from their respective eras, the Fiat carried adornment that may have set a record for costly accoutrements. No, I'm not talking about the four Ferrari flags that flapped at each of the truck's corners; I mean the cars. Thanks to three generous owners, two 1958 250 Testa Rossas and a 1959 250 TR took time off from their Laguna Seca racing activities, so they could be displayed on the car carrier. Depending upon the daily market adjustment, we're talking about $12-14 million worth of cargo!

The transporter's caretaker, Tony Garmey invited us to come back another time to the West Coast for a closer look. Climbing up into the Fiat's gargantuan cab I'm struck by the contrast of austere bare metal and Bakelite set off with accents of flashy red leather piping. The engine cover dominates the area and is topped by a chrome railing. Twin red leather bucket seats flank the engine cover, and behind is a convertible bench seat that doubles as a sleeping bunk. A side door reveals a workshop in the back half of the cab with room for spare racing parts.

When Tony fires up the six-cylinder diesel engine I feel like I am trapped in a washing machine filled with nuts and bolts. The noise never subsides, but as I contemplate the Fiat's bare-bones interior and significance to the Italian marque, the din seemed irrelevant. A hydraulically operated-winch makes pulling the low slung racing cars up the ramps a slow, but safe procedure.

While I had harbored illusions of adding this to my list of test-drives, after watching Tony's gyrations behind the massive wheel I'm happy to leave the driving to him. The four-speed non-syncromesh gearbox offers little pity for the unskilled. A second lever toggles between the two ratios in the split-rear axle. From the dashboard a lever sprouts for the air brakes, and another lowers the shield in front of the radiator on cold mornings.

Thanks to the diesel's low-end grunt, the Fiat moves resolutely away from each stop. But the gearing gives it a busy maximum speed of about 46 mph. Imagine this veteran chugging its way up Alpine passes as it carried racing cars bound for victory and show cars constructed to win the hearts of all. Life as a dramatic display cabinet for vintage Ferraris insures Fiat #003001 will continue as Bartoletti's most visible star.

1958 Ferrari Series I Pininfarina 250 GT. (DA)

1958 Ferrari 250 Pininfarina Cabriolet Series I s/n 0873. (WG)

1958 Ferrari 250 Pininfarina Cabriolet Series I s/n 0873. (WG)

Ferrari 250 Testa Rossa circa 1960. (DG)

TYPE 250 GT (LWB) — V-12 — Production of the long-wheelbase 250 GT (described in 1954-55 listing) continued into 1962. New for the 1960 model year, and continuing into 1964, was a short-wheelbase version. Tubular telescopic shocks replaced lever hydraulics in 1960, and overdrive was added to the all-synchro four-speed transmission.

TYPE 250 GT (SWB) — V-12 — This was a companion to the "interim" 250 GT berlinetta, which debuted early in 1959. Designed by Pininfarina, the short-wheelbase body was built by Scaglietti as a race/street two-seater with new rounded contours and a more aggressive look. Wheelbase was nearly eight inches

shorter than the LWB edition, at 94.5 inches. For the street or Lusso versions, the standard steel body had aluminum doors, hood, and trunklid. Most competition bodies were all-aluminum. Under the hood was the Colombo V-12 design, with spark plugs now outside of the heads and new coil-type valve springs replacing the former hairpin-type. Moving the spark plugs allowed for better flow through all of the intake ports. Twin distributors at the rear of the engine returned. The 2953-cc engine produced as much as 280 horsepower at 7000 rpm. Six axle ratios were offered, from 3.44:1 to 4.57:1. Brakes were disc all around. Top speeds reached as high as 150 mph, and a 250 GT SWB could accelerate from zero to 60 mph in seven seconds or less. Borrani center-lock wire wheels were standard.

During 1959, a Spyder California (with Scaglietti body) debuted on the SWB chassis to replace the LWB Spyder, which was similar in appearance. The SWB berlinetta (coupe), on the other hand, did not resemble its LWB predecessors. Several differences were evident between the two. Front-fender air outlets, for one, had three vertical bars on the LWB, two on the SWB (though some of each series had none at all). Short-wheelbase Spyders had a horizontal ridge between their tail lamps; long-wheelbase 250 GTs did not. Both versions had headlamps behind clear plastic covers.

Perhaps the most pure design ever to be created by Pininfarina appeared late in 1962 at the Paris show—the 250 GT/L, better know as Berlinetta Lusso (luxury). While it was penned by Pininfarina, construction was handled by Scaglietti. This car was meant for those cultured clients who longed for the looks of the legendary GTO, but required more civilized road manners. Its front end was similar to the SWB model, while the Kamm-style tail resembled that of the 250 GTO racing coupe, with round tail lamps. The most unusual feature may well be the absence of a vent window in the driver's door, despite the appearance of one on the passenger's side. Overall, the new fastback profile had a thin-pillar roofline, with aluminum hood, doors, and trunklid. The rear fenders did not have the GTO's high haunches as equal size tires were fitted front and rear. At the center of the dashboard was a large speedometer and tachometer, with five gauges ahead of the steering wheel. Lusso was the final 250 GT version.

TYPE 250 GTE/GT 2+2 — V-12 — Some buyers may have felt excluded from purchasing a Ferrari due to their need for a back seat. While the new 2+2-seat version offered the promise of accommodations for three passengers, the two in back faced a mighty tight squeeze. All former 2+2s (bodied by Touring, Ghia, or Vignale) in the early 1950s were one-offs, not production models. The 2+2 was 12 inches longer, and two inches wider than the 250 GT. Wheelbase was 102.3 inches (same as the

1960 Ferrari Type 250 GT LWB Spyder California. (DA)

250 GT LWB), but the engine, pedals, seat, and front floorboard were moved forward to create the rear-seat area. The new block casting meant that 2+2 engines could not be swapped with those of the two place cars. Initially named 250 GTE, the notchback coupe had coil springs in the front suspension and twin headlamps. Body design and construction of the body were by Pininfarina. Minor appearance revisions in 1962 brought a name change to 250 GT 2+2. Before long, it would evolve into the 330 GT America, and 330 GT 2+2. The 2953-cc V-12 (similar to that used in other roadgoing 250 models) produced 240 horsepower, working through a four-speed (plus overdrive) gearbox.

TYPE 400 SUPERAMERICA — V-12 — This final evolution of the America/Superamerica series wore custom bodywork styled and built by Pininfarina. Most were coupes. Wheelbases started at 95.3 inches, then grew to 102.3 inches as Series II in 1962. Mechanical details were similar to the former 410. Under the hood the heavy Lampredi 4.9-liter engine was replaced by a new version of the Colombo V-12 that displaced 3967 cc and produced a claimed 400 bhp initially with its 9.8:1 compression ratio and three Weber 46 DCF carburetors. A single dry-plate clutch replaced the multi-disc unit. Laycock de Normanville electric overdrive was included with the all-synchro four-speed gearbox. Koni telescopic shocks replaced the earlier lever-type units. Borrani center-lock wire wheels were standard.

The 400 Superamerica prototype appeared at the 1959 Turin show, wearing a boxy body with squarish grille, wraparound windshield, and quad headlamps. The production model at the Brussels show in January 1960 was considerably different, with its Farina-styled cabriolet body. A few production cabrios came with a

1960 Ferrari Type 250 GT LWB Spyder California. (DA)

1961 Ferrari 250 SWB. (DG)

lift-off steel top. Series II was inspired by the Superfast II seen at the 1960 Turin show, which Pininfarina said he'd created with wind tunnel help. Its fastback body was tapered at each end, with retracting headlamps fitted to the long nose and partly-skirted back wheels. In winter 1961-62 a hood scoop was added, skirts dropped, and headlamps exposed (with clear plastic lenses), to create the PF Coupe Aerodinamico. That body was used for all later 400s.

Note: Starting with the 400 Superamerica, model numbers indicated total engine displacement in deciliters (1/10 of a liter), rather than the number of cubic centimeters per cylinder as before.

I.D. DATA: All 250 GT SWB models had odd (touring) serial numbers.

Model	Body Type & Seating	Engine Type/CID	P.O.E. Price	Weight (lbs.)	Prod. Total
TYPE 250 GT					
250 GT LWB	2-dr Coupe-2P	V12/180	12600	N/A	Note 1
250 GT SWB	2-dr Coupe-2P	V12/180	N/A	N/A	Note 2
California	2-dr Conv-2P	V12/180	13600	N/A	Note 2
TYPE 250 GT 2+2					
250 GT	2-dr Coupe-2+2P	V12/180	12600	2822	Note 3
TYPE 400 SUPERAMERICA					
400	2-dr Coupe	-2PV12/242	N/A	2822	Note 4

Note 1: Approximately 2,500 Type 250 GTs (long-wheelbase) were produced over the full model run; see 1954-55 listing for breakdown details.

Note 2: Production of the 250 GT SWB over the full model run (through 1964) included 175 Berlinettas, 57 Spyder Californias (into early 1963 only), and 351 Berlinetta Lussos.
Note 3: A total of 299 Type 250 GT 2+2s Series I were produced from 1960-61. A total of 355 Type 250 GT 2+2s Series II were produced from 1961-62.
Note 4: As many as 56 Type 400 Superamericas were produced from 1960-64, including six cabrios (in 1960), 14 Series I SWB coupes, and 36 Series II LWB coupes.
Body Style Note: As usual, Ferraris came in a wide variety of body styles, open and closed, from different coachbuilders.
Weight Note: Figures shown are approximate (or averages).

ENGINE [Base V-12 (250 GT)]: 60-degree, single-overhead-cam, "vee" type 12-cylinder (Colombo). Aluminum alloy block and heads. Displacement: 180 cid (2953 cc). Bore & stroke: 2.87 x 2.31 in. (73 x 58.8 mm). Compression ratio: 9.2:1. Brake horsepower: (250 GT SWB, 250 GT 2+2) 240 at 7000 rpm; (racing 250 GT SWB) 280 at 7000 rpm. Seven main bearings. Three twin-choke Weber carburetors.

ENGINE [Base V-12 (400 Superamerica)]: 60-degree, single-overhead-cam, "vee" type 12-cylinder (Colombo). Aluminum alloy block and heads. Displacement: 242 cid (3967 cc). Bore & stroke: 3.03 x 2.80 in. (77 x 71 mm). Compression ratio: 9.8:1 (later, 8.8:1). Brake horsepower: 400 at 6750 rpm (later, 340 at 7000 rpm). Seven main bearings. Three Weber 46 DCF carburetors.

CHASSIS: Wheelbase: (250 GT LWB) 102.3 in.; (250 GT SWB) 94.5 in.; (250 GT 2+2) 102.3 in.; (400 Series I) 95.3 in.; (400 Series II/III) 102.3 in. Overall Length: (250 GT LWB) 185 in. typical; (250 GT SWB) 174 in. typical;

(250 GT 2+2) 185 in.; (400) 172 in. typical. Height: (250 GT LWB) 53 in. typical; (250 GT SWB) 48 in.; (250 GT 2+2) 51.5 in. Width: (250 GT LWB) 67 in. typical; (250 GT SWB) 64 in.; (250 GT 2+2) 65-67.3 in. Front Tread: (250 GT SWB/2+2) 53.3 in. Rear Tread: (250 GT SWB) 53.1 in.; (250 GT 2+2) 54.7 in.

TECHNICAL: Layout: front-engine, rear-drive. Transmission: four-speed all-synchro manual (plus overdrive in 250 GT 2+2 and 400 Superamerica). Steering: worm and peg. Suspension (front): upper/lower A-arms with coil springs. Suspension (rear): rigid axle with parallel trailing arms and semi-elliptic leaf springs. Brakes: front/rear disc. Body Construction: separate body on tubular steel ladder-type frame.

PERFORMANCE: Top Speed: (250 GT LWB) 124-155 mph; (250 GT SWB) 140-156 mph; (250 GT 2+2) 115+ mph; (400) 140-160+ mph. Acceleration (0-60 mph): (250 GT LWB) 7.0-8.0 sec.; (250 GT SWB) about 6.5-7.0 sec.; (250 GT 2+2) 8.0 sec. Acceleration (quarter-mile): (250 GT 2+2) 16.3 sec.

ADDITIONAL MODELS: If Ferraris became known for their ability to transport their owners to the track, offer some lively competition, and then be driven safely home, the GTO is the epitome of this idea. Ferrari produced the 250 GTO racing car through 1964, after its debut in February 1962. The 2953-cc V-12 produced 300 bhp at 7500 rpm, using 9.8:1 compression and six Weber carburetors. This was the final front-engine race version.

1960 Ferrari Type 250 GT SWB Spyder California. (DA)

1961 Ferrari 250 SWB. (DG)

GTO stood for Gran Turismo Omologato, meaning homologated (sanctioned) for racing. Top speed of the coupe was 176 mph, and a total of 38 or 39 were built on a 102.4-inch wheelbase. The 250 GTO wore no bumpers and had no cockpit insulation. Sliding plastic side windows were used, along with a plastic back window. The engine even lacked an air filter. The GTO offered its owner unparalleled performance in its day.

Manufacturer: Automobili Ferrari S.p.A. SEFAC, Maranello (Modena), Italy.

Distributor: Luigi Chinetti Motors Inc., New York City.

HISTORY: Ferrari's Type 500 Superfast, produced from 1964-66, evolved from the Superfast II show car that appeared at the Turin show in 1960; and the subsequent Superfast III show car at the 1962 Geneva Salon.

From 1956-60, Ferrari took 1-2-3 victories at the Tour de France. In 1961, Ferraris earned 1-2-3-4 positions, with 250 GT berlinettas. Ads promoted the Spyder California as a car that could be "driven in normal daily use, or raced."

A 2+2 Ferrari was used as the course marshal's car at the Le Mans in 1960, and formal announcement of the new 250 GTE came at the Paris show in October of that year. It was phased out in late 1963, to be replaced by the 330 GT series.

1962 Ferrari 400 Superamerica. (DG)

The 250 GT California Spyder;
A Unique Combination of Style and Speed

1960 Ferrari Type 250 GT SWB Spyder California. (DA)

Few automobiles have ever offered up the visual excitement that a Ferrari California Spyder generates. The wire wheels, flowing lines, and delicate chrome accents can be likened to a visual poem in metal. Conceived by the United States Ferrari importer for his well-heeled clients, the California Spyder was a great success in the Hollywood hills, and across the country.

When you delve back into the early annals of Ferrari history, some questions are more definitely answered than others. While the suggestion to make an open version of Ferrari's competition Berlinetta is generally credited to West Coast importer John von Newman, other folks

1962-64 Ferrari 250 GT engine. (DG)

say that Luigi Chinetti on the East Coast was the one to turn his dream into reality. Perhaps the nomenclature of a later Spyder, the 275 GTB/4 NART Spyder, is a response to this confusion. With Chinetti's North American Racing Team included in the model designation, there could be no mistake whose baby this one was.

Just to add to the confusion, Ferrari also produced 36 250 GT Pinin Farina (the name change to Pininfarina was still in the future) Series I cabriolets from 1957 to 1959, 201 Series II cabs from 1959-1962, and even six 400 Superamerica Short Wheelbase Pinin Farina Cabriolets between 1959 and 1962. While similar in overall appearance, these convertibles were aimed more towards the Ferrari buyers who favored luxury over speed. The Spyder California was meant to be equally at home on the track, or carving up Mulholland Drive.

And these convertibles did make respectable racers. The 1959 24 Hours of Le Mans saw Bob Grossman and Fernando Tararo drive their Spyder California to fifth place overall. The following year, Ferrari scored a first in GT class, and ninth overall with another pair of privateers at the Twelve Hours of Sebring. Despite the fact that the California was actually heavier than the Berlinetta, it acquitted itself quite well in various races throughout the world.

There was even a convertible before the Pinin Farina cars broke cover. Carrozzeria Boano is credited with the first 250 GT convertible. As early as 1957, prototypes of an open-top version of the 250 GT berlinettas were constructed. It was at the December 19, 1958, annual press conference in Modena that the news of the California Spyder was made public.

Forty-seven examples were constructed between the middle of 1958 and February 1960. These cars all had the 102-inch wheelbase, and came in both steel (street) bodies and aluminum skins for those intending to race their cars. The aluminum cars all had external gasoline filler caps. Many of the Californias had covered headlights, the rest did not. There seems to be no rhyme or reason as to which cars got which front-end treatment. The final fifteen of these featured rear fenders whose flanks did not rise up quite so far. (Please don't call them tailfins!) In addition to a slightly revised deck lid, these cars also were fitted with Girling disc brakes, instead of the aluminum drums worn by the early cars.

At the March 1960 Geneva Auto Salon, the new short wheelbase California Spyder was revealed, along with three other new models. The 250 GT Pinin Farina coupe and cabriolet were displayed with a Scaglietti-designed berlinetta. Just as a Scaglietti berlinetta shown at the 1959 Paris Salon had been shortened, the new California Spyder SWB was built on a 94.5-inch wheelbase. The tidier dimensions made for a more nimble car, and it boasted improved handling.

While Pinin Farina designed both the long and short wheelbase cars, Scaglietti in Modena assembled the body. At the time, the other 250 GT body shells were being built in Turin. Production continued until February of 1963 when a total of 104 California Spyders had been crafted; 47 LWB and 57 SWB cars.

The chief thrill of any Ferrari, be it a California Spyder or the latest 360 Modena, is the engine. While a few of the early cars may have been fitted with the inside plug engine, the later 128C, with its sparkplugs on the exhaust side of the heads, is what you'll find in most of these cars. The 2953 cc V-12 had aluminum heads and block, and came topped by three DCL3 Weber two-barrel carburetors. Output is quoted at 260, 270, and even 280, all at a lofty 7000-rpm. Every car was equipped with a four-speed transmission, and they could run up to between 126 and 167 mph, depending on the rear end ratio.

In a period when American cars sported tailfins that stretched to the stratosphere, and wore enough chrome to plate a battleship, the California Spyder was a delightful model of restraint. The windshield was set at what was then a rakish angle. A delicate band of chrome framed it, and certainly a rollover test had never even crossed the designers' minds. On the short wheelbase models, a shallow hood scoop was also ringed in chrome. Like the covered headlight issue, the inclusion or omission of the chrome side vents seemed to have no pattern. All cars rode on center knock-off Borrani wheels, including the competition aluminum body cars.

While the inside may not have been as ornately fitted as the PF Cabs of the day, they were a far cry away from being spartan. A large wood-rimmed steering wheel dominated the cockpit. The tall chrome shift lever sported a shift knob that resembled a chrome cue ball. A sizeable speedometer and tachometer nestled under individual hoods, directly in front of the driver. Four ancillary gauges and a clock stood in a line in the middle of the dashboard, each ringed in chrome. The bucket seats were fairly narrow, but the idea of side bolstering in a streetcar was still off in the future.

There was no doubt that Ferrari had a hit on their hands. One enthusiastic owner was movie star James Coburn. When he wasn't starring in Westerns, or making a name for himself in *Our Man Flint*, Coburn enjoyed driving his silver 250 GT SWB California Spyder (complete with the headlight covers and the side vents). He would keep the gleaming silver rocket for 25 years, until a divorce forced him to pare down his collection.

So even if you weren't "In Like Flint," or even in the Golden State, the California Special remains a high water mark in Ferrari style and speed.

1962-64 Ferrari 250 GTO. (DG)

250 GTO: The Greatest Street Ferrari Ever Raced

1962 Ferrari 250 GTO. (DG)

With a total production of only 39 cars, the 1962-1964 Ferrari 250 GTO's significant impact on the auto world was disproportionate to its minimal production numbers. When the Federation Internationale Automobile (FIA) announced that the World Manufacturer's Championship would be decided by homologated Grand Touring cars for the 1962 season, rather than the faster sport prototype cars, they played right into Enzo Ferrari's hands. Ferrari was in the habit of building lightweight,

high power versions of his grand touring cars, and his experience with the 250 GT SWB (Short Wheelbase Berlinetta) provided a road map for the creation of what many people consider to be his masterpiece, the GTO.

Giotto Bizzarrini is credited with much of the development work on this classic Ferrari. As an alumnus, he had access to the wind tunnel at the University of Pisa, where he spent many hours testing and reshaping the GTO's sensuous body. The 250 GT SWB offered great acceleration and handling, but when it came time to stretch its legs on the racecourse, the blunt-nose coupe was limited by aerodynamics to 155 mph.

As a result, the GTO's nose was stretched out and lowered. The back end was finished with a short spoiler molded into the tail. Despite its curvaceous figure, the GTO was one of the first steps in the direction of the wedge shape that became the standard form for racing cars in the ensuing decades. Numerous slots and scoops were added to good effect. Three holes above the small, elliptical opening in the nose gulped additional air for the hungry engine, and they could be closed off for operation in cooler temperatures. Slots behind the front wheels helped to exhaust the heat that built up in the engine compartment, and the cutouts in the aft fenders worked to keep the rear disc brakes from overheating. Despite all the interruptions to the smooth flow of air, the GTO could now touch 170 mph with the proper rear axle ratio.

The Type 128F V-12 had proved itself in the Testa Rossa, and it served in good stead for "Grand Touring" duty as well. The 3.0-liter Colombo engine had a dry sump oil system and was fitted with six 38 DCN Weber carburetors. No air cleaner kept out road debris; instead, twelve gleaming velocity stacks ensured a straight shot down the ravenous throats of the fuel mixers. The aluminum engine was fitted with magnesium cam covers finished in the traditional black wrinkle paint. Output is said to have been 300 bhp at 7500 rpms. The first three GTOs were originally fitted with 4.0-liter engines as prototypes. Adapted from the 400 Super America, these motors were said to produce an additional 100 bhp. These cars can be recognized by their taller hood bulge.

In order for a car to become homologated, the manufacturer had to submit a detailed series of specifications for a car whose actual or intended production exceeds 100 units in 12 consecutive months. Ferrari successfully argued that the GTO was simply a 250 GT SWB fitted with a different body. The vehicle's name originated with the phrase "Grand Touring Omologato" (homologated). While the Ferrari sport racers of the day were fitted with an independent rear suspension, the GTO kept its live rear end, just to prove that it was indeed an evolution of the 250 GT road car.

The GTO was first shown at the February 24, 1962, open house held in the Ferrari factory. Its display alongside the 1962 Ferrari Formula One car spoke to the car's true intentions. There were no bumpers, sound deadening, or insulation inside the car. The rear window was made of Plexiglas and the side windows were also plastic and slid open. The "passenger's" feet had to share the foot well with the battery, an oil tank, and a frame brace. The trunk could be fitted with a spare tire, but you'd best not have brought any suitcases for your "road trip," they wouldn't fit. Yet, the interior was remarkably tidy for a racing car. There were no wires or relays on display in the cockpit, the doors were covered with rudimentary trim, and the gauges even had chrome bezels.

Ferrari, Bizzarrini, and the boys got it right at the very beginning. The one-month-old car took Phil Hill and Olivier Gendebien to first in GT class and second overall in the 1962 running of the 12 Hours of Sebring. That year's Le Mans produced a similar result, and the GTO went on to win the Manufacturer's World Championship in 1962, 1963, and 1964. The five 1964 cars were known as Series II and rode a bit lower than the earlier vehicles.

Weighing only 2,474 pounds, including a full tank of 35.1 gallons of gasoline, the GTO was a very quick car for its day. *Car and Driver* put American racing legend, Dan Gurney, behind the wheel of one in 1984; he produced a 0-60 mph time of 5.8 seconds, and the quarter mile flashed by in 14.4 seconds at 108 mph. Because of the numerically high rear end ratio of 4.25:1 on this particular sample, top speed was limited to *only* 144 mph.

Whether the GTO was ever intended

to be used on the street remains a moot point. It served Ferrari's purpose of winning races when it was new. It also established a cultural icon for the Ferrari shape of the sixties. And it is now one of the most sought after Ferraris on the auction block, with prices frequently exceeding the $6,000,000 mark. This is the car that forced Carroll Shelby to build and refine the Cobra. What more is there to say?

1962-64 Ferrari 250 GTO. (DG)

1962 Ferrari 400 Superamerica. (DG)

1962-64 Ferrari 250 GT Berlinetta Lusso. (DG)

1963

TYPE 250 LM — V-12 — When Ferrari claimed that you could drive his car to the track, win the race, and then drive home again he wasn't far from wrong. The 250LM was clearly a racing car. Luigi Chinetti's North American Racing Team (NART) took first place at the 1965 24 Hours of Le Mans with their customer 275 LM. (A slightly larger engine version.) This was also Ferrari's first mid-engined roadgoing GT model, and it was derived from the 250P racing prototype that appeared in March 1963. Ferrari wanted to compete in production racing, and the 250 LM was the ace up his sleeve. He wanted to convince the FIA that this sleek, mid-engined car was merely a variation of the 250 GT series. The car was well suited to the task of winning races and with optimum gearing, it could reach speeds of 170 mph and beyond. Scaglietti built most of the bodies as closed coupes, but a few open race roadsters were produced. In all, no more than 40 were built in both the 250 LM and 275 LM configurations, from 1963-65.

1962-1964 Ferrari 250 GT Berlinetta Lusso engine. (MC)

The Colombo-derived V-12 engine sat inches behind the driver's ear. Except for the first example, all were 3.3-liter in size, and produced 320 horsepower. The multi-tube chassis, was almost identically constructed as Ferrari's racecars were. The 250 LM had coil springs with tubular A-arms all around, and a 95-inch wheelbase. Four-wheel disc brakes were installed (inboard at the rear). A multi-disc clutch was mounted on the flywheel between engine and transaxle (later versions put the clutch behind the transaxle, for easier access in the pits). The non-synchro five-speed had all-indirect gearing, which helped allow the engine to be positioned even lower. Pininfarina designed the Berlinetta body, and its windshield and side windows would go on to be used in the Series II 250 GTOs. Both had a "flying buttress" roof, with sloping sail panels alongside a vertical back window. It looked like no other Ferrari, with a low grille below the front-end crease and headlamps behind clear covers. Radiator, oil cooler, and oil reservoir were all in the nose. All 250/275 LMs were right-hand drive, with a bare minimum of passenger space. Still, they came fully equipped for the road, including lights, horn, and even a spare tire strapped above the transaxle. Besides having the nimbleness inherent in a mid-engined design, with weight down to 1874 pounds, the 2.2-liter engine moved the 250 LM along quite briskly.

TYPE 250 GT (SWB) — V-12 — Production of the short-wheelbase 250 GT continued through 1964; see previous listing for details.

TYPE 250 GT 2+2 — V-12 — Production of Ferrari's 2+2 continued with little change; see previous listing for details.

TYPE 330 AMERICA — V-12 — After phase-out of the 250 GT 2+2 in late 1963 came 50 "interim" models with a new Type 209 4.0-liter engine, many displaying an "America" rear nameplate. Those became known as the 330 America.

TYPE 400 SUPERAMERICA — V-12 — In an effort to keep costs down and provide more luxurious accommodations; the luxury/performance Ferrari received a stretch so it could share the 102.5-inch wheelbase of the 2+2 coupe and cabriolet. A reduction in compression to 8:8:1 and the use of three Weber 40 DCL carburetors reduced the horsepower to a more tractable 340. This was considered to be more in keeping with the SA's mission.

I.D. DATA: Not available.

Model	Body Type & Seating	Engine Type/CID	P.O.E. Price	Weight (lbs.)	Prod. Total
TYPE 250 GT					
250 GT SWB	2-dr Coupe-2P	V12/180	12950	2400	Note 1
California	2-dr Conv-2P	V12/180	12950	N/A	Note 1
TYPE 250 GT 2+2					
250 GT	2-dr Coupe-2+2P	V12/180	12900	2820	Note 2
TYPE 250 LM					
250 LM	2-dr Coupe-2P	V12/180	N/A	1874	Note 3
TYPE 400 SUPERAMERICA					
400	2-dr Coupe-2P	V12/242	N/A	2860	Note 4

Note 1: Production of the 250 GT SWB over the full model run (through 1964) included 175 Berlinettas, 57 Spyder Californias, and 350 Berlinetta Lussos.
Note 2: A total of 950 Type 250 GT 2+2s were produced from 1960-63.
Note 3: Approximately 32 Type 250/275 LM racing coupes were produced between 1963-66.
Note 4: As many as 54 Type 400 Superamericas were produced from 1960-64, including six cabrios (in 1960), 29 Series I coupes, and 19 Series II coupes.
Body Style Note: As usual, Ferraris came in a wide variety of body styles, open and closed, from different coachbuilders.
Weight Note: Figures shown are approximate (or averages).

ENGINE [Base V-12 (250 GT)]: 60-degree, single-overhead-cam, "vee" type 12-cylinder (Colombo). Aluminum alloy block and heads. Displacement: 180 cid (2953 cc). Bore & stroke: 2.87 x 2.31 in. (73 x 58.8 mm). Compression ratio: (250 GT 2+2) 8.8:1. Brake horsepower: (250 GT 2+2) 240 at 7000 rpm; (250 GT SWB) 280 at 7000 rpm. Seven main bearings. Three twin-choke Weber carburetors.

ENGINE [Base V-12 (initial 250 LM)]: 60-degree, single-overhead-cam, "vee" type 12-cylinder (Colombo). Aluminum alloy block and heads. Displacement: 180 cid (2953 cc). Bore & stroke: 2.87 x 2.31 in. (73 x 58.8 mm). Compression ratio: 9.7:1. Brake horsepower: 300 at 7500 rpm. Seven main bearings. Six 38 DCN Weber carburetors.

Note: All subsequent 250 LMs had a 3286-cc engine; see next listing.

ENGINE [Base V-12 (330 America)]: 60-degree, single-overhead-cam, "vee" type 12-cylinder. Aluminum alloy block and heads. Displacement: 242 cid (3967 cc). Bore & stroke: 3.03 x 2.80 in. (77 x 71 mm). Compression ratio: 8.8:1. Brake horsepower: 300 at 6000/6600 rpm. Seven main bearings. Three Weber 40 DCZ/6 carburetors.

ENGINE [Base V-12 (400 Superamerica)]: 60-degree, single-overhead-cam, "vee" type 12-cylinder (Colombo). Aluminum alloy block and heads. Displacement: 242 cid (3967 cc). Bore & stroke: 3.03 x 2.80 in. (77 x 71 mm). Compression ratio: 9.8:1/8.8:1. Brake horsepower: 400 at 6750 rpm or 340 at 7000 rpm. Seven main bearings. Three Weber 46DCF carburetors (340 bhp).

CHASSIS: Wheelbase: (250 GT SWB) 94.5 in.; (250 GT 2+2) 102.3 in.; (250 LM) 94.5 in.; (400 Series I) 95.3 in.; (400 Series II/III) 102.3 in. Overall Length: (250 GT SWB) 174 in. average; (250 GT 2+2) 183.6 in. average; (250 LM) 161 in.; (400) 172 in. average. Height: (250 GT SWB) 48 in.; (250 GT 2+2) 55.4 in.; (400) 51.5 in. Width: (250 GT SWB) 64 in.; (250 GT 2+2) 67.3 in.; (400) 66 in. Front Tread: (250 GT SWB) 55 in.; (250 GT 2+2) 53.3 in.; (250 LM) 53.1 in. Rear Tread: (250 GT SWB) 54.5 in.; (250 GT 2+2) 54.9 in.; (250 LM) 52.7 in. Standard Tires: (250 GT SWB) 185x15. Specifications for the 50 330 America's were the same as the 250 GTE 2+2.

TECHNICAL: Layout: front-engine, rear-drive except (250 LM) mid-engine, rear-drive. Transmission: four-speed all-synchro manual (plus overdrive in 250 GT 2+2 and 400 Superamerica) except (250 LM) non-synchro, all-indirect five-speed manual. Steering: worm and peg. Suspension (front): upper/lower A-arms with coil springs. Suspension (rear): rigid axle with parallel trailing arms and semi-elliptic leaf springs except (250 LM) upper/lower A-arms with coil springs. Brakes: front/rear disc. Body Construction: separate body on tubular steel ladder-type frame.

PERFORMANCE: Top Speed: (250 GT) 124-155

mph; (250 LM) 160 mph (factory claimed 183 mph); (400) 140-160+ mph. Acceleration (0-60 mph): (250 GT SWB) about 6.5-7.0 sec.; (250 LM) 6.5 sec. estimated; (250 GT 2+2) 8.0 sec.

ADDITIONAL MODELS: Production of the 250 GTO racing coupe continued until 1964.

Manufacturer: Automobili Ferrari S.p.A. SEFAC, Maranello (Modena), Italy.

Distributor: Luigi Chinetti Motors, New York City.

HISTORY: Ferrari started experimenting with mid-engine racecars in 1960. The 250P used a racing version of the 3.0-liter V-12 with six DCN Weber carburetors from the front-engine Testa Rossa. Its chassis came from V-6/V-8 Dino mid-engine racers. John Surtees soon broke the lap record at Monza driving a 250P. In November 1963, the 250 LM (for Le Mans) closed version appeared at the Paris Salon. The first one came to the U.S. in late 1963, and was raced by the North American Racing Team of Luigi Chinetti (Ferrari's U.S. distributor). After a lack of significant success, it caught fire at Sebring and was destroyed. Later editions fared much better, including the 1965 NART entry driven by Masten Gregory and Jochen Rindt that finished first at Le Mans in 1965.

1963 Ferrari Superfast IV (400 Superamerica 1-off). (WG)

Ferrari 250LM:
The Little Berlinetta That Could ... Win Le Mans

Today we accept the mid-engine car's place at the top of the sportscar pecking order. There was a time when the idea of putting "the cart before the horse" was heresy. Enzo Ferrari used the previous phrase to justify why his cars would continue with the engines in front of the driver. As first Cooper, then Lotus, demonstrated the advantages for a racing car having its engine behind the driver, Ferrari came around to the new order.

There was an experimental V-6-engined Ferrari F-1 car as early as 1960, and Phil Hill won the 1961 World Championship for Drivers in a mid-engined car. It's clear that Ferrari could be taught new tricks. In March of 1963, Ferrari raced the mid-engined 250P and won the 12 hours of Sebring. The car also went on to win the 24 hours of Le Mans that year.

The other force that shaped the subject of this story was the Commission Sportive Internationale (CSI) rules regarding what constitutes a production car. Ferrari successfully argued that the 250 GTO (Grand Tour Omologato) was not a new car, but merely an evolution of his highly successful 250 GT SWB (Short Wheel Base). The CSI's rules called for 100 examples to be manufactured for a variation to be eligible for competition. After Enzo had finished his smoke and mirrors routine, the GTO was eligible to compete against production-based cars, and it cleaned up. This was despite the protests of Ford, Carroll Shelby, and others. Only 39 GTOs were ever produced.

So when Ferrari unveiled his 250 LM Berlinetta, he dutifully submitted it as the next step in the evolution of the GTO. This time the protests were loud enough that the CSI relented, and late in the summer of 1964, they put the little coupe in with the big boys, where it competed against the much larger, and faster prototypes such as the Ford GT40, and Ferrari's own 275P and 330P. Ferrari was so miffed at this turn of events, that when the CSI didn't give him his way, he ran his Formula One cars at the remaining races painted in white and blue. The cars would have been painted red like all Italian racecars wore in those days; instead they wore the livery of Luigi Chinetti's North American Racing Team. In theory this showed his own national automobile club the extent of his displeasure at their failing to help him secure the homologation.

The 250 LM was Ferrari's first "road-going" mid-engine car. While its intent was clearly to win races, it did come equipped with such road equipment as a horn, turn signals, and passenger seat. Inside, the 250 LM offered none of the luxuries you find in the real road-going Ferraris of its day. Few people would enjoy any type of a road trip in a 250 LM. Because the long engine also had a transmission and differential stretched out behind it, the short 94.5-inch wheelbase left little room in the cockpit for its occupants. Their feet were stretched out so far forward that they had to be canted quite acutely inward to clear the wheel arches. Add in the heat created by the plumbing for the front mounted radiators, and you had an environment more like a sauna than a Grand Touring Automobile.

The 250 LM also suffered from another form of identity crises. While the first LM did indeed have 250 ccs per cylinder, resulting in a 2953-cc engine; subsequent examples all carried a 3286-cc V-12, whose individual cylinders were much closer to 275 cc. At the time, folks took to calling the new cars 275 LMs, although Ferrari never officially changed the designation. This was the same engine design that appeared in the soon-to-follow 275 GTB and 275 GTS. Both of these were front-engined cars, so it's clear that Ferrari never intended the 250 LM to be the beginning of his mid-engine conversion.

Perhaps the best success of the 250 LM was the beauty of the Pininfarina lines. The nose contains a wide grille flanked by those obligatory turn signals. (On some cars, these openings were modified for fog lights or front brake ducts.) The headlight covers helped to smooth the flow of air over the shapely fenders. The steeply raked windshield flowed into a roof that terminated in a pair of graceful flying buttresses. The rear fenders rose above the rear deck and tapered to a terminus featuring a small raised lip of a spoiler. Two rear grilles, for exhausting hot air, separated the pair of round taillights, and centered between them was a license plate holder. It even came equipped with tiny chrome lights. A wide grille was set below the "bumper" line and a pair of twin tailpipes completed this classic Pininfarina design.

Quick access for the drivetrain was achieved by lifting the top half of the rear end in one piece. Once the assembly was propped up, the sight that greeted you was enough to set any racing fan's pulse soaring. Working back from the Plexiglas rear window, the long V-12 sat nestled in the center of a steel tubing framework. Behind it, the transaxle stretched out even further. The battery most frequently resided atop the framework that supported the aft end of the lower

bodywork. The 250 LM had four-wheel disc brakes, (another innovation that Enzo was slow to adopt), the rear discs were inboard and snuggled right up against the transmission. Large, hand-formed fuel and oil tanks nearly completed the cramped compartment. The only other item to be squeezed into this tight package was the spare tire that perched atop the transaxle back when Ferrari was still keeping up the charade of the 250 LM as a street car.

There is a happy ending to the little Berlinetta's story—and it came at the 1965 Le Mans. Competition for the pole and overall win was primarily between Ford's GT40 and Ferrari's own P4. Luigi Chinetti's lists of entries included a 250 LM driven by Masten Gregory, and rising Formula One star Jochen Rindt. Gregory was well known for his habit of stepping out of crashing racecars and emerging unscathed. Rindt would become known for being the first (and so far only) posthumous winner of the World Driver's Championship.

The boys' plan was to run the older, slightly heavy coupe as hard as they could, as if they were in a sprint race, instead of one lasting all day and night. Rather than having the car break and getting to go home early, our heroes moved up steadily as the more powerful cars dropped out. When the checkered flag was waved at 4 p.m., the little racing (I mean street) car had collected Ferrari's sixth straight Le Mans victory. It would be the last one for Ferrari while Enzo was alive.

1964 Ferrari 330P. (DG)

TYPE 250 LM/275 LM — V-12 — When a 250 LM entered the Le Mans race in April 1964, it was with a 3286-cc engine rather than the original 2953 cc; the result of a 4 mm bore increase. That accounted for the unofficial name change to 275 LM, yet Ferrari did not use that designation for homologation purposes. During 1964, this car took first and second spots at the 12 Hours of Reins race; second in the Tourist Trophy; first at Elkhart Lake; first at Mont Tremblant; and 1-2 at the Coppa Inter-Europa. It won 10 major races in all, and finished second in six. After 1964, all racing was under private auspices.

TYPE 250 GT (SWB) — V-12 — Production of the short-wheelbase 250 GT halted in 1964.

1964 Ferrari 330P. (DG)

TYPE 275 GTB/GTS — V-12 — The 275 street series represented several milestones for Ferrari. While the 250 LM's mid-engine position was a bit too extreme for street use in the mid-Sixties, Ferrari had the idea of moving the transmission to the back of the car. Combining the transmission and rear axle into a single transaxle gave the 275 Series much better weight distribution. Both the fastback berlinetta coupe (GTB) and the open Spider (GTS) versions were first shown at the Paris Salon in October 1964—their production would continue through 1966. Rather than being a chopped top version of the berlinetta, the 275 GTS used entirely different body panels and had a different mission. The coupe was intended for those Ferrari owners who stressed performance and was a sports/racer. Buyers for the GTS convertible were more impressed by comfort and wanted a car that was suitable for touring. Both vehicles rode on a 94.5-inch wheelbase, continued with Ferrari's tradition of a multi-tube chassis, and carried a Colombo-derived 3286-cc 200.5-cid V-12, as suited their different clientele. That engine produced 260 horsepower in the Spider, or 280 bhp in the berlinetta. If you chose the GTB, your options included three or six Weber carburetors, a race-inspired quick fill gas cap, and Borrani wire wheels. The most rarely chosen option was to distain the steel body (with aluminum hood, doors, and trunk lid) in favor of the lighter one made fully of aluminum. The better to impress your friends and neighbors with your sporty intent. Some consider the 275 GTB to be the most sensuous Ferrari ever to be offered for the road. The 275 may be the epitome of the classic "long hood and short deck" look. Pininfarina designed the coupe bodies, and Scaglietti built them. The GTB evolved from two classic beauties, the 250 GT Berlinetta Lusso, and the 250 GTO. Pininfarina styled the Spider and produced the body, which was evolved from the 330 GT 2+2. Standard Campagnolo alloy disc wheels went on all models, with Borrani wires optional. Initially a thin propeller shaft riding in center bearings transmitted power. The fully independent suspension consisted of unequal-length A-arms and coil springs, front and rear. Disc brakes were installed all around.

At the 1965 Frankfurt show, the Series II GTS lost its chrome headlamp surrounds and left-door vent wing, while adding external trunk hinges and a hood bulge (over the carburetors). Then, at that year's Paris show, the GTB on display had a lower and longer nose and larger back window. Those changes allow division of the Series I and II into "short-nose" and "long-nose" versions.

TYPE 330 GT 2+2 — V-12 — If you are looking for a bargain Ferrari today, the 330 GT 2+2 offers genuine V-12 panache at a surprisingly low price. Replacing the 250 GT 2+2, the new four-passenger coupe evolved from the 330 America. Not everyone attending the January 1964 press conference that announced its birth was impressed by the Pininfarina design, an opinion shared by a number of people once the new model entered the market. Some disliked the bulbous styling, with quad round headlamps in tapered oval housings. Outboard of the wide crosshatch grille were round amber park lights. Examples built from 1965 on wore two headlamps, with modified side vents and a new protruding nose.

Wheelbase was 104.2 inches. Beneath the hood was a 3967-cc 242-cid V-12 engine producing 300 horsepower. A five-speed manual gearbox was standard by 1965, but 1964 models used a four-speed with overdrive. Koni adjustable shocks with concentric coil springs augmented the rear semi-elliptic leafs. Early efforts were made at making Ferraris safer by having separate braking systems for front and rear. Alloy wheels became standard in 1965, with center-lock Borrani wires optional at extra cost (instead of standard as in early models). About 1,080 were produced over the full model run through 1968, in addition to the 50 Type 330 GTE Americas built in 1963.

TYPE 400 SUPERAMERICA — V-12 — Production of this model, introduced in 1960, continued into 1966; see previous listings for details.

TYPE 500 SUPERFAST — V-12 — Similar to the 400 Superamerica, the new Superfast (which evolved from the Superfast II show car seen at the Turin event in 1960) was longer and heavier than the 400, with a bigger and more powerful engine. Wheelbase was 104.3 inches; overall length around 190 inches. Power came from a 4962-cc (303-cid) V-12, producing 400 horsepower. Bore and stroke were identical to the 410 Superamerica. The rather unique engine was a long-block like the Lampredi, but had removable heads (like the Colombo design) with pressed-in cylinder liners. Dunlop disc brakes went on all four wheels. Appearance was similar to the 400, but with exposed headlamps and a squared-off tail (Kamm-style). Bodies were built by Pininfarina. Borrani wire wheels held 205/15 tires. A total of about 37 were built, in Series I and II, through early 1967.

Note: Some directories continued to list the 250 GT 2+2 coupe, though production ceased after 1963; see previous listing for details.

I.D. DATA: Not available.

Model	Body Type & Seating	Engine Type/CID	P.O.E. Price	Weight (lbs.)	Prod. Total
TYPE 250 GT					
250 GT SWB	2-dr Coupe-2P	V12/180	12950	2540	Note 1
TYPE 250 LM (275 LM)					
250 LM	2-dr Coupe-2P	V12/200	N/A	1874	Note 2
275 GTB/GTS					
275 GTB	2-dr Coupe-2P	V12/200	13900	2550	Note 3
275 GTS	2-dr Conv Cpe-2P	V12/200	14500	2750	Note 4
330 GT 2+2					
330 GT	2-dr Coupe-2+2P	V12/242	14200	3040	Note 5
TYPE 400 SUPERAMERICA					
400	2-dr Coupe-2P	V12/242	17800	2860	Note 6
TYPE 500 SUPERFAST					
500	2-dr Coupe-2P	V12/303	24400	3200	Note 7

Note 1: Production of the 250 GT SWB over the full model run (through 1964) included 175 Berlinettas, 57 Spyder Californias, and 350 Berlinetta Lussos.

Between 35 and 40 Type 250/275 LM racing coupes were produced in 1963-65.
Note 3: About 453 Type 275 GTB coupes were produced in all (253 Series I and 200 Series II), from 1964-66.
Note 4: About 200 Type 275 GTS convertibles were produced through 1966.
Note 5: About 1,080 Type 330 GT 2+2s were produced from 1964-68.
Note 6: As many as 34 Type 400 Superamericas were produced from 1960-64, including 10 cabrios (in 1960), 20 Series I coupes, and 4 Series II coupes.
Note 7: About 36 Type 500 Superfast coupes (24 Series I and 12 Series II) were produced from 1964-67.
Body Style Note: As usual, Ferraris came in a variety of body styles, open and closed, from different coachbuilders.
Weight Note: Figures shown are approximate (or averages).

ENGINE [Base V-12 (250 GT)]:
60-degree, single-overhead-cam, "vee" type 12-cylinder (Colombo). Aluminum alloy block and heads. Displacement: 180 cid (2953 cc). Bore & stroke: 2.87 x 2.31 in. (73 x 58.8 mm). Compression ratio: 9.2:1. Brake horsepower: 280 at 7000 rpm. Seven main bearings. Three twin-choke Weber carburetors.

ENGINE [Base V-12 (250/275 LM)]:
60-degree, single-overhead-cam, "vee" type 12-cylinder. Aluminum alloy block and heads. Displacement: 200.5 cid (3286 cc). Bore & stroke: 3.03 x 2.31 in. (77 x 58.8 mm). Compression ratio: 9.7:1. Brake horsepower: 320-330 at 7000-7500 rpm. Seven main bearings. Six 38 DCN Weber carburetors.

ENGINE [Base V-12 (275 GTB/GTS)]:
60-degree, single-overhead-cam, "vee" type 12-cylinder. Aluminum alloy block and heads. Displacement: 200.5 cid (3286 cc). Bore & stroke: 3.03 x 2.31 in. (77 x 58.8 mm). Compression ratio: 9.2:1. Brake horsepower: (GTS) 260 at 7000/7500 rpm; (GTB) 280 at 7000/7500 rpm. Seven main bearings. Three Weber 40 DCZ/6 carburetors (six-carb setup available).

ENGINE [Base V-12 (330 GT 2+2)]:
60-degree, single-overhead-cam, "vee" type 12-cylinder. Aluminum alloy block and heads. Displacement: 242 cid (3967 cc). Bore & stroke: 3.03 x 2.80 in. (77 x 71 mm). Compression ratio: 8.8:1. Brake horsepower: 300 at 6000/6600 rpm. Seven main bearings. Three Weber 40 DCZ/6 carburetors.

ENGINE [Base V-12 (400 Superamerica)]:
60-degree, single-overhead-cam, "vee" type 12-cylinder (Colombo). Aluminum alloy block and heads. Displacement: 242 cid (3967 cc). Bore & stroke: 3.03 x 2.80 in. (77 x 71 mm). Compression ratio: 8.8:1. Brake horsepower: 340 at 7000 rpm. Seven main bearings. Three Weber 46 DCF carburetors.

ENGINE [Base V-12 (500 Superfast)]:
60-degree, single-overhead-cam, "vee" type 12-cylinder. Aluminum alloy block and heads. Displacement: 302.7 cid (4962 cc). Bore & stroke: 3.46 x 2.68 in. (88 x 68 mm). Compression ratio: 8.8:1. Brake horsepower: 400 at 6500 rpm. Seven main bearings. Three Weber 40 DCZ/6 carburetors.

1965-1967 Ferrari 330 GT 2+2 Series II. (MC)

CHASSIS: Wheelbase: (250 GT SWB) 94.5 in.; (250/275 LM) 94.5 in.; (275 GTB/GTS) 94.5 in.; (330 GT 2+2) 104.2 in.; (400 Series II/III) 102.3 in.; (500) 104.3 in. Overall Length: (250 GT SWB) 174 in. average; (250/275 LM) 161 in.; (275 GTB/GTS) 171.3 in.; (330 GT 2+2) 189.4-190.5 in.; (400) 172 in.; (500) 190-194 in. Height: (250 GT SWB) 48 in.; (275 GTB) 49 in.; (275 GTS) 51.5 in.; (330 GT 2+2) 53 in.; (400) 51.5 in.; (500) 52.4 in. Width: (250 GT SWB) 64 in.; (275 GTB) 67 in.; (275 GTS) 66 in.; (330 GT 2+2) 70.5 in.; (400) 66 in.; (500) 71 in. Front Tread: (250 GT) 55 in.; (250/275 LM) 53.1 in.; (275 GTB/GTS) 54.2 in.; (330 GT 2+2) 55.2 in.; (500) 55 in. Rear Tread: (250 GT) 54.5 in.; (250/275 LM) 52.7 in.; (275 GTB/GTS) 54.8 in.; (330 GT 2+2) 54.7 in.; (500) 54.5 in. Standard Tires: (250 GT) 185x15; (275 GTB) 205x14; (275 GTS) 195x14; (500) 205x15.

TECHNICAL: Layout: front-engine, rear-drive except (250/275 LM) mid-engine, rear-drive. Transmission: four-speed all-synchro manual (plus overdrive in 250 GT 2+2 and 400 Superamerica) except (250/275 LM) non-synchro, all-indirect five-speed manual; (275 GTB/GTS) five-speed manual rear transaxle; (330 GT 2+2) four-speed w/overdrive or five-speed. Steering: worm and roller. Suspension (front): upper/lower A-arms with coil springs. Suspension (rear): rigid axle with parallel trailing arms and semi-elliptic leaf springs except (250/275 LM, 275 GTB/GTS) upper/lower A-arms with coil springs. Brakes: front/rear disc. Body Construction:

separate body on tubular steel ladder-type frame. Fuel Tank: (275 GTB) 21.4 gal.; (330 GT) 19.8 gal.

PERFORMANCE: Top Speed: (250 GT) 124-155 mph; (250 LM) 160 mph typical (137-183 mph); (275 GTB) 148 mph; (275 GTS) 143 mph; (330 GT 2+2) 115-125 mph; (400) 140-160+ mph. Acceleration (0-60 mph): (250 GT SWB) about 6.5-7.0 sec.; (250/275 LM) 6.5 sec. estimated; (275 GTB) 7.5 sec. or less.

Manufacturer: Automobili Ferrari S.p.A. SEFAC, Maranello (Modena), Italy.

Distributor: Luigi Chinetti Motors, New York City.

HISTORY: Development of the 500 Superfast began with a series of show cars. Following the Superfast II show car of 1960, a Superfast III had appeared at the March 1962 Geneva Salon. That one wore slimmer roof pillars, and had a thermostatically-controlled radiator cover, hidden headlamps, and partial rear skirts. Then came Superfast IV, with the same look but sporting four exposed headlamps. That model would later be sold in the U.S. Late in 1962 came the production Series II Superamerica on a 102.3-inch wheelbase, lacking the former hood scoop but showing a bulge over the carburetors. That led to the 500 Superfast, seen at Geneva in March 1964.

1964 Ferrari Type 500 Superfast. (DA)

1965 Ferrari Type 275 GTB/C. (DA)

1965 Ferrari Type 275 GTB/C. (DA)

Ferrari's Three Seater: An Automotive Fantasy Realized

c.1965 Ferrari 365P 3-seat prototype. (DG)

Soon after the 365 P *Berlinetta Speciale* made its debut at the 1966 Paris Salon, *Road & Track* spoke to many men's fantasy. The cartoon showed a distinguished gentleman seated in the center driver's seat while a blonde and a redhead scrapped on the side of the road. I prefer the image of its current owner, the urbane Luigi Chinetti Jr., arriving at a Concours with two beautiful women seated happily on either side.

Today a factory Ferrari racing car typically commands in excess of a million dollars. But, in the mid-Sixties, last season's racers were more frequently relegated to the scrap pile than turned into cash. The 1965 P2 racing car, chassis # 8971, was granted a kinder fate.

It is reported that the white three-seater is the first car that young Sergio penned on his own, when he started working for his father, Giovanni Batista at *Pininfarina Carrozzeria*. Gianni Agnelli, President of Fiat, received a second

Berlinetta Speciale; the silver car sported a jaunty rear spoiler.

After debuting in Paris, the car traveled to Earl's Court in London, then jumped across the pond to wow the crowds at the Los Angeles, San Francisco and New York shows. For several decades, this Ferrari was the centerpiece of the Luigi Chinetti Motors showroom. Can you imagine the delight of a young pilgrim venturing into the hallowed ground of Luigi's Greenwich, CT showroom? Not only did a ring of glamorous powerplants encircle the display area, but spotlighted among the Ferrari F1s and other exotica was a car whose very layout defied convention. With the driver positioned in the middle of the car, its mid-engined nimbleness could be experienced to the fullest. Truly this was the stuff of adolescent dreams!

For this application the 4.4-liter engine #217P is detuned. Three Weber carburetors flow *benzene* to the V-12, instead of the original half dozen. Twin distributors fire only one spark plug per cylinder, but the hand-welded oil tanks speak of the engine's dry sump racing heritage. The transaxle stretches out behind the engine for easy access in the pits, or to make the onlookers swoon when the long trunk lid is raised.

It's easier to enter from the left side door, the better to avoid entanglement with the chrome shift lever sprouting out of the floor by the driver's right knee. The initial impression is one of astonishingly good visibility; perhaps the best of any mid-engine car. A fixed glass sunroof combined with three windows on each side, and a wraparound rear window allows the interior to be flooded with natural light.

All the better to see the 8,000-rpm tachometer and the 300-kph speedometer nestled into pods smack dab in the center of the dash. The speedometer also contains the oil pressure gauge and shows less than 8,000 kilometers to date. The tachometer is redlined at 7,000 rpm and includes water and oil temperature gauges in its bottom quadrant. For a 37-year old show car the interior is remarkably well finished. A swath of leather starts at the belt line and is set off by a wide band of chrome beneath it.

The *Speciale* utilizes the typical Ferrari starting drill. After you turn the ignition key to on, you wait until the clicking of the electric fuel pumps has slowed, indicating that the fuel system is now pressurized. Pump the gas pedal a couple of times, engage the starter and be prepared for the "WHAMP" the heralds the symphony that is a Ferrari engine. It takes a while to get used to the

c.1965 Ferrari 365P 3-seat prototype. (DG)

center seating position. Surprisingly it is the right fender placement that makes the novice driver most nervous. The impression from the smooth, powerful engine overwhelms any misgivings that the vintage steering and chassis might cause.

The *Berlinetta Speciale's* current caretaker, Wayne Carini of Carini Carrozzeria, related his favorite memory of the car. At the 2001 Concours Italiano, Luigi Chinetti Jr. drove the car to the podium flanked by Piero Ferrari and Sergio Pininfarina. Here were the offspring of the gusty racer who imported all the original Ferraris into the US, the son of Enzo, and the progeny of the man responsible for some of the best designs ever to grace a Ferrari chassis. As Sergio explained how the *Berlinetta Speciale* foreshadowed cars such as the 246 Dino you could feel the shiver of electricity run through the crowd. What better conveyance for the triumvirate sons of Ferrari?

c.1965 Ferrari 365P 3-seat prototype. (DG)

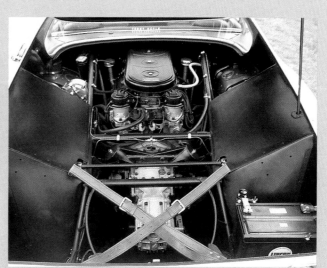
c.1965 Ferrari 365P engine. (DG)

1966-70 Ferrari 330 GTC. (DG)

1966

TYPE 275 GTB/GTS — V-12 — While many Ferraris received minor updates throughout their production runs, the 275 Series had a somewhat major change, despite it not being visible from above. After the January 1966 Brussels show, a closed torque tube replaced the original open driveshaft. This was considered to be a more reliable method of transmitting power from the engine to the transaxle. With its more powerful engine, the berlinetta coupe could exceed 167 mph, while the Spider convertible was capable of speeds beyond 149 mph. (As always, speeds varied with axle gearing.) Coupes had light cast alloy wheels, while convertibles wore wire wheels with alloy rims. In autumn 1966, a twin-cam head was added to the 275's engine, turning it into the 275 GTB/4 (below).

Meanwhile, a special competition 275 GTB/C berlinetta, introduced in spring 1966, had a lightweight aluminum body, Plexiglas windows, dry-sump lubrication, plus special camshafts, carburetors, pistons, and valves. Because only 12 were manufactured, this is one of the most coveted examples of Ferrari's 1960s engineering.

TYPE 275 GTB/4 — V-12 — With the addition of new twin-cam cylinder heads to the 3.3-liter 275 GTB engine in late 1966, the model received a new designation, the GTB/4 that was rated at 300 horsepower (DIN). Introduced at the Paris show that year, the GTB/4 berlinetta coupe became the first roadgoing Ferrari with a dual-overhead-camshaft engine. Appearance was similar to the basic 275 series. Whereas the basic GTB had a thin "rope drive" propeller shaft, the GTB/4 put the engine, propeller shaft cover, transmission, and differential into a single bolted-together unit. The GTB/4 was capable of 155 mph speeds, and approximately 330 were produced. Luigi Chinetti dreamed of combining the 275 GTB/4's performance with the GTS's top-down motoring capabilities, and the result was ten 275 GTS/4

Background: 1966 Ferrari GTC. Foreground: 1966 Ferrari GTS. (DG)

NART Spyder convertibles built in 1967. The first to be produced (#9437) was cream in color and used to great effect by Steve McQueen in *The Thomas Crown Affair* film. All of the open models were sold in the U.S.

TYPE 330 GT 2+2 — V-12 —

The two-headlight Series II 330 GT 2+2s have fared much better in the modern market place. Although their specifications are not substantially different, they command a stiff premium over the quad headlight model. A five-speed gearbox had replaced the early four-speed (with overdrive) in 1965, matching other Ferrari models. Otherwise, the four-place Ferrari coupe continued with little change. Top speed of the Pininfarina-styled coupe was advertised as 152.2 mph.

TYPE 330 GTC/GTS — V-12 —

Those hoping for a dramatic revolution in the next Ferrari model were in for a disappointment. Except for a larger engine, the new 330 coupe and convertible were very similar to the 275 series. The Pininfarina designed coupe body was more subdued, less rakish than the 275 GTB that it replaced. The 330 GTC mixed the 275 GTS tail with a front end similar to the 400 Superamerica. It was essentially a blend of 275 GTB chassis and 330 GT 2+2 engine. The classic "eggcrate" grille stood at the end of a pointed, tapered snout, with twin bumperettes alongside the grille. Exposed headlamps sat above small lower nacelles. Horizontal ribs went on sail panels, and vent wings were installed. Three air-intake slots sat on the rear of front fenders, behind the tops of front wheels. Identifying model script was evident on the rear deck, and a Ferrari insignia was ahead of the hood.

Debuting at the Geneva show in March 1966, the 330 GTC (Gran Turismo Coupe) had a front-mounted 3967-cc V-12 engine that was rated at 300 horsepower at 7000 rpm and used a five-speed rear transaxle. All-independent suspension and all-disc brakes kept the 330 GTC at the forefront of automotive design. The wheelbase was 94.5 inches, and the car measured 173.2 inches overall. As on late examples of the 275 GTB, the driveshaft passed through a torque tube. Air conditioning was optional. A 330 GTS convertible joined the coupe at the October 1966 Paris show. With a top speed claimed to be 150 mph, the 330 GTC could accelerate to 60 mph in about seven seconds and run the quarter-mile in under 15 seconds. Options included a hardtop for the convertible and Campagnolo alloy wheels.

TYPE 400 SUPERAMERICA — V-12 —

This would be the final year for the 400.

TYPE 500 SUPERFAST — V-12 —

Also in its final season, the Series II Superfast switched to a five-speed gearbox and had suspended pedals and new engine mounts. As for appearance, a trio of air outlets replaced the 11 small cowl louvers found on Series I models. Advertised top speed of the Pininfarina-styled coupe was 173.9 mph, and it was reported to hit 104 mph in second gear.

I.D. DATA: Not available.

Model	Body Type & Seating	Engine Type/CID	P.O.E. Price	Weight (lbs.)	Prod. Total
275 GTB/GTS					
275 GTB	2-dr Coupe-2P	V12/200	13900	2425	Note 1
275 GTS	2-dr Conv Cpe-2P	V12/200	14500	2536	Note 2
275 GTB/4	2-dr Coupe-2P	V12/200	15700	2300	Note 3
330 GT 2+2					
330 GT	2-dr Coupe-2+2P	V12/242	14200	3040	Note 4
330 GTC/GTS					
330 GTC	2-dr Coupe-2P	V12/242	17100	2866	Note 5
330 GTS	2-dr Conv Cpe-2P	V12/242	N/A	3250	Note 6
TYPE 400 SUPERAMERICA					
400	2-dr Coupe-2P	V12/242	N/A	2860	Note 7
TYPE 500 SUPERFAST					
500	2-dr Coupe-2P	V12/303	29300	3087	Note 8

Note 1: About 453 Type 275 GTB coupes were produced in all (253 Series I and 200 Series II) from 1964-67.

Note 2: About 200 Type 275 GTS convertibles were produced from 1964-66.

Note 3: About 330 Type 275 GTB/4 coupes were produced in 1966-68 (plus 10 special NART Spyder convertibles).

Note 4: About 1,080 Type 330 GT 2+2s were produced from 1964-68.

Note 5: About 600 Type 330 GTC coupes were produced from 1966-68.

Note 6: About 99 Type 330 GTS convertibles were produced from 1966-68.

Note 7: As many as 34 Type 400 Superamericas were produced from 1960-64, including 10 cabrios (in 1960), 20 Series I coupes, and 4 Series II coupes.

Note 8: About 36 Type 500 Superfast coupes (24 Series I and 12 Series II) were produced from 1964-67.

Body Style Note: As usual, Ferraris came in a variety of body styles, open and closed, from different coachbuilders.

Price Note: The 500 Superfast was listed for as little as $24,400 in the U.S.

Weight Note: Figures shown are approximate (or averages).

Production Note: A total of 700 Ferraris were built in 1966.

ENGINE [Base V-12 (275 GTB/GTS)]:

60-degree, single-overhead-cam, "vee" type 12-cylinder. Aluminum alloy block and heads. Displacement: 200.5 cid (3286 cc). Bore & stroke: 3.03 x 2.31 in. (77 x 58.8 mm). Compression ratio: 9.2:1. Brake horsepower: (GTS) 260 DIN at 7600 rpm (280 SAE at 7500 rpm); (GTB) 280 DIN (310 SAE) at 7500 rpm. Torque: 217 lbs.-ft. at 5000 rpm. Seven main bearings. Three Weber 40 DCZ/6 carburetors (six-carb setup available in 320-bhp competition engine).

ENGINE [Base V-12 (275 GTB/4)]:

60-degree, dual-overhead-cam, "vee" type 12-cylinder. Aluminum alloy block and heads. Displacement: 200.5 cid (3286 cc). Bore & stroke: 3.03 x 2.31 in. (77 x 58.8 mm). Compression ratio: 9.2:1. Brake horsepower: 300 at 8000 rpm. Seven main bearings. Six Weber 40 DCN 17 carburetors.

ENGINE [Base V-12 (330 GT 2+2)]:

60-degree, single-overhead-cam, "vee" type 12-cylinder. Aluminum alloy block and heads. Displacement: 242 cid (3967 cc). Bore & stroke: 3.03 x 2.80 in. (77 x 71 mm). Compression ratio: 8.8:1. Brake horsepower: 300 at 6600/7000 rpm. Torque: 288 lbs.-ft. (241 DIN) at 5000 rpm. Seven main bearings. Three Weber 40 DCZ/6 carburetors.

ENGINE [Base V-12 (330 GTC/GTS)]:

60-degree, single-overhead-cam, "vee" type 12-cylinder (Colombo). Aluminum alloy block and heads. Displacement: 242 cid (3967 cc). Bore & stroke: 3.03 x 2.80 in. (77 x 71 mm). Compression ratio: 8.8:1. Brake

1966-1967 Ferrari 330P3/4 out in the rain at a recent Mille Miglia. (DG)

horsepower: 300 at 7000 rpm. Seven main bearings. Three Weber two-barrel carburetors.

ENGINE [Base V-12 (400 Superamerica)]:
60-degree, single-overhead-cam, "vee" type 12-cylinder (Colombo). Aluminum alloy block and heads. Displacement: 242 cid (3967 cc). Bore & stroke: 3.03 x 2.80 in. (77 x 71 mm). Compression ratio: 8.8:1. Brake horsepower: 340 at 7000 rpm. Seven main bearings.

ENGINE [Base V-12 (500 Superfast)]: 60-degree, single-overhead-cam, "vee" type 12-cylinder. Aluminum alloy block and heads. Displacement: 302.7 cid (4962 cc). Bore & stroke: 3.46 x 2.68 in. (88 x 68 mm). Compression ratio: 8.8:1. Brake horsepower: 400 (DIN) at 6500 rpm. Torque: 351 lbs.-ft. (DIN) at 4750 rpm. Seven main bearings. Six Weber 40 DCZ/6 two-barrel carburetors.

CHASSIS: Wheelbase: (275 GTB/GTS) 94.5 in.; (330 GT 2+2) 104.2 in.; (330 GTC/GTS) 94.5 in.; (400 Series II/III) 102.3 in.; (500) 104.3 in. Overall Length: (275 GTB) 170.3 in.; (275 GTS) 171.3 in.; (330 GT 2+2) 189.4-190.5 in.; (330 GTC/GTS) 173.2 in.; (400) 172 in.; (500) 189.8 in. Height: (275 GTB) 49 in.; (275 GTS) 49.2

in.; (330 GT 2+2) 53.5 in.; (330 GTC) 51.2 in.; (330 GTS) 49.2 in.; (400) 51.5 in.; (500) 50.4 in. Width: (275 GTB) 67.9 in.; (275 GTS) 65.9 in.; (330 GT 2+2) 69 in.; (330 GTC) 65.75 in.; (330 GTS) 65.9 in.; (400) 66 in.; (500) 70.1 in. Front Tread: (275 GTB/GTS) 54.3 in.; (275 GTB/4) 55.2 in.; (330 GT 2+2) 55 in.; (330 GTC/GTS) 55.2 in.; (500) 55 in. Rear Tread: (275 GTB/GTS) 54.7 in.; (275 GTB/4) 55.8 in.; (330 GT 2+2) 54.7 in.; (330 GTC/GTS) 55.8 in.; (500) 54.7 in. Standard Tires: (275 GTB) 205x14; (275 GTS) 185x14; (330 GT 2+2) 205x15; (330 GTC/GTS) 205x14; (500) 205x15.

TECHNICAL: Layout: front-engine, rear-drive. Transmission: (400) four-speed all-synchro manual plus overdrive; (330 GT 2+2, 500) five-speed manual; (275 GTB/GTS, 330 GTC/GTS) five-speed manual in rear transaxle. Standard Final Drive Ratio: (275 GTB) 3.30:1 or 3.555:1; (330 GT 2+2) 4.25:1; (500) 3.778:1. Steering: worm and roller. Suspension (front): upper/lower A-arms with coil springs. Suspension (rear): (330 GT 2+2, 400, 500) rigid axle with parallel trailing arms and semi-elliptic leaf springs; (275 GTB/GTS, 330 GTC/GTS) upper/lower A-arms with coil springs. Brakes: front/rear disc. Body Construction: separate body on tubular steel ladder-type frame.

MAJOR OPTIONS: Limited-slip differential. Competition engine (275 GTB). 195x14 tires (275 GTB). Various gearbox ratios (275 series).

PERFORMANCE: Top Speed: (275 GTB) 152 mph; (275 GTS) about 144 mph; (275 GTB/4) 155 mph; (330 GT 2+2) as much as 151 mph; (330 GTC) 145-150 mph; (400) 140-160+ mph; (500) up to 174 mph. Acceleration (0-60 mph): (275 GTB) 5.9-7.5 sec.; (275 GTS) 6.5 sec.; (330 GTC) 7.0 sec.; (330 GT 2+2) 6.8 sec. Acceleration (quarter-mile): (275 GTS) 14.0 sec. (95 mph); (330 GTC) 14.6-14.9 sec. (about 95 mph); (330 GT 2+2) 16.0 sec. (102 mph).

Manufacturer: Automobili Ferrari S.p.A. SEFAC, Maranello (Modena), Italy.

Distributor: Luigi Chinetti Motors, New York City.

HISTORY: Paul Frere, writing about the 330 GTC in *The Motor* (Britain) in 1966, was most surprised by "the silence of the engine," though its handling was unchanged, as "close to being as neutral as one could want." Frere was pleased by "the solidness with which it changes direction, particularly in S-bends, where it tracks with about the same precision as a modern race car."

1966-67 Ferrari 275 GTB/4. (DG)

1964-1966 Ferrari 275 GTS. (MC)

1967 Ferrari Type 275/GTS N.A.R.T. Spyder. (DA)

DINO 206 GT — V-6 — The Dino was Ferrari's first attempt at introducing a secondary marque, since the Dino carried no Ferrari name or prancing-horse insignia on its body. The all-alloy engine was built by Fiat, and the Dino (named for Enzo Ferrari's deceased son) was put into production automobiles to make it eligible for Formula Two racing. The Dino nameplate first appeared at the 1965 Paris Salon on the Dino 206S Speciale coupe. It carried avant-garde styling by Pininfarina and sported a mid-engine twin-cam, 2.0-liter V-6. That showcar's Ferrari-designed engine was nonfunctional. A second Dino prototype, the Dino Berlinetta GT was displayed at the 1966 Turin show. The production version was introduced at the next year's Turin event and would carry the first transverse-mounted mid-engine offered by Ferrari.

Anyone in doubt about the car's origin had only to listen to the V-6's exhaust snarl to be convinced that this was

indeed a Ferrari. The low, curvaceous body, built by Scaglietti to Pininfarina specifications, had its headlamps deeply set back into front-fender nacelles, with a tiny grille opening in the short, sloping, and protruding nose. Alongside the grille were long wraparound bumperettes. Most examples had covered headlamps. A bulged look was evident above front wheels; and to some extent, at the rears as well. A trio of small slots sat on each side of the hood, near the front. An upright back window stood between twin "flying buttress" roof extensions. Front vent wings and trapezoidal rear quarter windows were installed. Wheelbase was 90 inches, and the Dino measured 165 inches long. With its race-inspired 1987-cc V-6 rated 180 horsepower (DIN), a Dino was capable of 140 mph. The five-speed gearbox was mounted in the rear transaxle. Produced until late 1969 in this original form, most Dinos were sold in Europe.

TYPE 275 GTB/4 and GTS/4 NART — V-12 — Production of the twin-cam 3286-cc coupe and convertible continued with little change, into 1968.

TYPE 330 GT 2+2 — V-12 — Ferrari's 2+2 coupe continued with little change, but was soon to be replaced by the new 365 GT 2+2.

TYPE 330 GTC/GTS — V-12 — Introduced a year earlier, the 3967-cc coupe and convertible continued with little change into 1970.

TYPE 365 GT 2+2 — V-12 — Replacing the 330 GT 2+2, the larger-engined fastback coupe appeared at the 1967 Paris Salon, ready to become Ferrari's biggest and poshest model yet. Riding a 104.2-inch wheelbase, the Superfast-style coupe penned by Pininfarina, measured 196 inches long and weighed close to two tons at the curb. The low, rounded nose displayed an elliptical eggcrate-patterned grille (similar to that of the 330 GTC), with headlamps in lower nacelles. Parking lights were built into bumperettes, and a Ferrari emblem graced the nose of the hood. European models had clear plastic headlamp covers contoured to fender shape. "Ferrari" lettering went on the decklid. Slim "A" and "B" pillars, large tapered rear quarter windows, front vent wings, and flush door handles helped complete the car's look. A Kamm-type tail contained three round tail lamps in each housing on the rear panel.

Optional Borrani wires could replace standard Cromodora alloy disc wheels, and starting in 1968 the five-spoke wheels from the Daytona would become standard. Other standard equipment included power brakes/steering, power windows, air conditioning, pleated leather upholstery, full carpeting, and a radio. Needle-type gauges sat ahead of the driver, with controls in a center console. As usual, this Ferrari rode a multi-tube steel frame, and had all-independent suspension. Self-leveling rear suspension, a "first" for the marque, had been developed in concert with Koni. The 4390-cc Colombo-derived V-12 developed 320 hp (DIN) using three downdraft carburetors, driving a five-speed gearbox. A 365 GT 2+2 could accelerate to 60 mph in just over seven seconds. Production continued into 1971, with about 800 built in all. During its three-year life, this model accounted for half of Ferrari production.

I.D. DATA: Not available.

Model	Body Type & Seating	Engine Type/CID	P.O.E. Price	Weight (lbs.)	Prod. Total
206 DINO GT					
206 Dino	2-dr Coupe-2P	V6/121	N/A	1980	Note 1
275 GTB/4					
275 GTB/4	2-dr Coupe-2P	V12/200	N/A	2425	Note 2
330 GT 2+2					
330 GT	2-dr Coupe-2+2P	V12/242	14200	3040	Note 3
330 GTC/GTS					
330 GTC	2-dr Coupe-2P	V12/242	14200	2867	Note 4
330 GTS	2-dr Conv Cpe-2P	V12/242	14200	2640	Note 5
365 GT 2+2					
365 GT	2-dr Coupe-2+2P	V12/268	N/A	3236	Note 6

1967 Ferrari Type 275/GTS N.A.R.T. Spyder. (DA)

1966-67 Ferrari 275 GTB/4. (DG)

Note 1: As many as 153 Type 206 Dino GT coupes were produced from 1967-69.
Note 2: About 330 Type 275 GTB/4 coupes were produced in 1966-68 (plus 10 special NART Spyder convertibles).
Note 3: About 1,080 Type 330 GT 2+2s were produced from 1964-68.
Note 4: About 600 Type 330 GTC coupes were produced from 1966-68.
Note 5: About 99 Type 330 GTS convertibles were produced from 1966-68.
Note 6: About 801 Type 365 GT 2+2 coupes were produced from 1968-71.
Weight Note: Figures shown are approximate (or averages).
Production Note: A total of 706 Ferraris were built in 1967.

ENGINE [Base V-6 (206 Dino GT)]: 65-degree, dual-overhead-cam, "vee" type six-cylinder. Aluminum alloy block and heads. Displacement: 121 cid (1987 cc). Bore & stroke: 3.39 x 2.24 in. (86 x 57 mm). Compression ratio: 9.7:1. Brake horsepower: 180 (DIN) at 8000 rpm. Torque: 138 lbs.-ft. (DIN) at 6500 rpm. Four main bearings. Three Weber two-barrel carburetors.

ENGINE [Base V-12 (275 GTB/4)]: 60-degree, dual-overhead-cam, "vee" type 12-cylinder. Aluminum alloy block and heads. Displacement: 200.5 cid (3286 cc). Bore & stroke: 3.03 x 2.31 in. (77 x 58.8 mm). Compression ratio: 9.2:1. Brake horsepower: 300

at 8000 rpm. Seven main bearings. Six Weber two-barrel carburetors.

ENGINE [Base V-12 (330 GT 2+2, 330 GTC/GTS)]: 60-degree, single-overhead-cam, "vee" type 12-cylinder. Aluminum alloy block and heads. Displacement: 242 cid (3967 cc). Bore & stroke: 3.03 x 2.80 in. (77 x 71 mm). Compression ratio: 8.8:1. Brake horsepower: 300 DIN (345 SAE) at 7000 rpm. Seven main bearings. Three Weber two-barrel carburetors.

ENGINE [Base V-12 (365 GT 2+2)]: 60-degree, single-overhead-cam, "vee" type 12-cylinder (Colombo). Aluminum alloy block and heads. Displacement: 268 cid (4390 cc). Bore & stroke: 3.19 x 2.80 in. (81 x 71 mm). Compression ratio: 8.8:1. Brake horsepower: 320 at 6600 rpm. Seven main bearings. Three Weber carburetors.

CHASSIS: Wheelbase: (206 Dino GT) 90.0 in.; (275 GTB/4) 94.5 in.; (330 GT 2+2) 104.2 in.; (330 GTC/GTS)

94.5 in.; (365 GT 2+2) 104.2 in. Overall Length: (206 Dino GT) 165 in.; (275 GTB/4) 173.6 in.; (330 GT 2+2) 189.4 in.; (330 GTC/GTS) 173.2 in.; (365 GT 2+2) 196 in. Height: (206 Dino GT) 43.9 in.; (275 GTB/4) 50.8 in.; (330 GT 2+2) 52 in.; (330 GTC) 51.2 in.; (330 GTS) 49.2 in.; (365 GT 2+2) 53 in. Width: (206 Dino GT) 66.9 in.; (275 GTB/4) 68.9 in.; (330 GT 2+2) 69 in.; (330 GTC) 65.75 in.; (330 GTS) 65.9 in.; (365 GT 2+2) 70.5 in. Front Tread: (206 Dino GT) 56.1 in.; (275 GTB/4) 55.2 in.; (330 GT 2+2) 55.3 in.; (330 GTC/GTS) 55.2 in.; (365 GT 2+2) 56.6 in. Rear Tread: (206 Dino GT) 55.1 in.; (275 GTB/4) 55.8 in.; (330 GT 2+2) 55.0 in.; (330 GTC/GTS) 55.8 in.; (365 GT 2+2) 57.8 in. Standard Tires: (206 Dino GT) 185x14; (275 GTB/4) 205x14; (330 GT 2+2) 205x15; (330 GTC/GTS) 205x14; (365 GT 2+2) 205x15.

TECHNICAL: Layout: front-engine, rear-drive except (Dino) mid-engine, rear-drive. Transmission: (330 GT 2+2) five-speed manual; (206 Dino GT, 275 GTB/4, 330 GTC/GTS, 365 GT 2+2) five-speed manual in rear transaxle. Steering: worm and roller. Suspension (front): upper/lower A-arms with coil springs. Suspension (rear): (330 GT 2+2) rigid axle with parallel trailing arms and semi-elliptic leaf springs; (206 Dino GT, 275 GTB/4, 330 GTC/GTS, 365 GT 2+2) upper/lower A-arms with coil springs. Brakes: front/rear disc. Body Construction: separate body on tubular steel ladder-type frame.

PERFORMANCE: Top Speed: (206 Dino GT) 142 mph; (275 GTB/4) 165+ mph; (330 GT 2+2) as high as 150+ mph; (330 GTC) 145-150 mph; (365 GT 2+2) 140-145+ mph. Acceleration (0-60 mph): (206 Dino GT) about 7.1 sec.; (330 GTC) 7.0 sec.; (365 GT 2+2) 7.1 sec. Acceleration (quarter-mile): (330 GTC) 14.6-14.9 sec. (about 95 mph).

Manufacturer: Automobili Ferrari S.p.A. SEFAC, Maranello (Modena), Italy.

Distributor: Luigi Chinetti Motors, New York City.

1967 Ferrari Type 330 GTC. (DA)

1967 Ferrari 330 GTS s/n 9781. (WG)

1967 Ferrari 330 GTS s/n 9781. (WG)

1967 Ferrari Type 330 GTC. (DA)

1967 Ferrari 330 Speciale (one of only two built). (WG)

1967 Ferrari 275 GTB/4 s/n 9838. The car has a remarkable 8000+ original miles. (WG)

1967 Ferrari 275 GTB/4 s/n 9838. (WG)

1968 Ferrari Type 275 GTB/4 Berlinetta. (DA)

1968

DINO 206 GT — V-6 — Dino production in this form continued with little change into 1969.

275 GTB/4 — V-12 — Production of the twin-cam version of the 275 series continued into early 1968.

TYPE 330 GT 2+2 — V-12 — This was the final year for the four-seat Ferrari with 3967-cc V-12, which was replaced by the 365 GT 2+2 series.

TYPE 330 GTC/GTS — V-12 — This was the final year for the coupe and convertible with 3967-cc V-12 engine.

TYPE 365 GTC/GTS — V-12 — Starting in 1968, a larger engine went into the former 330 GTC/GTS, resulting in a model number change. A 4-mm bore increase (to 81 mm) boosted displacement of the V-12 to 4390 cc (267.8 cid), developing 320 horsepower at 6600 rpm. Production would continue into 1970.

TYPE 365 GT 2+2 — V-12 — Introduced in 1967, the 2+2 coupe with 4390-cc V-12 engine would remain in production into 1971.

TYPE 365 GTB/4 "DAYTONA" — V-12 — One of Ferrari's most popular models debuted at the Paris Salon in 1968, soon acquiring the "Daytona" nickname. This would be the final front-engine, two-seat production Ferrari. Pininfarina designed the fastback coupe, but bodies were built by Scaglietti. Layout and chassis were essentially that of the former 275 GTB/4, with 94.5-inch wheelbase, but power came from the new 4390-cc V-12 engine. Using an 8.8:1 compression ratio and six Weber carburetors, that twin-cam engine produced 352 hp. A five-speed manual transaxle was mounted in the rear. Early models had full-width plastic headlamp covers. That layout was illegal in the U.S., so imported versions had hidden headlamps. From 1970 onward, all Daytonas wore concealed headlamps. A small blackout eggcrate rectangular grille was flanked by rubber-tipped bumperettes. Wraparound amber park/signal lights were installed. The smooth, frill-free shape displayed a horizontal bodyside crease just below the level of the top of the wheel wells. Bumperettes at the rear were black-tipped, to match the front units. Two round tail lamps were mounted on each side. Aluminum was used for the doors, hood, and trunklid. Cromodora five-spoke light alloy wheels were standard. Ranking as Ferrari's most costly production model up to that time, the Daytona was also the fastest, capable of hitting 174 mph. It could run the quarter-mile in 13.8 seconds, reaching 107.5 mph, and accelerate to 60 mph in 5.9 seconds. More than 1,400 examples would be produced over the full model run, which began in 1969 and continued into 1974. Most were closed coupes, but about 127 Spider convertibles were built. A handful of racing berlinetta coupes had all-aluminum bodies, with engines producing up to 405 bhp.

I.D. DATA: Not available.

Model	Body Type & Seating	Engine Type/CID	P.O.E. Price	Weight (lbs.)	Prod. Total
206 DINO GT					
206 Dino	2-dr Coupe-2P	V6/121	N/A	1980	Note 1
275 GTB/4					
275 GTB/4	2-dr Coupe-2P	V12/200	14900	2315	Note 2
330 GT 2+2					
330 GT	2-dr Coupe-2+2P	V12/242	14900	3040	Note 3
330 GTC/GTS					
330 GTC	2-dr Coupe-2P	V12/242	14900	2866	Note 4
330 GTS	2-dr Conv Cpe-2P	V12/242	14900	2646	Note 5
365 GTC/GTS					
365 GTC	2-dr Coupe-2P	V12/268	N/A	2976	Note 6
365 GTS	2-dr Conv Cpe-2P	V12/268	15000	2976	Note 7
365 GT 2+2					
365 GT	2-dr Coupe-2+2P	V12/268	N/A	3483	Note 8
365 GTB/4 "DAYTONA"					
365 GTB/4	2-dr Coupe-2P	V12/268	N/A	2650	Note 9

Note 1: As many as 153 Type 206 Dino GT coupes were produced from 1967-69.
Note 2: About 330 Type 275 GTB/4 coupes were produced from 1966 into early 1968 (plus 10 special NART Spyder convertibles).
Note 3: About 1,080 Type 330 GT 2+2s were produced from 1964-68.
Note 4: About 600 Type 330 GTC coupes were produced through 1968.
Note 5: About 99 Type 330 GTS convertibles were produced through 1968.
Note 6: About 150 Type 365 GTC coupes were produced from 1968-69.
Note 7: About 14 Type 365 GTS convertibles were produced from 1966-67.
Note 8: About 801 Type 365 GT 2+2 coupes were produced from 1968-71.
Note 9: About 1,383 Type 365 GTB/4 coupes (not including convertibles) were produced from 1968-74.
Weight Note: Figures shown are approximate (or averages).

ENGINE [Base V-6 (206 Dino GT)]: 65-degree, dual-overhead-cam "vee" type six-cylinder. Aluminum alloy block and heads. Displacement: 121 cid (1987 cc). Bore & stroke: 3.39 x 2.24 in. (86 x 57 mm). Compression ratio: 9.7:1. Brake horsepower: 180 (DIN) at 8000 rpm. Torque: 138 lbs.-ft. (DIN) at 6500 rpm. Four main bearings. Three Weber 40 DCN/4 two-barrel carburetors.

ENGINE [Base V-12 (275 GTB/4)]: 60-degree, dual-overhead-cam "vee" type 12-cylinder. Aluminum alloy block and heads. Displacement: 200.5 cid (3286 cc). Bore & stroke: 3.03 x 2.31 in. (77 x 58.8 mm). Compression ratio: 9.2:1. Brake horsepower: 300 (DIN) at 8000 rpm. Torque: 217 lbs.-ft. at 6000 rpm. Seven main bearings. Six Weber two-barrel carburetors.

ENGINE [Base V-12 (330 GT 2+2, 330 GTC/GTS)]: 60-degree, single-overhead-cam "vee" type 12-cylinder. Aluminum alloy block and heads. Displacement: 242 cid (3967 cc). Bore & stroke: 3.03 x 2.80 in. (77 x 71 mm). Compression ratio: 8.8:1. Brake horsepower: 300 DIN (345 SAE) at 7000 rpm. Torque: 241 lbs.-ft. at 5000 rpm. Seven main bearings. Three Weber DCZ/6 or 40 DFI two-barrel carburetors.

ENGINE [Base V-12 (365 GTC/GTS, 365 GT 2+2)]: 60-degree, single-overhead-cam "vee" type 12-cylinder (Colombo). Aluminum alloy block and heads. Displacement: 268 cid (4390 cc). Bore & stroke: 3.19 x 2.80 in. (81 x 71 mm). Compression ratio: 8.8:1. Brake horsepower: 320 (DIN) at 6600 rpm. Torque: 268 lbs.-ft. at 5000 rpm. Seven main bearings. Three Weber carburetors.

ENGINE [Base V-12 (365 GTB/4)]: 60-degree, dual-overhead-cam "vee" type 12-cylinder. Aluminum alloy block and heads. Displacement: 268 cid (4390 cc). Bore & stroke: 3.19 x 2.80 in. (81 x 71 mm). Compression ratio: 8.8:1. Brake horsepower: 352 at 7500 rpm. Torque: 365 lbs.-ft. at 5500 rpm. Seven main bearings. Six Weber 40 DCN 20 twin-choke carburetors.

CHASSIS: Wheelbase: (206 Dino GT) 90.0 in.; (275 GTB/4) 94.5 in.; (330 GT 2+2) 104.2 in.; (330 GTC/GTS) 94.5 in.; (365 GT 2+2) 104.2 in.; (365 GTC/GTS) 94.5 in.; (365 GTB/4) 94.5 in. Overall Length: (206 Dino GT) 165 in.; (275 GTB/4) 173.6 in.; (330 GT 2+2) 189.4 in.; (330 GTC) 176 in.; (330 GTS) 174.4 in.; (365 GT 2+2) 196 in.; (365 GTC/GTS) 176 in.; (365 GTB/4) 174 in. Height: (206 Dino GT) 43.9 in.; (275 GTB/4) 47.2 in.; (330 GT 2+2) 52 in.; (330 GTC) 51.2 in.; (330 GTS) 49.2 in.; (365 GT 2+2) 53 in.; (365 GTC/GTS) 51.2 in.; (365 GTB/4) 49.0 in. Width: (206 Dino GT) 66.9 in.; (275 GTB/4) 67.9 in.; (330 GT 2+2) 69 in.; (330 GTC) 65.8 in.; (330 GTS) 65.9 in.; (365 GT 2+2) 70.5 in.; (365 GTC/GTS) 65.7 in.; (365 GTB/4) 69.3 in. Front Tread: (206 Dino GT) 56.1 in.; (275 GTB/4) 55.2 in.; (330 GT 2+2) 55.3 in.; (330 GTC/GTS) 55.2 in.; (365 GT 2+2) 56.6 in.; (365 GTC/GTS) 55.2 in.; (365 GTB/4) 56.7 in. Rear Tread: (206 Dino GT) 55.1 in.; (275 GTB/4) 55.8 in.; (330 GT 2+2) 55 in.; (330 GTC/GTS) 55.8 in.; (365 GT 2+2) 57.8 in.; (365 GTC/GTS) 55.8 in.; (365 GTB/4)

1968 Ferrari Dino 206 GT. (DA)

56.1 in. Standard Tires: (206 Dino GT) 185x14; (330 GTC/GTS) 205x14; (365 GT 2+2) 205x15; (365 GTC/GTS) 215x15; (365 GTB/4) 215x15.

TECHNICAL: Layout: front-engine, rear-drive except (Dino) mid-engine, rear-drive. Transmission: (330 GT 2+2) five-speed manual; (206 Dino GT, 330 GTC/GTS, 365 GT 2+2, 365 GTC/GTS, 365 GTB/4) five-speed manual in rear transaxle. Standard Final Drive Ratio: (206 Dino) 3.41:1; (275 GTB/4) 3.55:1; (330 GT) 4.25:1 (330 GTS) 3.44:1; (365 GT 2+2) 4.25:1. Steering: (Dino) rack and pinion; (275/330 GTB/4) worm and roller; (365 GT 2+2) recirculating ball. Suspension (front): upper/lower A-arms with coil springs. Suspension (rear): (330 GT 2+2) rigid axle with parallel trailing arms and semi-elliptic leaf springs; (206 Dino GT, 275 GTB/GTS, 330 GTC/GTS, 365 GT 2+2, 365 GTC/GTS, 365 GTB/4) upper/lower A-arms with coil springs. Brakes: front/rear disc. Body Construction: separate body on tubular steel ladder-type frame.

MAJOR OPTIONS: Air conditioning (330 GTC/GTS). Wire wheels (330 GTC/GTS, 365 GT 2+2).

PERFORMANCE: Top Speed: (206 Dino GT) 142-146 mph; (275 GTB/4) 166 mph; (330 GT 2+2) 115-125 mph; (330 GTC) 145-152 mph; (330 GTS) 149 mph; (365 GT 2+2) 140-152 mph; (365 GTB/4) 174 mph. Acceleration (0-60 mph): (206 Dino GT) about 7.1 sec.; (330 GTC) 7.0 sec.; (365 GT 2+2) 7.1 sec.; (365 GTB/4) 5.9 sec. Acceleration (quarter-mile): (330 GTC) 14.6-14.9 sec. (about 95 mph).

Manufacturer: Ferrari S.p.A. SEFAC, Maranello (Modena), Italy.

Distributor: Luigi Chinetti Motors, New York City and Greenwich, Connecticut.

1968 Ferrari Dino 206 GT. (DA)

1969 Ferrari Type 365 GTS/4 Daytona Spyder. (DA)

DINO 206 GT — V-6 — Never a strong seller, the 206 ceased production to make way for the much more popular Dino 246.

DINO 246 GT — V-6 — Externally there was little to distinguish the Dino 246 from the 206. Unlike the 206, a version for the United Sates was prepared. Larger rectangular units replaced the diminutive round side marker lights, and all U.S. editions had Cromodora alloy wheels with five-bolts instead of the center knock off hubs. The changes under the engine cover were much more significant. A larger, and more reliable 2418-cc (148-cid) V-6 was fitted; both bore and stroke were increased. This resulted in a rating of 195 bhp for the European version with a top speed of 146 mph quoted by the factory. For the United States, an air pump and a change in the timing netted a rating of 180 bhp. While this might not seem like a lot for a 2700-lb. car, the engine's willingness to rev, and the delightful melody

emanating from the four chrome tailpipes makes it seem like much more. The prototype appeared early in 1969, production commenced later that year, and did quite well through 1971 and 1972. Like the Dino 206, it had a tubular steel chassis, fully independent suspension, and front/rear disc brakes. Wheelbase grew 2.1 inches, however, now measuring 92.1 inches. Bodies were built by Scaglietti, while the transverse-mounted engines came from Fiat (but had been designed at Ferrari). Some engine components were manufactured at the Ferrari facility. As before, the extremely low fastback profile featured bulged front fenders, and the car wore no Ferrari name or insignia. On the dashboard, eight instruments sat in an elliptical binnacle just ahead of the driver. Production continued into 1973.

TYPE 365 GTC/GTS— V-12 — Production of the coupe and convertible with a 4390-cc engine continued with little change into 1970.

TYPE 365 GT 2+2 — V-12 — Affectionately know as the Queen Mother of Ferraris, this 2+2 offers the largest rear seat of any Ferrari ever made. If you want a Ferrari that comes very close to having seating for four, this is your car. Luigi Chinetti supplied the factory with six General Motors automatic transmissions to be fitted to U.S. spec cars. These six cars offer a rare, but not necessarily desirable Ferrari driving experience. Production of the four-seat Ferrari with 4390-cc V-12 continued into 1971, with little change. Standard equipment included air conditioning, power steering, power windows, and an AM/FM radio.

TYPE 365 GTB/4, 365 GTS/4 "DAYTONA" — V-12 —

It's hard to believe a car that many consider the most desirable road Ferrari didn't sell well when it was new. The Spyder version of the 365 GTB appeared on the stand at the 1969 Frankfurt Auto Show. Add an easy-to-use convertible top to the already stunning long hood/short deck Daytona and you have the making of an instant classic. Of the 150 Daytona Spyders (365 GTS/4) produced, approximately 100 of them were imported into the U.S. Today they must number well over 200, as the conversion from coupe to spyder was carried out my several U.S. coachbuilders. Be sure to check the serial number for authenticity as those imported into the U.S. were stamped "365GTB/4" on the manufacturer's plate. While the original design specified four headlights under clear covers, this version did not comply with U.S. lighting regulations. The elegant solution was the now familiar popup headlights.

I.D. DATA: Not available.

Model	Body Type & Seating	Engine Type/CID	P.O.E. Price	Weight (lbs.)	Prod. Total
206 DINO GT					
206 Dino	2-dr Coupe-2P	V6/121	13400	1980	Note 1
246 DINO GT					
246 Dino	2-dr Coupe-2P	V6/148	13900	2380	Note 2
365 GTC/GTS					
365 GTC	2-dr Coupe-2P	V12/268	N/A	3350	Note 3
365 GTS	2-dr Conv Cpe-2P	V12/268	N/A	3450	Note 4
365 GT 2+2					
365 GT	2-dr Coupe-2+2P	V12/268	18900	3483	Note 5
365 GTB/4 "DAYTONA"					
365 GTB/4	2-dr Coupe-2P	V12/268	19700	3600	Note 6
365 GTS/4	2-dr Conv Cpe-2P	V12/268	N/A	N/A	Note 7

Note 1: About 153 Type 206 Dino GT coupes were produced from 1967-69.
Note 2: About 2,487 Type 246 Dino GT coupes were produced from 1969-74.
Note 3: About 150 Type 365 GTC coupes were produced from 1968-1969.
Note 4: About 14 Type 365 GTS convertibles were produced through 1970.
Note 5: About 801 Type 365 GT 2+2 coupes were produced from 1968-71.

1969 Ferrari Type 365 GTS/4 Daytona Spyder. (DA)

1971-72 Ferrari 365 GTC/4. (WG)

Note 6: About 1,383 Type 365 GTB/4 coupes were produced from 1968-74.
Note 7: About 121 Type 365 GTS/4 convertibles were produced from 1969-73.
Price Note: Figures shown were valid during 1969. The 365 GT 2+2 sold for $21,700 in 1970; the 365 GTB/4 "Daytona" coupe listed for $20,500 in 1970-71.
Weight Note: Figures shown are approximate (or averages).
Production Note: Approximately 730 Ferraris were built in 1969, followed by 850 in 1970, and 1,246 in 1971 (including 832 Dinos and 326 Type 365 GT/GTB).

ENGINE [Base V-6 (206 Dino GT)]: 65-degree, dual-overhead-cam "vee" type six-cylinder. Light alloy (Silumin) block and heads. Displacement: 121 cid (1987 cc). Bore & stroke: 3.39 x 2.24 in. (86 x 57 mm). Compression ratio: 9.3:1. Brake horsepower: 180 (DIN) at 8000 rpm. Torque: 138 lbs.-ft. at 6500 rpm. Four main bearings. Three Weber 40 DCN/4 two-barrel carburetors.

ENGINE [Base V-6 (246 Dino GT)]: 65-degree, dual-overhead-cam "vee" type six-cylinder. Cast-iron block and light alloy heads. Displacement: 148 cid (2418 cc). Bore & stroke: 3.64 x 2.36 in. (92.5 x 60 mm). Compression ratio: 9.0:1. Brake horsepower: 195 (DIN) at 7600 rpm. Torque: 167 lbs.-ft. at 5500 rpm. Four main bearings. Three Weber 40 DCNF/6 or 40 DCNF/7 carburetors.

ENGINE [Base V-12 (365 GTC/GTS, 365 GT 2+2)]: 60-degree, single-overhead-cam "vee" type 12-cylinder (Colombo). Aluminum alloy block and heads. Displacement: 268 cid (4390 cc). Bore & stroke: 3.19 x 2.80 in. (81 x 71 mm). Compression ratio: 8.8:1. Brake horsepower: 320 (DIN) at 6600 rpm. Torque: 268 lbs.-ft. at 5000 rpm. Seven main bearings. Three Weber 40 DFI carburetors.

ENGINE [Base V-12 (365 GTB/4, GTS/4)]: 60-degree, dual-overhead-cam "vee" type 12-cylinder. Aluminum alloy block and heads. Displacement: 268 cid (4390 cc). Bore & stroke: 3.19 x 2.80 in. (81 x 71 mm). Compression ratio: 8.8:1. Brake horsepower: 352 at 7500 rpm. Torque: 319 lbs.-ft. DIN (365 SAE) at 5000-5500 rpm. Seven main bearings. Six Weber 40 CDN2A or DCN20 twin-choke carburetors.

CHASSIS: Wheelbase: (206 Dino GT) 90.0 in.; (246 Dino GT) 92.1 in.; (365 GT 2+2) 104.3 in.; (365 GTC/GTS) 94.5 in.; (365 GTB/4) 94.5 in. Overall Length: (206 Dino GT) 165 in.; (246 Dino GT) 163.4 in.; (365 GT 2+2) 195 in.; (365 GTC/GTS) 174-176 in.; (365 GTB/4) 171-174 in. Height: (206/246 Dino GT) 43.9 in.; (365 GT 2+2) 53 in.; (365 GTC/GTS) 50.5 in.; (365 GTB/4) 49 in. Width: (206/246 Dino GT) 66.9 in.; (365 GT 2+2) 70 in.; (365 GTC/GTS) 65.5 in.; (365 GTC/4) 70.1 in.; (365 GTB/4) 68-70 in. Front Tread: (206/246 Dino GT) 56.1

in.; (365 GT 2+2) 56.6 in.; (365 GTC/GTS) 55.2 in.; (365 GTB/4) 56.7 in. Rear Tread: (206 Dino GT) 55.1 in.; (246 Dino GT) 56.3 in.; (365 GT 2+2) 56.6 in.; (365 GTC/GTS) 55.8 in.; (365 GTB/4) 56.1 in. Standard Tires: (206 Dino GT) 185x14; (246 Dino GT) 205x14; (365 GTB/4, GTS/4) 215/70x15.

TECHNICAL: Layout: front-engine, rear-drive except (Dino) mid-engine, rear-drive. Transmission: five-speed manual in rear transaxle. Standard Final Drive Ratio: (Dino 246 GT) 3.62:1. Steering: (Dino 206/246) rack and pinion; (365 GTB/4) worm and roller; (365 GT 2+2) recirculating ball. Suspension (front): unequal-length A-arms with coil springs (anti-roll bar on 206/246 Dino, 365 GTB/4, 365 GTS/4). Suspension (rear): (365 GTC/GTS) unequal-length A-arms with coil springs; (365 GT 2+2) unequal-length A-arms with coil springs and hydropneumatic self-leveling; (206/246 Dino, 365 GTB/GTS) unequal-length A-arms with coil springs and anti-roll bar. Brakes: front/rear disc. Body Construction: separate body on tubular steel frame.

MAJOR OPTIONS: Air conditioning: GTB/4 ($800). AM/FM radio: GTB/4 ($320).

PERFORMANCE: Top Speed: (206 Dino GT) 142-146 mph; (246 Dino GT) 140-146 mph; (365 GT 2+2) 140-152 mph; (365 GTB/4) 174-180 mph. Acceleration (0-60 mph): (206 Dino GT) about 7.1 sec.; (246 Dino GT) 8.0 sec.; (365 GT 2+2) 7.1 sec.; (365 GTB/4) 5.9 sec.; (365 GTC/4) 6.9 sec.

Manufacturer: Ferrari S.p.A. SEFAC, Maranello (Modena), Italy.

Distributor: Luigi Chinetti Motors, Greenwich, Connecticut.

HISTORY: Fiat used the same 1987-cc V-6 engine installed in the Dino 206 GT in its own front-engined Fiat Dino Coupe and Spyder. The relationship was no surprise, since Fiat bought a controlling interest in Ferrari in 1969.

1971-72 Ferrari 365 GTC/4. (WG)

Ferrari 365 GTB/4 Daytona;
Meeting the Challenge the Old-Fashioned Way

1969 Ferrari Type 365 GTB/4 Daytona. (DA)

No car is designed and sold in a vacuum. When it comes to a purely ego-gratifying purchase like a Ferrari, this is especially true. When upstart Italian manufacturer, Lamborghini, first unveiled the Miura chassis and engine at the 1965 Turin show, then the completed car the following spring in Geneva, many enthusiasts thought that glorious cars such as the Ferrari 275 GTB and the Jaguar XKE were relics from the past. So when the 365 GTB/4 was unveiled at the 1968 Paris Salon, many considered this brand-new car already outdated.

The easiest way to silence those critics was to put them behind the wheel of what *Road & Track* called "... the best sports car in the world. Or the best GT. Take your pick." While Ferrari would later bow to the winds of change with the 365 GTB/4's replacement, the mid-engined Boxer, there are many Ferrari fans that consider the front engine/rear drive 365 GTB/4 the last of the "true Ferraris."

While the purchase of Ferrari by Italian automotive giant, Fiat, may have caused some softening of the racing-oriented focus, it is doubtful the company would have survived very far into the Seventies without Fiat's heavy infusion of capital.

One look at the achingly long hood and the curvaceous rear quarters was enough to set the heart of any Seventies schoolboy aflutter. The leading edge features thin chrome bumpers flanking a classic Ferrari "eggcrate" grille. European models were built with a Plexiglas strip that stretched from one broad amber turn signal to the other, covering four round headlights. U.S. lighting regulations prohibited any such arrangement, so American cars had popup headlights that left a more uncluttered nose when they were recessed.

A "blood strake" runs down each side of every 365 GTB/4 from the back of the front wheel well, and wraps around the rear end. Pininfarina outdid himself with the design of some of the details, such as the petite, yet elegant chrome lever atop the doors. No big-grab handle mars the smooth and flowing side view; only the keyholes, the side of his front marker lights and his signature badges interrupt. In back, there are again two thin strips of rubber-edged chrome bumpers that accent the chrome license plate light, the four round taillights, and the four sharp-cut, chrome exhaust tips.

Lifting the front-hinged hood reveals a powerplant that proved its mettle in endurance races throughout the 1970s. In fact, this model is more commonly known as the Daytona, in recognition of its remarkable success at this classic, American 24-hour endurance contest. The four-cam, 4.4-liter engine makes 352 brake horsepower at a lofty (for its day) 7500 rpms. Six 40 DCN 20 Weber carburetors stand in tight formation down the middle of the V-12's valley. The bottom of the engine was kept shallow by the inclusion of a race-tested, dry sump oil system. Packaging the transmission with the final drive in a transaxle was an additional innovation gained from Ferrari's racing expertise. Just as with the 275 GTB, it provided a nearly equal weight distribution for better handling.

As you slide into the leather bucket, take a moment to adjust the tilt mechanism. Instead of a more conventional, adjustable backrest, the entire pleated bucket tilts to suit your preference. In front of you is a hooded instrument binnacle, chock-full of useful information. The large speedometer reaches all the way up to 200 mph (300 kph) and the chrome-ringed, 8000-rpm tachometer invites you to rev the Daytona's engine to its 7500-rpm redline. Between the speedometer and tach sit gauges for water temperature, amps, oil pressure, and oil temperature. On the ends of the cluster are a clock and a fuel gauge. Lack of time, or gas, might be the only reason you would want to pull over once your test drive has commenced.

Ferraris of this vintage have their own peculiar starting drill. Twist the key in the ignition, wait until the clicking stops or slows (signifying that the twin Bendix electric fuel pumps have pressurized the system), pump the gas pedal a couple of times and, "WHOOMPP!" Much has been written about the "tearing silk" sound of a Ferrari V-12 engine, but the example in a Daytona is among the finest ever made for aural gratification.

Grab hold of the black ball atop the chrome shift lever and slot down and to the left for first gear. It takes practice to maneuver the lever through the chrome shift gate, and when the transaxle is cold, the gears are particularly reluctant to engage. The Momo leather or Nardi wood steering wheel feels a bit large in diameter at first. Then you become glad for the additional leverage it provides as you discover that the non-power assisted steering is only one of the components that has earned Daytona the label, "a man's car." The clutch, too, requires a firm push and careful modulation for smooth engagement.

Once under way, the Daytona delights in the immediacy of the controls. As the oil temperature gauge stirs from its slumber, the engine revs pick up more quickly. The smoothness of the V-12 is as impressive as the massive torque the engine provides. After a short time behind the wheel, the prancing horse that rears up on the yellow horn button seems to whisper, "Now's the time to hit it." Given a full throttle, the Daytona will accelerate to 120 mph in under 18 seconds. If you have the proper road and the requisite courage, achieving the factory's advertised top speed of 173 mph is easily accomplished.

Even when the opportunity for a high-speed run is not available, this Ferrari enchants its pilot with a smooth ride, powerful acceleration, and confidence-inspiring handling. The 215/70x15 Michelin XWXs were considered to be huge tires when the Daytona was new. Today they look remarkably tall, and their small contact patch means that traction can be lost quite dramatically in a moment of carelessness. The four-wheel, vented disc brakes were state-of-the-art at the time, but the nearly 3,600 pounds of metal, fluids, and leather mean that stops will take a bit longer than modern pilots have become accustomed to.

With its place atop the sales chart of its day, stunning good looks, and fabulous sound, the Daytona will remain a desirable Ferrari for years to come. Coupes were selling for a quarter of a million dollars at the height of Ferrari fever in 1989/90. It was not unheard of for the even more rare Spider versions to change hands for $500,000 and more. Now that prices have dropped to between one-half to one-third of those heady numbers, it seems like the perfect time to invest in what many consider to be the ultimate Ferrari coupe and roadster.

1971 Ferrari 365 GTB/4 Daytona s/n 14233. (WG)

The Dino 246 WAS a True Ferrari

1969-74 Ferrari Dino 246 GTS. (DG)

Alfredo Ferrari, better known as Dino, was the only legitimate heir to Enzo Ferrari. His tragically early death would have an everlasting influence on both Enzo's life and the Ferrari lineup that followed.

Alfredo was trained as an engineer in Switzerland, and he was being groomed by his father to succeed Enzo when the time came to hand over control of the company. Enzo Ferrari was so devoted to his son that he even retired from driving racing cars, so that his Dino would not suffer the same heartbreak he had from losing his parents early in life. The Dino

line of Ferraris became a touching tribute to the boy who died in 1956 at the tender age of twenty-four.

Dino's interest in smaller, V-6 configured engines helped influence his father's use of those in some of his racing cars. But the story of the Dino road cars begins with the 1965 Pininfarina *Berlinetta Speciale* Dino 206S, first displayed at the Paris show that year. Following that, the 1966 Turin show car's proportions came much closer to the production version, with hints of the two-off, three-seater around the rear windows and decklid. Tacked-on front and rear wings worn by the 1967 Frankfurt show car were just some of what made that example more of a styling exercise, rather than a part of the Dino 246's direct lineage.

Before Fiat bought an interest in Ferrari, the two collaborated on the design and production of a 2.0-liter V-6 engine. In order to compete in Formula Two, a manufacturer had to produce 500 or more engines upon which their racing version could be based. This was a lofty number for a company that spent most of their production capacity on the popular V-12 motors. Fiat agreed to build the Ferrari designed V-6 motor, in return for their being able to use it in the Fiat Dino Coupe and Spyder. This allowed Ferrari to not only use the engine for competition purposes, but also to install it in the 206 Dino.

The appearance of the first street Ferrari with its engine placed amidships should have been cause for celebration among the *cognoscenti*. Yet, when the car debuted in 1967, it was as if Enzo had disowned the little car, or at least was trying to keep it a good distance away from his V-12 automobiles. The Ferrari name did not appear anywhere on the car. Instead, a Dino script was on the nose, tail, horn button, and camshaft covers. While the 2.0-liter's 180 horsepower seemed like small potatoes compared to the powerful engines in the V-12 cars, the 1969 debut of the very similar 2.4-liter Dino 246 addressed some of the complaints.

There were little or no gripes about the styling. One would be hard pressed to point to another street Ferrari possessing such a curvaceous shape. All four fenders rise up in such a way that the remaining bodywork seems even more delicate. The side air intakes are masterfully sculpted into the doors and rear fenders. The hood sits low, nestled between front fenders whose deeply faired-in headlights seem to be lifted right from the powerful P3 and P4 racing cars.

The rear end terminates with a sharply cut, Kamm-style abruptness. The wraparound rear window is an inspired touch that provides exceptional visibility for a mid-engined automobile. On the Dino 246 GT coupe, the sail panels contain rear quarter windows that add to the airiness in the cockpit. On the later Dino 246 GTS, the flying buttresses each have three small vents that echo those on the front hood and engine cover. When one lifts off the roof panel and stores it behind the seats, one almost has a convertible. Fourteen-inch Campagnolo alloy wheels complete this Italian masterpiece. The Dino 206s had triple-eared, knock-off hub spinners, while the Dino 246s used a more modern, five-bolt wheel.

The Dino's doors open with the same delicate handle used to great effect on the Daytona. The interior is not as luxurious as its larger siblings. But, what it lacks in opulence it more than makes up for with the properly placed tools a good driver needs. The deeply hooded instrument binnacle has gauges for water temperature, amps, and both oil pressure and temperature in its center. These are flanked by a large, chrome-ringed speedometer and matching tachometer, with a clock and the fuel gauge on either end.

The dashboard is covered in the flat finish "mouse hair" material that was in vogue at the time. While it did a great job of keeping glare and reflections to a minimum, it's the bane of Ferrari restorers. Easily damaged by water and sun, its short life is only rivaled by the difficulty in obtaining it today. The small-diameter, thick-rimmed Momo steering wheel seems perfectly sized for this compact car. Having most of the vehicle's weight over the rear wheels helps to make the steering feel both direct and highly communicative. It also eliminates the need for power assist.

The engine is not at all temperamental, and fires to life with a twist of the key and a stab of the gas pedal. If you are not too broad of beam, the one-piece buckets offer a reassuring grasp of your posterior. This is important, because the Dino 246 delights in hard cornering. The 195-horsepower engine sounds more potent than it feels, but the independent suspension delivers on the mid-engine promise of racecar-like handling.

A low polar moment of inertia is the scientific explanation for this delightful feeling. Think of trying to spin a dumbbell from side to side, and then picture how much easier the task is if the weights on the ends are moved to the center. That's the principle behind the Dino's quick reflexes. Certainly the 205/70x14-inch Michelin XWX tires were adequate in their day, but now they appear laughably small compared to a modern sportscar. So, the Dino's nimble handling is not a function of wide and sticky tires. Rather, it's the mid-engine placement and the attention to suspension design that make the Dino such a pleasure to drive.

The Dino 308 GT4 came after the Dino 246, but it never truly replaced the beloved icon. It, too, wore the Dino badge instead of the Ferrari logo. While today's manufacturers have been known to introduce new car lines to sell their up-market models, Ferrari's example of trying to reach further down the scale was highly successful with its products, even if the Dino brand did not last. Despite this, the Dino brand remains a lasting tribute to a father's beloved son.

1969-74 Ferrari Dino 246 GTS. (DG)

1972-1973 Ferrari 365 GTC/4. (MC)

1972

A significant change in the distribution of Ferraris in the United States took place this year. Luigi Chinetti forged a partnership with Al Garthwaite to form Chinetti-Garthwaite Imports of Paoli, Pennsylvania for distribution of Ferraris in the Eastern U.S. About a year before this, Bill Harrah established Modern Classic Motors in Reno, Nevada as the western distributor. The result was a significant boost in sales.

DINO 246 GT/GTS — V-6 — Continuing the tradition of offering open-air motoring to his clients, Ferrari also offered a 246 GTS Dino. The lift-off roof panel was stored behind the seats, and featured a surprisingly quiet airflow above the cockpit. Rear visibility suffered some as the GTS had metal panels with three small louvers, instead of the coupe's small rear quarter windows.

TYPE 365 GTB/4, 365 GTS/4 "DAYTONA" — V-12 — Luigi Chinetti's North American Racing Team continued to run "Daytonas" at Le Mans, Watkins Glen, and of course, Daytona Speedway. Their success helped to promote model popularity in the U.S even further. Production of the two "Daytona" models continued into 1974; see previous listings for additional details.

TYPE 365 GTC/4 — V-12 — When the 365 GTC/4 was introduced at the Geneva Show in March 1971; many people scratched their heads. This 2+2 was too small to replace the 365 GT 2+2. This car was offered for those who wanted Ferrari performance and more touring comfort than was offered by the Daytona. Mechanically it was very similar to the 365GTB/4 but with some significant differences. The C4 had a wet sump, versus the Daytona's more race-oriented dry sump oil system. The B's six downdraft Webbers were replaced by six side drafts that allowed for a lower hood line, and a conventional five-speed transmission was directly behind the engine, versus the Daytona's more sporting transaxle. Most of the C4s that were imported into the U.S. were produced in 1972.

365 GT4 2+2 — V-12 — Although it was not destined for sale in the U.S., a new four-seat Ferrari debuted at the October 1972 Paris show as successor to the 365 GT 2+2 (which actually ceased production more than a year earlier). While the chassis layout, suspension, brakes, and steering were similar to the GTC/4, it offered a much more upright profile. The GT4 2+2's wheelbase was two inches longer than the 365 GT 2+2, but this model was markedly shorter overall and it weighed considerably more. Interior dimensions were noticeably wider. Six horizontal Weber carburetors fed a 268-cid (4390-cc) four-cam V-12, and provided plenty of "wow" factor when the hood was lifted. Horsepower was rated 320 at 6200 rpm, and it hooked to a five-speed manual gearbox. Five-spoke Cromodora alloy wheels were standard, as were air conditioning, power steering, and power brakes. Not a typical Ferrari in appearance, the 365 GT4 had a body by Scaglietti

1972 Ferrari 246 GTS Dino s/n 04462. (WG)

I.D. DATA: Not available.

Model	Body Type & Seating	Engine Type/CID	P.O.E. Price	Weight (lbs.)	Prod. Total
246 DINO					
GT	2-dr Coupe-2P	V6/148	13900	2380	Note 1
GTS	2-dr Targa Cpe-2P	V6/148	14500	2381	Note 2
365 GTB/4 "DAYTONA"					
365 GTB/4	2-dr Coupe-2P	V12/268	25350	2646	Note 3
365 GTS/4	2-dr Conv Cpe-2P	V12/268	28275	2646	Note 4
365 GTC/4					
365 GTC/4	2-dr Coupe-2P	V12/268	27250	3197	Note 5
365 GT4 2+2					
365 GT4	2-dr Coupe-2+2P	V12/268	N/A	3307	Note 6

Note 1: About 2,487 Type 246 Dino GT coupes were produced from 1969-73.
Note 2: About 2,487 Type 246 Dino GT coupes were produced from 1969-74. About 1,274 Type 246 Dino GTS Targa coupes were produced from 1972-73.
Note 3: About 1,383 Type 365 GTB/4 coupes were produced from 1968-74.
Note 4: About 127 Type 365 GTS/4 convertibles were produced from 1969-74.
Note 5: Approximately 500 Type 365 GTC/4 coupes were produced in 1971-72.
Note 6: A total of 525 Type 365 GT4 2+2 coupes (sometimes called sedans) were produced from 1972-75.
Weight Note: Figures shown are approximate (or averages).
Production Note: A total of 1,843 Ferraris (330 of them 365 GT/GTB) were built in 1972.

ENGINE [Base V-6 (246 Dino GT)]: 65-degree, dual-overhead-cam "vee" type six-cylinder. Cast-iron block and light alloy heads. Displacement: 148 cid (2418 cc). Bore & stroke: 3.64 x 2.36 in. (92.5 x 60 mm). Compression ratio: 9.0:1. Brake horsepower: 195 (DIN) at 7600 rpm. Torque: 167 lbs.-ft. (DIN) at 5500 rpm. Four main bearings. Three Weber 40 DCNF 13 two-barrel carburetors.

ENGINE [Base V-12 (365 GTB/4, GTS/4)]: 60-degree, dual-overhead-cam, "vee" type 12-cylinder. Aluminum alloy block and heads. Displacement: 267.8 cid (4390 cc). Bore & stroke: 3.19 x 2.80 in. (81 x 71 mm). Compression ratio: 8.8:1. Brake horsepower: 352 (DIN) at 7500 rpm. Torque: 319 lbs.-ft. at 5000 rpm. Seven main bearings. Six Weber 40 DCN-20 twin-choke carburetors.

ENGINE [Base V-12 (365 GT4 2+2, GTC/4)]: Same as 4390-cc V-12 above, except Brake horsepower: (GT4) 320 at 6200 rpm; (GTC/4) 320-340 DIN at 6200-6800 rpm. Torque: 312/319 lbs.-ft. at 4600 rpm. Seven main bearings. Six Weber 38 DCOE twin-choke carburetors.

CHASSIS: Wheelbase: (246 Dino GT) 92.1 in.; (365 GTB/4, GTS/4) 94.5 in.; (365 GT4) 106.3 in.; (365 GTC/4) 98.4 in. Overall Length: (246 Dino GT) 163.4 in.; (365 GTB/4) 174 in.; (365 GT4 2+2) 189.4 in.; (365 GTC/4) 179.9 in. Height: (246 Dino GT) 43.9 in.; (365 GTB/4) 49.8 in.; (365 GT4 2+2) 51.6 in.; (365 GTC/4) 50 in. Width: (246 Dino GT) 66.9 in.; (365 GTB/4) 69.3 in.; (365 GT4 2+2) 70.7 in.; (365 GTC/4) 70.1 in. Front Tread: (246 Dino GT) 56.1 in.; (365 GTB/4) 56.7 in.; (365 GT4 2+2) 57.9 in.; (365 GTC/4) 57.9 in. Rear Tread: (246 Dino GT) 56.3 in.; (365 GTB/4) 56.1 in.; (365 GT4 2+2) 59.1 in.; (365 GTC/4) 57.9 in. Standard Tires: (246 Dino GT) 205x14; (365 GTB/4, GTS/4, GTC/4) 215/70x15; (365 GT4 2+2) 215/70VR15.

TECHNICAL: Layout: (Dino) mid-engine, rear-drive; (365 series) front-engine, rear-drive. Transmission: (Dino, 365 GTB/4, 365 GTS/4) five-speed manual in rear transaxle; (365 GT4) five-speed manual. Standard Final Drive Ratio: (365 GTB/4) 3.30:1. Steering: (Dino) rack and pinion; (365 GTB/4) worm and roller; (365 GTC/4) recirculating ball. Suspension (front): unequal-length A-arms with coil springs with anti-roll bar. Suspension (rear): (246 Dino, 365 GTB/4, 365 GTS/4) unequal-length A-arms with coil springs and anti-roll bar; (365 GT4 2+2) unequal-length A-arms with coil springs, anti-roll bar and hydraulic self-leveling. Brakes: front/rear disc. Body Construction: separate body on tubular steel frame.

PERFORMANCE: Top Speed: (246 Dino GT) 140-146 mph; (365 GTB/4) 174 mph; (365 GT4 2+2) about 145 mph; (365 GTC/4) 152-163 mph. Acceleration (0-60 mph): (246 Dino GT) 7.9-8.0 sec.; (365 GTB/4) 5.9 sec.; (365 GTC/4) 7.3 sec. Acceleration (quarter-mile): (246 Dino GT) 15.25-15.9 sec. (87-92 mph); (365 GTB/4) under 14 sec.; (365 GTC/4) 15.7 sec. (91 mph).

Manufacturer: Ferrari S.p.A. SEFAC, Maranello (Modena), Italy.

Distributor: Chinetti-Garthwaite, Paoli, Pennsylvania; or Modern Classic Motors, Reno, Nevada.

HISTORY: Testing the Dino 246 coupe, *Road & Track* advised readers that its engine was "noisy in the extreme. The sounds are exciting to be sure: busy tappets, whining cam chains and transfer drive, a raucous exhaust system...Even on a slow run to the corner drugstore, the Dino seems to be working, snarling, racing. The exhaust note at low speeds gives away its 6-cylinder configuration, but as the engine climbs into its effective rev range...it takes on the characteristic Ferrari sounds despite having only half the number of cylinders." *Motor Trend* called the Dino "pleasurably sensual." This author would lean much more towards *Motor Trend's* description of the sound. No one buys a Dino 246 as a grocery getter.

Ferrari 365 GTC/4: The 2+2s Get No Respect

In the world of Ferrari collectors, it's common knowledge that the 2+2 models are always worth less than comparable two seaters. With most collectible cars, a convertible will always be worth more than a sedan or coupe body. This can be easily explained by the comparative rarity of drop-top models to their fixed-roof siblings, and the convertible's higher initial price tag. But shouldn't a car that offers the added convenience of a rear seat suitable for luggage or small children be worth more, not less? Take the example of the 365 GTB/4 Daytona Berlinetta and its sister car, the 365 GTC/4 Coupe.

In the early 1970s, when they were new, the Daytona went for about $24,000; the C4 carried a sticker of around $26,000. Both cars used a state-of-the-art, 4.4-liter V-12 with such complexities as double overhead camshafts, dual distributors with twin points and even dual oil filters. Where the Daytona's six Weber two-barrel carburetors were nestled in the "V" of the engine, the C4 had six-side-draft Webers bolted directly to the outboard cam covers. This permitted an even lower hood line than the Daytona's already sleek nose.

As befits its lineage of racing coupes, the Daytona used a dry-sump oil system, and had its gearbox combined with the rear end for better weight distribution. The more pedestrian, Grand Touring-oriented C4 had its five-speed transmission directly behind the engine, and carried its oil supply in the more conventional location, the oil pan. The C4 also came standard with air-conditioning and a Becker Mexico radio—niceties that were optional on the Daytona.

Where the Daytona's styling is almost universally praised, the C4 has come under some criticism for one of its more innovative touches. Prior to the C4, Ferrari bumpers were more decorative than protective. The C4's low nose wears a black urethane bumper that wraps all

the way around. The same material is used at the rear for a full width cushion. The front bumper blends in well on dark color cars, but on light color examples the contrast can be a bit unattractive.

The low hood wears two large ducts for exhausting hot air, like the Daytona does. While the door handles are not the miniature pieces of jewelry that the Dino and Daytona wear, they still accent a side view that offers plenty of sex appeal. A delicate character line sweeps up from the nose, runs along the top of the fender, and then fades into the front of the door. This same line is picked up at the back of the door and adds a graceful note to the trunk, fender, and roof junction. Six round taillights, a prancing horse emblem, and four chrome tipped exhaust pipes give the rear end the proper Ferrari look.

Inside, the C4 offers significantly more room than many other Ferraris. The large rear quarter windows give it one of the brightest spaces to contemplate the elegance within. Connolly leather hides cover all the seating surfaces, and the wide center console is topped by a board that resembles a NASA control panel from a Sixties space launch. There is a thick, chrome shift lever topped by a black ball shift knob, but instead of the more typical Ferrari chrome shift gate, a more traditional black boot surrounds the lever's entry into the gearbox. Various unlabeled toggle switches are mixed in with levers for the heating and air conditioning system. The only upper air outlets are four round vents whose rotation theoretically allows them to double as both defroster and face portals for cool and hot air. The radio, too, resides in the console.

The wide, flat front seats were obviously shaped more for grand touring gallops than hard cornering cosseting. The best thing to say about the tiny rear seats is that they fold down to form a nicely carpeted luggage shelf.

This author agrees with the majority

of reviews that a C4 is a much nicer car than the Daytona for everyday driving. The standard power steering means that every outing does not turn into an upper body workout. While the engines are essentially the same, there is something about the collection of mufflers, pipes, and resonators under the C4 that allow it to produce what's been called the best rendition of the classic V-12 aria that any Ferrari has ever produced. Sure, a racing V-12 will be both louder and more feral, but the song that emanates from a C4 offers just the right balance between soul-stirring raucousness and sophisticated crooning. Perhaps the C4's side-draft Webers are the key to this singer's perfection?

Driving a C4 is a pleasure that everyone should experience. Once the engine and gearbox are up to temperature, sprints from 0-60 take between six and seven seconds. The C4 was never geared for drag strip work, so the pleasures of its engine are better exploited as the speed rises. It's entirely possible to see 156 mph in an example that is in a peak state of tune. But, you don't need to go that fast to enjoy this Ferrari. The engine offers so much torque that downshifts are more a matter of choice than necessity. The V-12 pulls the somewhat heavy car with an alacrity that seems even greater than it is, thanks to the marvelous soundtrack.

It was produced at a pivotal time in the Ferrari chronicles. Along with the Daytona and Dino, these three were the last Ferraris designed when Enzo Ferrari owned the company. It would be untrue to say that the steeds from Maranello were tamer under Fiat's watch, but many manufacturer's glory days were at the beginning of the 1960s, and the end of the 1970s. The U.S. regulations put a stranglehold on horsepower, and the initial attempts to meet bumper regulations now look crude.

So, while the C4 offers most of the same driving pleasures of a Daytona, its prices languish at a level only one half or less than its Berlinetta brother. It offers a useable trunk, and with only 500 made (compared to 1,504 for the 365 GTB/4 and GTS/4 production), it has the added cachet of lower volume.

Road & Track may have said it best in their 1972 road test, "The Ferrari for the mature enthusiast."

Have you grown up yet?

1973 Ferrari 365 Boxer. (FSpA/WG)

1973

DINO 246 GT/GTS — V-6 —
Despite their not wearing any Ferrari logos, the Dino 246 models continued to be highly desirable cars. Several U.S. Dinos came equipped with more intricately designed Campagnolo road wheels. These cars also had mildly flared fenders. Another popular option was the Daytona-style seats that feature longitudinal bolsters. Cars equipped with both options were known as having "flares and chairs."

DINO 308 GT4 — V-8 —
This car was a bold step for Ferrari. In one model the company introduced their first V-8 power road car, and the first mid-engine with 2+2 seating. The difficulty in fitting four people and an engine in the relatively short 100.4-inch wheelbase might have been overcome. However, instead of being draped in the usual sensuous lines of a Pininfarina design, the 308 GT4 wore an angular body penned by Bertone. And, to make things even more difficult for the dealers, the car initially wore no Ferrari badges. The twin-cam, 2927-cc Ferrari-built V-8 engine with four Weber carburetors initially produced 250 horsepower in European trim. Thanks to an air pump and a change in the timing, U.S. cars made about 230 hp. A toothed-belt

cam drive replaced the usual chain arrangement. Hidden headlamps were installed, with amber rectangular parking lights inset in the black bumper. Air intakes stood aft of tapered rear quarter windows. A horizontal bodyside trim strip could separate two-tone paint jobs, and the "flying buttress" roofline gave this Dino a semi-fastback look.

TYPE 365 GTB/4, GTS/4 "DAYTONA" —
V-12 — Production of the popular "Daytona" would continue into 1974; see previous listings for additional details.

365 GT4 2+2 — V-12 — Production of the 4390-cc four-seater continued into 1975; see previous listings for additional details.

Note: Some American directories for 1973 continued to list the 365 GTC/4 coupe, priced at $27,250; see previous listing for details.

I.D. DATA: Not available.

Model	Body Type & Seating	Engine Type/CID	P.O.E. Price	Weight (lbs.)	Prod. Total
246 DINO					
GT	2-dr Coupe-2P	V6/148	14450	2380	Note 1
GTS	2-dr Targa Cpe-2P	V6/148	15255	2426	Note 2
DINO 308 GT4					
308 GT4	2-dr Coupe-2+2P	V8/179	N/A	2535	N/A
365 GTB/4 "DAYTONA"					
365 GTB/4	2-dr Coupe-2P	V12/268	25350	2646	Note 3
365 GTS/4	2-dr Conv Cpe-2P	V12/268	28275	2646	Note 4
365 GT4 2+2					
365 GT4	2-dr Coupe-2+2P	V12/268	N/A	3307	Note 5

Note 1: About 2,487 Type 246 Dino GT coupes were produced from 1969-73.
Note 2: About 1,274 Type 246 Dino GTS Targa coupes were produced from 1972-73.
Note 3: About 1,285 Type 365 GTB/4 coupes were produced from 1968-74.
Note 4: About 127 Type 365 GTS/4 convertibles were produced from 1969-74.
Note 5: A total of 470 Type 365 GT4 2+2 coupes (sometimes called sedans) were produced from 1972-75.
Weight Note: Figures shown are approximate (or averages).
Production Note: A total of 1,772 Ferraris (including 1,164 Dinos and 584 series 365) were built in 1973.

1973 Ferrari 365 Boxer interior. (FSpA/WG)

ENGINE [Base V-6 (246 Dino GT)]: 65-degree, dual-overhead-cam "vee" type six-cylinder. Cast-iron block and light alloy heads. Displacement: 148 cid (2418 cc). Bore & stroke: 3.64 x 2.36 in. (92.5 x 60 mm). Compression ratio: 9.0:1. Brake horsepower: 195 (DIN) at 7600 rpm. Torque: 167 lbs.-ft. at 5500 rpm. Four main bearings. Three Weber 40 DCNF 13 carburetors.

ENGINE [Base V-8 (Dino 308 GT4)]: 90-degree, dual-overhead-cam "vee" type eight-cylinder. Light alloy block and heads. Displacement: 179 cid (2927 cc). Bore & stroke: 3.19 x 2.80 in. (81 x 71 mm). Compression ratio: 8.8:1. Brake horsepower: 230 at 6600 rpm. Torque: 209 lbs.-ft. at 5000 rpm. Five main bearings. Four Weber 40 DCNF carburetors.

Note: European Dino 308 GT4 V-8 produced 250 bhp.

ENGINE [Base V-12 (365 GTB/4, GTS/4)]: 60-degree, dual-overhead-cam "vee" type 12-cylinder. Aluminum alloy block and heads. Displacement: 267.8 cid (4390 cc). Bore & stroke: 3.19 x 2.80 in. (81 x 71 mm). Compression ratio: 8.8:1. Brake horsepower: 352 (DIN) at 7500 rpm. Torque: 319 lbs.-ft. DIN (365 SAE) at 5000 rpm. Seven main bearings. Six Weber twin-choke carburetors.

ENGINE [Base V-12 (365 GT4 2+2)]: 60-degree, dual-overhead-cam "vee" type 12-cylinder. Aluminum alloy block and heads. Displacement: 267.8 cid (4390 cc). Bore & stroke: 3.19 x 2.80 in. (81 x 71 mm). Compression ratio: 8.8:1. Brake horsepower: 320 at 6200 rpm. Torque: 319 lbs.-ft. at 4600 rpm. Seven main bearings. Six Weber twin-choke carburetors.

CHASSIS: Wheelbase: (246 Dino GT) 92.1 in.; (Dino 308 GT4) 100.4 in.; (365 GTB/4, GTS/4) 94.5 in.; (365 GT4) 106.3 in. Overall Length: (246 Dino GT) 165 in.; (Dino 308 GT4) 170.1 in.; (365 GTB/4) 174 in.; (365 GT4 2+2) 189.4 in. Height: (246 Dino GT) 43.9 in.; (Dino 308 GT4) 46.5 in.; (365 GTB/4) 49.8 in.; (365 GT4 2+2) 51.6 in. Width: (246 Dino GT) 66.9 in.; (Dino 308 GT4) 70.9 in.; (365 GTB/4) 69.3 in.; (365 GT4 2+2) 70.7 in. Front Tread: (246 Dino GT) 56.1 in.; (Dino 308 GT4) 57.9 in.; (365 GTB/4) 56.7 in.; (365 GT4 2+2) 57.9 in. Rear Tread: (246 Dino GT) 56.3 in.; (Dino 308 GT4) 57.5 in.; (365 GTB/4) 56.1 in.; (365 GT4 2+2) 59.1 in. Standard Tires: (246 Dino GT) 205/70VR14; (Dino 308 GT4) 205/70VR14; (365 GTB/4, GTS/4) 215/70x15; (365 GT4 2+2) 215/70VR15.

TECHNICAL: Layout: (Dino) mid-engine, rear-drive; (365 series) front-engine, rear-drive. Transmission: (Dino, 365 GTB/4, 365 GTS/4) five-speed manual in rear transaxle; (365 GT4) five-speed manual. Steering: (Dino) rack and pinion; (365 GTB/4) worm and roller; (365 GT4 2+2) recirculating ball. Suspension (front): unequal-length A-arms with coil springs with anti-roll bar. Suspension (rear): (246/308 Dino, 365 GTB/4, 365 GTS/4) unequal-length A-arms with coil springs and anti-roll bar; (365 GT4 2+2) unequal-length A-arms with coil springs, anti-roll bar and hydraulic self-leveling. Brakes: front/rear disc. Body Construction: separate body on tubular steel frame.

PERFORMANCE: Top Speed: (246 Dino GT) 140 mph; (European Dino 308 GT4) 150+ mph; (365 GTB/4) 170+ mph; (365 GT4 2+2) 145-152 mph. Acceleration (0-60 mph): (246 Dino GT) 8.0 sec.; (European Dino 308 GT4) 6.4 sec.; (365 GTB/4) 5.9 sec.

Manufacturer: Ferrari S.p.A. SEFAC, Maranello (Modena), Italy.

Distributor: Chinetti-Garthwaite Imports Inc., Paoli, Pennsylvania; or Modern Classic Motors, Reno, Nevada.

1973 Ferrari 365 GTS/4 Daytona Spider. (WG)

1973 Ferrari 308 GT/4 production prototype rear view. (WG)

1973 Ferrari 308 GT/4 production prototype. (WG)

365GT4 BB, BB512, or BB512i:
They All Spell Ferrari Berlinetta Boxer

1973 Ferrari 365 Boxer. (FSpA/WG)

Today, many fans consider the Ferrari Daytona the ultimate expression of Ferrari magic. While its charms are undeniable, it suffered from a comparison to its cross-town rivals, the Lamborghini Miura, and the Maserati Bora. Some said that the Daytona proved that Enzo Ferrari was mired in the past with his refusal to launch a flagship Ferrari with its engine in the middle. At the 1971 Turin Auto Show, Ferrari answered his critics with a loud retort, the 365GT4 BB.

The Boxer's appearance was a smash hit with everyone. Pininfarina's latest creation seemed to epitomize the longer, lower, wider mantra that drove car design. As impressive as the sleek design was, there were plenty more "wows" generated when the rear-hinged engine cover was tilted back. An engine worthy of display in an art museum sat cradled in a framework of steel tubing. Beneath the black wrinkled-finished cam covers, two banks of six cylinders were set 180 degrees apart, so when the pistons moved up and down in their bores, one

could imagine two boxers throwing punches at one another. Sitting atop the engine were four Weber 401F3C triple-throat carburetors. Here was an engine that looked like it came right out of Ferrari's Formula One car plugged into a car made for galloping down the auto strata.

The "365" designation of the 4.391-liter engine came from the 365-cc displacement of a single cylinder. By using this size, various components (pistons, connecting rods, and valve train) from the 365 GTC/4 engine could be used as a cost-saving measure. The "4" stood for the four camshafts driven by belts, instead of the traditional Ferrari timing chains. Berlinetta was the typical Italian designation for a coupe. Ferrari quoted the prototype engine as making 380 horsepower.

It was announced at the following year's Turin show that production would soon begin. Eager buyers would have to wait another ten months before the first Boxer finally made its way into European showrooms. American buyers would have an even longer wait, as the tough new emissions and safety laws caused Ferrari to not go to the expense of having the Boxer federalized. Demand for the new Ferrari model was so strong that companies were formed to change the cars over to meet U.S. regulations. Amerispec's Dick Fritz used the expertise he developed as the service manager of Luigi Chinetti Motors, the premier Ferrari dealer in the country, to change and add the necessary components to bring the Boxer into compliance.

Ferrari used a mix of materials in constructing their new supercar. The doors, under tray, and both the nose and tail were crafted from aluminum. Fiberglass was chosen for the front and rear valances, and steel was the metal for the roof and framework. While Ferrari had used a flat twelve before, the first was a 1964 Formula One twelve-cylinder engine displacing only 1.5 liters. They had experimented with mid-engine layouts, placing the 250LM's engine longitudinally and the Dino 246's transversely across the

tight engine bay. Their concern over having so much weight in the tail of the car caused the inclusion of double coils at each of the rear corners.

There should have been more concern with the accuracy of the promotional material. While the Boxer prototype may have made 380 hp, concern for the engine's longevity forced a de-tuning to 360 hp. This might have been all right if they hadn't continued to claim a 188-mph top speed for this new Ferrari. *Road & Track* could only achieve 175 mph, and their 0-60 mph times were nearly two seconds slower than the factory's figures. Despite this controversy, 387 Boxers found their way into new homes.

By 1976, it was time for Ferrari to show that he was receptive to his customers suggestions. The engine's displacement was increased to 4,942 ccs, and a dry sump system was added for greater oil capacity. A twin plate clutch used two smaller discs to reduce the effort necessary when one wanted to stir

1973-1976 Ferrari 365 GT4/BB engine. (MC)

the chrome lever through its external gate. The body was two inches wider, rear the track increased by 1.7 inches, and the nine-inch rear wheels became standard equipment. Externally, a small chin spoiler reduced some of the high-speed wander that spooked those brave souls who ventured above 150 mph. At the rear, the six taillights and six exhaust tips were reduced to four, and the Boxer got a new name, 512BB. Now the engine displacement (5 liters) and the number of cylinders were proudly announced in the model designation. From 1976 through 1981, 929 512 BBis roared out of the Ferrari factory.

In a reversal of the usual procedure, the 512 BBi went into production several months before it was officially launched at the Frankfurt Auto Show in 1981. Bosch K-Jetronic fuel injection replaced the exotic, but easy to get out of synch carburetors. Once again, there was little or no change in the horsepower, but the power now peaked at lower rpms. More important for us Yankees, was the greater ease in getting the injected engine to pass the U.S. emissions test. Ferrari instituted a program in 1983 where North American dealers could sell the 512 BBi for delivery at the Ferrari factory, with the intention of having one of the conversion companies change the car, once the new owner had enjoyed a European vacation with his new Ferrari. This proved to be the most popular edition of the Boxer with 1,007 being sold between 1981 and 1984, when the Boxer stepped aside for its replacement, the Testarossa.

In today's market, Boxers are considered a bargain. It resides in a gray zone between the modern, trouble-free Ferraris and the classic older cars. Plus, all of them are called "gray-market" cars, because the factory never imported them. Like the 275 GTB/4, the Daytona, the 288 GTO, the F40, the F50, and the Enzo, the Boxer was the top of the line Ferrari in its day. While you can find Daytonas and 275s in the $100,000 to $200,000 range, you'll have to climb up above $325,000 to get into your own F40. F50s and Enzos are still so new that you might need $500,000 or more to take possession of one of these supercars.

The most desirable model is the carbureted 365 GTB/4; the song this engine sings is the closest thing you'll hear on the street to a Ferrari racing engine. Luggage space is minimal; so don't buy a Boxer if you don't know how to travel light. If you enjoy a lively driving tussle, the Boxer could be the Ferrari you're looking for.

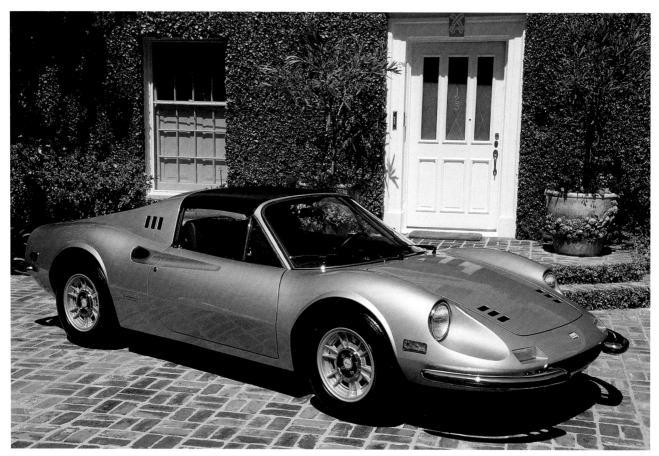

1974 Ferrari Dino 246/GTS. (DA)

1974

DINO 308 GT4 — V-8 — While production started in 1973 for the European market, it was late in 1974 before the first U.S. models were shipped. Dealers started selling the cars in early 1975.

TYPE 365 GTB/4, 365 GTS/4 "DAYTONA" — V-12 — This would be the final year of production for the popular "Daytona" duo.

TYPE 365 GT4 2+2 — V-12 — Introduced in 1972, the four-seat 365-series coupe continued with little change into 1975.

TYPE 365 GT4 BB — FLAT-12 — While cross-town rivals, Lamborghini and Maserati were turning out mid-engine supercars like the Muria and the Bora, Ferrari still clung to the traditional front-engine/rear drive layout for the premier Ferrari, the 365 GTB/4. Then, late in 1973, the first Berlinetta Boxer was shown. Although the 365 designation showed the same displacement per cylinder as the Daytona, the layout was completely different. The BB carried its new 4390-cc twin-cam engine behind the cockpit, ahead of the rear axle, and the cylinders were arranged on a 180-degree

plane for a lower center of gravity. The mid-engine twelve, with toothed-belt camshaft drive and four triple-barrel Weber carburetors, produced 344 hp (DIN) and 302 lbs.-ft. of torque. As usual, the body panels were steel; aluminum was used for the hood, doors and engine cover. New fiberglass lower panels were painted in matte black, giving the car an even lower look than its 49.8 inches. The entire front end hinged forward as a unit, as did the rear-hinged rear section. The long, tapered-forward nose held the radiator, spare tire, and minimal luggage. Hidden headlamps were used. Slight bulges were evident over the front wheels and the profile displayed a "flying buttress" roofline. Three tail lamps stood on each side of the back panel. Pininfarina was responsible for the styling, while Scaglietti built the bodies. No cars were officially imported into the U.S. by Chinetti-Garthwaite; instead they came in through the gray market and were modified by local shops such as Amerispec to meet emissions. The multi-tube chassis used square and rectangular sections instead of round and oval. Three axle ratios were available: 3.90:1, 3.75:1, and 3.46:1. With an achieved top speed of 175 mph, *Road & Track* in 1975 called the 365 GT4 BB "the fastest road car we've ever tested." As for acceleration, the coupe could hit sixty in 7.2-seconds and run the quarter-mile in 15.5-seconds, reaching 102.5 mph, though noting that the "Boxer is surprisingly heavy." They further explained that "1st gear is very tall and the clutch in our test car slipped badly," so test times might have been swifter yet. Before long, this "Boxer" would lead to the 512 BB/BBi.

Note: Thanks to unsold inventories, some American directories continued to list the Dino 246 GT coupe and GTS convertible, selling for $14,990 and $15,795 respectively, though production halted after 1973; and the 365 GTC/4 coupe at $28,220, that also ceased production.

I.D. DATA: Not available.

Model	Body Type & Seating	Engine Type/CID	P.O.E. Price	Weight (lbs.)	Prod. Total
DINO 308 GT4					
308 GT4	2-dr Coupe-2+2P	V8/179	N/A	2535	Note 1
365 GTB/4 "DAYTONA"					
365 GTB/4	2-dr Coupe-2P	V12/268	25350	2646	Note 2
365 GTS/4	2-dr Conv Cpe-2P	V12/268	28275	2646	Note 3
365 GT4 2+2					
365 GT4	2-dr Coupe-2+2P	V12/268	N/A	3307	Note 4
365 GT4 BB					
365 GT4 BB	2-dr Coupe-2P	H12/268	N/A	2469	Note 5

Note 1: About 2,826 Type 308 GT4 coupes were produced from 1973-80.
Note 2: About 1,383 Type 365 GTB/4 coupes were produced from 1968-74.
Note 3: About 121 Type 365 GTS/4 convertibles were produced from 1969-73.
Note 4: A total of 470 Type 365 GT4 2+2 coupes (sometimes called sedans) were

produced from 1972-75.
Note 5: About 387 Type 365 GT4 BB coupes were produced from 1973-76.
Weight Note: Figures shown are approximate (or averages).
Production Note: A total of 1,436 Ferraris (316 Dino, 764 Dino 308, 127 365 GT/GT4, and 229 BB) were built in 1974.

ENGINE [Base V-8 (Dino 308 GT4)]: 90-degree, dual-overhead-cam "vee" type eight-cylinder. Light alloy block and heads. Displacement: 179 cid (2927 cc). Bore & stroke: 3.19 x 2.80 in. (81 x 71 mm). Compression ratio: 8.8:1. Brake horsepower: 230 at 6600 rpm (possibly as high as 240 bhp available). Torque: 209 lbs.-ft. at 5000 rpm. Five main bearings. Four Weber 40 DCNF carburetors.

Note: European 308 GT4 V-8 produced 250 bhp.

ENGINE [Base V-12 (365 GTB/4, GTS/4)]: 60-degree, dual-overhead-cam "vee" type 12-cylinder. Aluminum alloy block and heads. Displacement: 267.8 cid (4390 cc). Bore & stroke: 3.19 x 2.80 in. (81 x 71 mm). Compression ratio: 8.8:1. Brake horsepower: 352 (DIN) at 7500 rpm. Torque: 319 lbs.-ft. DIN (365 SAE) at 5000 rpm. Seven main bearings. Six Weber 40 DCN-20 twin-choke carburetors.

1974 Ferrari Dino 246/GTS. (DA)

ENGINE [Base V-12 (365 GT4 2+2)]: Same as 4390-cc V-12 engine above, except Brake horsepower: 320 at 6200 rpm. Torque: 319 lbs.-ft. at 4600 rpm. Six Weber twin-choke carburetors.

ENGINE [Base Flat-12 (365 GT4 BB)]: Horizontally-opposed, dual-overhead-cam 12-cylinder. Aluminum alloy block and heads. Displacement: 267.8 cid (4390 cc). Bore & stroke: 3.19 x 2.80 in. (81 x 71 mm). Compression ratio: 8.8:1. Brake horsepower: 344 (DIN) at 7000 rpm. Torque: 302 lbs.-ft. at 3900 rpm. Seven main bearings. Four Weber triple-barrel carburetors.

CHASSIS: Wheelbase: (Dino 308 GT4) 100.4 in.; (365 GTB/4, GTS/4) 94.5 in.; (365 GT4 2+2) 106.3 in.; (365 GT4 BB) 98.4 in. Overall Length: (Dino 308 GT4) 170.1 in.; (365 GTB/4) 174 in.; (365 GT4 2+2) 189.4 in.; (365 GT4 BB) 171.6 in. Height: (Dino 308 GT4) 46.5 in.; (365 GTB/4) 49.8 in.; (365 GT4 2+2) 51.6 in.; (365 GT4 BB) 44.1 in. Width: (Dino 308 GT4) 70.9 in.; (365 GTB/4) 69.3 in.; (365 GT4 2+2) 70.7 in.; (365 GT4 BB) 70.9 in. Front Tread: (Dino 308 GT4) 57.9 in.; (365 GTB/4) 56.7 in.; (365 GT4 2+2) 59.1 in.; (365 GT4 BB) 59.1 in. Rear Tread: (Dino 308 GT4) 57.5 in.; (365 GTB/4) 56.1 in.; (365 GT4 2+2) 57.9 in.; (365 GT4 BB) 59.8 in. Standard Tires: (Dino 308 GT4) 205/70VR14; (365 GTB/4, GTS/4) 215/70VR15; (365 GT4 2+2) 215/70VR15; (365 GT4 BB) 215/70VR15.

TECHNICAL: Layout: (Dino, 365 GT4 BB) mid-engine, rear-drive; (others) front-engine, rear-drive. Transmission: (Dino, 365 GT4 BB, 365 GTB/4, 365 GTS/4) five-speed manual in rear transaxle; (365 GT4 2+2) five-speed manual. Steering: (Dino, BB) rack and pinion; (365 GTB/4) worm and roller; (365 GT4 2+2) recirculating ball. Suspension (front): unequal-length A-arms with coil springs and anti-roll bar. Suspension (rear): (308 Dino, 365 GTB/4, 365 GTS/4) unequal-length A-arms with coil springs and anti-roll bar; (365 GT4 BB) unequal-length A-arms with twin coil springs and anti-roll bar; (365 GT4 2+2) unequal-length A-arms with coil springs, anti-roll bar and hydraulic self-leveling. Brakes: front/rear disc. Body Construction: separate body on tubular steel frame.

PERFORMANCE: Top Speed: (European Dino 308 GT4) 150-155 mph; (365 GTB/4) 170+ mph; (365 GT4 2+2) about 145 mph; (365 GT4 BB) 175-188 mph. Acceleration (0-60 mph): (European Dino 308 GT4) 6.4 sec.; (365 GTB/4) 5.9 sec.; (365 GT4 BB) 7.2 sec. Acceleration (quarter-mile): (365 GT4 BB) 15.5 sec. (102.5 mph).

Manufacturer: Ferrari S.p.A. SEFAC, Maranello (Modena), Italy.

Distributor: Chinetti-Garthwaite Imports Inc., Paoli, Pennsylvania; or Modern Classic Motors, Reno, Nevada.

HISTORY: The new "BB" wasn't the first horizontally-opposed powerplant to come from Ferrari. A dozen 1.5-liter flat engines had been built in 1964 for Formula One purposes. The term "boxer" had been used earlier when referring to Volkswagen and Porsche engines, and other versions were used in Grand Prix and sports/racing vehicles. Ferrari's first roadgoing prototype, however, appeared at the Turin show in 1971. Production of the 365 GT4 BB began late in 1973, as a 1974 model.

Despite Three (or More) Strikes Against It, the 308 GT4 2+2 is Still a Bargain

Ferrari 308 GT4 circa 1974. (MC)

Everyone remembers his or her first love, and by comparison, the next suitor almost always seems lacking. For me, and many Ferrari fans in the early 1970s, the sensuous Dino 246 was that first love. As a 20-year old I could never imagine having enough money to buy a V-12 Ferrari, but the little jewel of a mid-engined, V-6 coupe seemed almost attainable. In the early '70s, Ferrari offered a varied and potent model line; the 365 GTB/4 Daytona, the 365 GTC/4 2+2, and the "junior Ferrari," the Dino 246 GT. By 1975, all the United States dealers had to offer was the just-introduced 308 GT4 2+2.

The 308 GT4 had three, no, make that five, strikes against it when it first hit the shores here in January of 1975:

1. It was either viewed as a replacement for the 246 Dino, in which case it fell woefully short in the desired sex appeal category. Or, it really wasn't a replacement for any of the three previous models due to its unusual nature.

2. Bertone, instead of Pininfarina, designed the 308 GT4's body. While Bertone had become known for such classic designs as the Lamborghini Miura, it was from the pens of Pininfarina shops that most all of the previous Ferraris had emerged.

3. This Ferrari was a 2+2, instead of the more popular two-seat sportscars.

Ferrari 2+2s always sold at a much slower rate than their sportier siblings.

4. All automobile manufacturers were having trouble meeting the twin demands of lower emissions and crash-worthy bumpers in the mid-Seventies. As a result, most every car from 1974-1976 offers inferior and temperamental performance compared with those cars before and after these dark days. And, the 308 GT4's initial attempts to meet U.S. bumper regulations look like tacked-on, last minute solutions.

5. Perhaps the biggest problem that faced the 308 GT4 here in the U.S. was its lack of Ferrari badges. Instead of the fabled prancing horse medallion, the 308 GT4 wore the Dino script on its nose and tail.

This may have had some small effect on limiting Dino 246 GT sales, but it was positively disastrous for the 308 GT4. Only 188 were sold in the U.S. in 1975. And, bear in mind that since the 400i was never officially imported into the U.S., this was the only new product the Ferrari dealers had to offer here.

When the car debuted at the Paris Auto Salon in October 1973, reaction was mixed. On the plus side, this was the first time that Ferrari had offered a V-8 engine in a street car. Also, this engine was mounted amidships, qualifying the 308 GT4 for another Ferrari first. While the

Campagnolo alloy wheels looked like a carry-over from the Dino 246 GT, the cars' shapes were totally different. The 246 offered smooth curves with voluptuous fenders that gave the little two-seater a lusty shape.

The wedge nose and angular style of the 308 GT4 were a sharp contrast, but did at least form a cohesive whole. However, the car's original lines were butchered by the battering ram bumpers hung on both ends of the Series I cars that made it to our shores. The 2927-cc V-8 engine lost something in its trip across the Atlantic—power. European models were rated at 255 DIN horsepower. (No, DIN does not stand for Deutschland Invented Number.) Testing a European 308 GT4 for *Road & Track*, Paul Frere managed to get a 0-60 mph time of 6.4 seconds, did the quarter mile sprint in 14.6 seconds, and reached a top speed of 152 mph. When the car was fitted with an air pump and revised timing, Ferrari rated the engine for 240 hp. *Road and Track's* test of a U.S. model yielded a 0-60 of 8 seconds, a 1/4 mile stroll of 16.1 seconds, and a top speed of only 138 mph.

By May of 1976, Ferrari was ready to address some of the criticisms for the 308 GT4. The U.S. bumpers were now smaller, air conditioning vents were added to the foot wells, and wider wheels and a deeper front spoiler were available as options. But the biggest, most profitable change cost the factory very little in research and development—a proper prancing stallion replaced the Dino badge on the nose. Even if the Dino script still adorned the rear deck lid, 308 GT4 owners could now proudly point to their car's proboscis and say, "See, it's a REAL Ferrari."

Tightening emissions standards led to the 1978 Series II engines being down rated to 230 hp, and the 1979 models could only muster 205 heavily burdened ponies.

Despite all these problems, the 308 GT4 is still a very desirable automobile. Because of all the aforementioned difficulties, prices for these Ferraris languish between $15,000 and $30,000.

This is significantly less than any V-12 model, except perhaps the 330 GT 2+2 with the under-loved, four-headlight setup.

Access to the cockpit is easier than many of its contemporaries, thanks to the long doors needed to gain entry to the very occasional rear seats. Most U.S. models came with all of the optional equipment standard. So, leather covers the seats as well as the door panels. The dashboard is a bit different in that the instrument binnacle angles back towards the driver at both ends. The right end contains the levers for the heating and ventilation system, the left has those great Ferrari toggle switches that control the less important functions.

The nearly 3.0-liter V-8 makes 3/4 of the correct sounds. Double overhead camshafts driven by belts produce the proper whirring noise, just inches behind the driver's head. Thanks to the cab-forward design, necessitated by the packaging of four people and a drivetrain between its compact 100.4-inch wheelbases, the view ahead offers far more road than hood paint. The 205/70x14-inch tires offer respectable amounts of grip for cars of this era. Once the four Weber 40 DCNF carburetors are properly synched, the 308 GT4 acquits itself so well in the drivability department that many owners use them as daily drivers.

The folks that I met who seemed to be getting the most enjoyment from their 308 GT4s were three fellows at Lime Rock who had long ago given up driving their 308s on the street, and had done the necessary modifications to make them enjoyable track cars. Strip out the interior, fit a roll cage, hop up the engine, and put on a sticky set of tires and you've got a bargain Ferrari, ready to infuse the driver's head with fantasies of Le Mans, even if the venue is only Lime Rock.

While it may not reside in the same stratosphere as Ferrari GTOs and 250 LMs, the 308 GT4 is a bargain for those folks looking to make the leap from Ferrari fan to Ferrari owner.

1975 Ferrari 308 GTB. (WG)

DINO 308 GT4 — V-8 — The Bertone-bodied eight-cylinder Dino continued with little change. Until the arrival of the 308 GTB in the fall of 1976, this was the only new model that US dealers were authorized to sell.

TYPE 308 GTB — V-8 — Thanks to the popularity of the television show *Magnum PI*, the 308 is still the image most people conjure up when someone mentions Ferrari. The fact that production of the 308, and its similar decedents, lasted for nearly 15 years, helped to make this the most popular Ferrari ever produced. Production is listed as 21,678 cars—more than all Ferraris produced for the first two decades of the company's illustrious career. The replacement for the Dino 246 first appeared at the Paris show in October 1975. Although it carried a Pininfarina design, the bodies were built by Scaglietti. Rather than the typical steel or aluminum, these early 308 GTB bodies were made of fiberglass; though construction would soon change to

steel. A wide eggcrate grille stood below the bumper, with Ferrari's prancing horse insignia rearing proudly in its center. Large amber-over-clear park/signal lights were set into the outboard ends of the bumper. Hidden headlamps and fenders were used, with a "flying buttress" fastback roofline and a low, squared-off nose. Perhaps the most distinctive of the body's features, though, were the large concave air-intake scoops that ran back from the center of each door, tapering gently outward as they entered the quarter-panel inlet opening. These provided air for the engine intake and helped to keep the mid-engine compartment cooler. Four large round tail lamps (two red, two amber) went in the Kamm-style tail. Mechanical details were similar to the 246 and 308 Dinos, with unequal-length A-arms and coil springs forming the suspension at each wheel. Wheelbase was 92.1 inches, as on the Dino 246. Power came from a four-cam 2927-cc (179-cid) V-8, nearly identical to the 308 GT4 engine. With four Weber carburetors, producing 240 hp (255 for European models) via 8.8:1 compression and hooked to a five-speed all-synchro transaxle.

TYPE 365 GT4 BB — FLAT-12 — Production of the "boxer" coupe with horizontally-opposed engine continued with little change.

Model	Body Type & Seating	Engine Type/CID	P.O.E. Price	Weight (lbs.)	Prod. Total
308 GTB4					
308 GT4	2-dr Coupe-2+2P	V8/179	22550	2535	Note 1
308 GTB					
308 GTB	2-dr Coupe-2P	V8/179	28500	3085	Note 2
365 GT4 BB					
365 GTB BB	2-dr Coupe-2P	H12/268	N/A	3420	Note 3

Note 1: About 2,826 Type 308 GT4 coupes were produced from 1973-80.
Note 2: About 3,665 Type 308 GTB (and 208 GTB) coupes were produced from 1975-80.
Note 3: About 387 Type 365 GT4 BB coupes were produced from 1974-76.
Weight Note: Figures shown are approximate (or averages).
Production Note: A total of 1,337 Ferraris (1,211 of them 308s) were built in 1975.

ENGINE [Base V-8 (Dino 308 GT4, 308 GTB)]:
90-degree, dual-overhead-cam "vee" type eight-cylinder. Light alloy block and heads. Displacement: 178.6 cid (2927 cc). Bore & stroke: 3.19 x 2.79 in. (81 x 71 mm). Compression ratio: 8.8:1. Brake horsepower: 240 at 6600 rpm. Torque: 195 lbs.-ft. at 5000 rpm. Five main bearings. Four Weber 40 DCNF two-barrel carburetors.

ENGINE [Base Flat-12 (365 GT4 BB)]:
Horizontally-opposed, dual-overhead-cam 12-cylinder. Aluminum alloy block and heads. Displacement: 267.8 cid (4390 cc). Bore & stroke: 3.19 x 2.80 in. (81 x 71 mm). Compression ratio: 8.8:1. Brake horsepower: 344 (DIN) at 7000 rpm. Torque: 302 lbs.-ft. at 3900 rpm. Seven main bearings. Four Weber triple-barrel carburetors.

CHASSIS:
Wheelbase: (Dino 308 GT4) 100.4 in.; (308 GTB) 92.1 in.; (365 GT4 BB) 98.4 in. Overall Length: (Dino 308 GT4) 176.7 in.; (308 GTB) 166.5 in.; (365 GT4 BB) 171.6 in. Height: (Dino 308 GT4) 47.6 in.; (308 GTB) 44.1 in.; (365 GT4 BB) 44.1 in. Width: (Dino 308 GT4) 71 in.; (308 GTB) 67.75 in.; (365 GT4 BB) 70.9 in. Front Tread: (Dino 308 GT4) 57.9 in.; (308 GTB) 57.9 in.; (365 GT4 BB) 59.1 in. Rear Tread: (Dino 308 GT4) 57.9 in.; (308 GTB) 57.5 in.; (365 GT4 BB) 59.8 in. Standard Tires: (Dino 308 GT4) 205/70VR14; (308 GTB) 205/70VR14 Michelin XWX; (365 GT4 BB) 215/70VR15.

TECHNICAL:
Layout: mid-engine, rear-drive. Transmission: five-speed manual in rear transaxle. 308 GTB gear ratios: (1st) 3.58:1; (2nd) 2.37:1; (3rd) 1.69:1; (4th) 1.24:1; (5th) 0.95:1. Standard Final Drive Ratio: (308 GTB) 3.71:1 or 4.06:1. Steering: rack and pinion. Suspension (front): unequal-length A-arms with coil springs and anti-roll bar. Suspension (rear): (308 Dino, 308 GTB) unequal-length A-arms with coil springs and anti-roll bar; (365 GT4 BB) unequal-length A-arms with twin coil springs and anti-roll bar. Brakes: front/rear disc. Body Construction: separate body (fiberglass on 308 GTB) on tubular steel frame.

PERFORMANCE:
Top Speed: (European Dino 308 GT4) 150+ mph; (308 GTB) up to 150 mph estimated; (365 GT4 BB) 175 mph. Acceleration (0-60 mph): (European Dino 308 GT4) 6.4 sec.; (308 GTB) 8.2 sec.; (365 GT4 BB) 7.2 sec. Acceleration (quarter-mile): (308 GTB) 17.0 sec. (90.8 mph); (365 GT4 BB) 15.5 sec. (102.5 mph).

ADDITIONAL MODELS:
In order to save on taxes a 1991-cc engine was fitted to the GT4 and became known as the 208GT4 2+2. This model can be recognized by the small NASA duct below the side air intake.

Manufacturer: Ferrari S.p.A. SEFAC, Maranello (Modena), Italy.

Distributor: Chinetti-Garthwaite Imports, Paoli, Pennsylvania; and Modern Classic Motors, Reno, Nevada.

HISTORY:
By this time, Ferrari had 40 dealers in the U.S.

1975 Ferrari 308 GTB. (WG)

Ferrari 308:
You Don't Have to Be a Private Investigator to Drive One

1975-76 Ferrari 308 GTB. (MC)

Thanks to Tom Selleck's television show, *Magnum P.I.*, the 308 GTB and 308 GTS are easily the most recognized Ferraris in the world. If you showed photos of exotic cars to the general public, this is the car they could quickly pick out as the Ferrari. The knowledgeable enthusiast also loved this car, which was the first non-V-12 engine vehicle to wear the prancing horse proudly on its nose.

When the 308 GTB was unveiled at the October 1975 Paris Auto Salon, the *tifosi* breathed a sigh of relief. The last new Ferrari, the Dino 308 GT4, had been designed by Bertone and its styling was not loved by all. For the 308 GTB, Ferrari had gone back to the pen of Pininfarina, and once again had the coachwork built by Scaglietti. Sergio Pininfarina stated that the inspiration for the car came from his 1965 Paris Auto Salon Dino Berlinetta Speciale. Many observers saw traces of both the beautiful Dino 246 GT and the potent Berlinetta Boxer in the 308 GTB's lines.

Because the 308 GTB was a proper two-seater, its wheelbase was eight inches shorter than the 308 GT4 2+2's, and its weight was 200 pounds less. It used the same 2927-cc engine as the 308 GT4 2+2. Its aluminum block had an 81 mm bore, and the pistons rode up and down in a 71 mm stroke, creating an 8.8:1 compression ratio. Four Weber 40 DCNF two-barrel carburetors flowed enough fuel that the European cars carried a 255 horsepower rating.

The European magazine, *Autosport*, was able to flog their tester to 60 mph in a scant 5.8 seconds. Paul Frere saw a top speed of 154 mph in his example. Here in the states, *Motor Trend* could only muster an eight second 0-60 walk, and *Car and Driver* didn't do much better at 7.9 seconds. No, the American testers were not inept; the relatively new emissions standards caused a power loss of 50 ponies, so that only 205 were available for stateside duty. Also, while European cars had the race-proven dry sump oil system, American cars used a more conventional oil pan for the oil supply.

Still, the 308 GTB got good reviews. Aside from falling in love with its exotic shape, those who had a chance to slide behind the leather Momo Prototipo steering wheel delighted in the response from this Italian power plant. The sound of the carbureted engine might not be as awesome as the "ripping canvas" song a Ferrari V-12 makes, but it was potent enough to thrill. When pushed to the limit, the 308 GTB tended towards benign understeer, and its high-speed stability inspired confidence. Perhaps the biggest complaint came from Ferrari's first use of a fiberglass body on a road car. It's not that the build quality suffered any—Ferrari owners didn't like being lumped into the category with Corvettes as "plastic cars."

After 712 "glass cars" were made, Ferrari switched back to the more common steel bodies in 1977, and an additional 2,185 308 GTBs were made. The other news in 1977 was the Frankfurt Auto Show introduction of the 308 GTS. Just as the Dino 246 was available with a lift-off roof, the 308 GTB got a Targa-top sibling. The roof conveniently fit behind the seats, so it could be replaced in case your route didn't allow you to run fast enough to keep those pesky raindrops flowing over your mount. Black louvers covered the rear quarter windows on the GTS model. Proving even more popular than the GTB, the 308 GTS accounted for 3,219 sales for Ferrari between 1977 and 1980.

Ferrari also had a two-liter V-8 version of the 308 for home market sale. The tax breaks involved were sufficient enough that 300 buyers lined up to purchase 208 GTBs and GTSs. The later models were turbocharged, and had 220 horsepower, a significant boost from the original 170 hp.

Bosch K-Jetronic fuel injection was the big news for 1980, and the 308 siblings added an "i" to their names. Between 1980 and 1982 the GTSi outsold the GTBi almost three to one (1,473 versus 494.) While U.S. cars were rated at the same 205 horsepower, there were some changes to the interior. Better bucket bolstering led the list, and the oil temperature gauge and clock were no longer hidden behind the left knee of the driver. Now they could be more easily read atop one another, just forward of the shift lever. This was helpful, because like many Ferraris, the 308 required significant effort to move the chrome wand through the gated shift pattern when the car was cold. Once the oil temperature gauge showed some movement, an experienced hand could easily snap off shifts.

The final change to the model line came with the introduction of the four-valves-per-cylinder heads. While today this is a feature commonly found even in economy cars, this was a very high-tech, race-inspired effort for Ferrari in 1982. Thanks also to a boost in compression to 9.2:1, the 308 *Quattrovalvole* now carried a horsepower rating of 230 (240 for European cars). *Road & Track* was able to sprint a 308 QV to 60 mph in 6.8 seconds. *Motor* saw their European car hit 60 mph in only 5.7 seconds. There was also a small spoiler added between the two sail panels, just behind the roof. Produced from 1982 to 1985, Ferrari sold 748 308 GTB QVs and once again significantly more Targa models; 3,042.

The similar-in-appearance 328 models replaced the 308 Series in 1985. The most obvious change was that the now body-color bumpers were more smoothly integrated into the nose and tail. Thanks to an increase in displacement to 3185 ccs, American models now had 260 horsepower. Ferrari even offered anti-lock brakes for the last six months of production in 1989. Everyone likes an open Ferrari, and 6,068 owners removed their 328 GTS tops whenever possible, while the 1,344 individuals who bought 328 GTBs between 1985 and 1989 had to content themselves with a marginally stiffer chassis.

If there was ever a car that could be called the "everyman's Ferrari," the 308/328 Series qualifies. Enough were produced that prices for good examples hover between new Toyota Camry prices and $57,000 for an excellent 1989 GTS. Tom Selleck showed us the way to make a Ferrari part of your every day driving experience.

1975-1976 Ferrari 308 GTB. (MC)

1976 Ferrari Type 512BB. (DA)

1976-79

DINO 308 GT4 — V-8 — The Dino badges gave way in May 1976 to the familiar "prancing horse," that went on the nose, wheel hubs, and steering wheel. Standard equipment on U.S. models included air conditioning, power windows, power antenna, leather steering wheel, limited-slip differential, rear defroster, and tinted glass. From late 1978 to 1979, every U.S. model was fitted with a sliding steel sunroof.

TYPE 308 GTB/GTS — V-8 — Keeping with the tradition of offering his clients open-air motoring,

1976 Ferrari Type 512BB. (DA)

Ferrari debuted the Targa-topped 308 GTS at the 1977 Frankfurt show. It became very popular and quickly outpaced the sales of its closed-coupe brethren. Like the 246 Dino GTS, its removable roof section could be stored behind the seats. The rear quarter windows were replaced by louvered panels. After the initial run of 712 fiberglass cars, Ferrari turned to steel for the remainder of the model run starting in April of 1997. All U.S. cars came well equipped with air conditioning, power windows, power antenna, tinted glass, and a rear-window defroster. The only remaining option for the dealer to install was the customer's choice of radio.

TYPE 365 GT4 BB — FLAT-12 — Introduced in 1974, the flat-engined "boxer" model ceased production in 1976 and was replaced by the 512 BB.

TYPE 400i — V-12 — Many of the Ferrari traditionalists were shocked when Ferrari's four-seat replacement for the 365 GT4 2+2 debuted at the 1976 Paris show with an automatic transmission. The General Motors unit was a Turbo Hydra-Matic with a three-speeds. Thankfully, the customary five-speed manual was available; this model was designated the 400i; with automatic, it became the 400i A. The V-12's stroke was increased to 78 mm, for displacement total of 4823 cc

1977 Ferrari 308 GTB. (FSpA/WG)

(294 cubic inches.) The latest Bosch K-Jetronic fuel injection replaced the more glamorous appearing six side-draft Webers. Horsepower grew by 20, to 340 at 6500 rpm. Body changes included restyled tail lamps, a modest front lip spoiler, and wheel lug nuts (replacing the former knock-off hubs). Front seats slid forward on their tracks when the seatbacks were tilted for easier access to the rear. A new quadraphonic four-speaker radio included a tape player. Ferrari never certified the 400i for sale in the U.S., though occasional examples crept in via the "grey market."

TYPE 512 BB — FLAT-12 —

Although it was still not legal for sale in the U.S., Ferrari continued to develop their flag ship model. The model designation changed from 365 GT4 BB (365 cc per cylinder) to BB512 (five liters and a twelve cylinder engine). The 4942-cc (302-cid) V-12 engine had an extra millimeter of bore and 7-mm greater stroke; horsepower remained the same, but torque was increased for better drivability. The 512BB entered production about two months before its actual debut at the October 1976 Paris show. Appearance was similar to the 365 GT4 BB, with the addition of a small front chin spoiler and NACA ducts (on lower bodysides ahead of back wheels). Perhaps the easiest way to tell the 512BB from its predecessor is the four tail lamps installed, versus six on the 365 GT4 BB.

I.D. DATA: Ferrari's Vehicle Identification Number is embossed on a metal plate attached to the steering column, and stamped in right frame member to rear of engine (under the hood). A prefix identifying the model is followed by a five-digit sequential production number.

Model	Body Type & Seating	Engine Type/CID	P.O.E. Price	Weight (lbs.)	Prod. Total
DINO 308 GT4					
308 GT4	2-dr Coupe-2+2P	V8/179	24935	2930	Note 1
308 GTB/GTS					
308 GTB	2-dr Coupe-2P	V8/179	26445	3160	Note 2
308 GTS	2-dr Targa Cpe-2P	V8/179	N/A	3225	Note 2
365 GT4 BB					
365 GT4 BB	2-dr Coupe-2P	H12/268	N/A	3420	Note 3
400i					
400i	2-dr Coupe-2+2P	V12/294	N/A	3748	Note 4
512 BB					
512 BB	2-dr Coupe-2P	H12/302	85000	3800	Note 5

Note 1: About 2,826 Type 308 GT4 coupes were produced from 1973-80.
Note 2: About 712 Type 308 GTB coupes were produced from 1975-77. About 2,185 Type 308 GTB coupes were produced from 1976-80.
Note 3: About 387 Type 365 GT4 BB coupes were produced, from 1973-76.
Note 4: About 501 Type 400 GTs were produced in 1976-79.
Note 5: About 929 Type 512 BB coupes were produced, from 1976-81.
Weight Note: Figures shown are approximate (or averages).
Price Note: Figures shown were valid in 1977, except for the 512 BB in 1978. In 1979, the Dino 308 GT4 sold for $35,652; the 308 GTB for $40,290; the 308 GTS for $36,010.
Production Note: A total of 1,427 Ferraris were built in 1976, followed by 1,798 in 1977, 1,939 in 1978, and 2,308 in 1979.

ENGINE [Base V-8 (Dino 308 GT4, 308 GTB/GTS)]:

90-degree, dual-overhead-cam "vee" type eight-cylinder. Light alloy block and heads. Displacement: 178.6 cid (2927 cc). Bore & stroke: 3.19 x 2.79 in. (81 x 71 mm). Compression ratio: 8.8:1. Brake horsepower: 240 at 6600 rpm (later, 205 bhp). Torque: 195 lbs.-ft. at 5000 rpm (later, 181 lbs.-ft.). Five main bearings. Four Weber 40 DCNF two-barrel carburetors.

ENGINE [Base Flat-12 (365 GT4 BB)]:

Horizontally-opposed, dual-overhead-cam 12-cylinder.

1978 Ferrari 512 BB. (FSpA/WG)

1978 Ferrari 512 BB interior. (FSpA/WG)

1978 Ferrari 512 BB. (FSpA/WG)

1979 Ferrari Dino 308 GT4. (DG)

1979 Ferrari Dino 308 GT4 interior. (DG)

Aluminum alloy block and heads. Displacement: 267.8 cid (4390 cc). Bore & stroke: 3.19 x 2.80 in. (81 x 71 mm). Compression ratio: 8.8:1. Brake horsepower: 344 (DIN) at 7000 rpm. Torque: 302 lbs.-ft. at 3900 rpm. Seven main bearings. Four Weber triple-barrel carburetors.

ENGINE [Base V-12 (400i)]: 60-degree, dual-overhead-cam "vee" type 12-cylinder. Aluminum alloy block and heads. Displacement: 294.2 cid (4823 cc). Bore & stroke: 3.19 x 3.07 in. (81 x 78 mm). Compression ratio: 8.8:1. Brake horsepower: 325-340 at 6000-6500 rpm. Torque: 347 lbs.-ft. at 3600 rpm. Seven main bearings. Bosch K-Jetronic fuel injection.

ENGINE [Base Flat-12 (512 BB)]: Horizontally-opposed, dual-overhead-cam 12-cylinder. Aluminum alloy block and heads. Displacement: 302 cid (4942 cc). Bore & stroke: 3.23 x 3.07 in. (82 x 78 mm). Compression ratio: 9.2:1. Brake horsepower: 360 (DIN) at 6200 rpm. Torque: 333 lbs.-ft. at 4600 rpm. Seven main bearings. Four Weber triple-barrel carburetors.

CHASSIS: Wheelbase: (Dino 308 GT4) 100.4 in.; (308 GTB/GTS) 92.1 in.; (365 GT4 BB) 98.4 in.; (400i) 106.3 in.; (512 BB) 98.4 in. Overall Length: (Dino 308 GT4) 176.7 in.; (308 GTB/GTS) 172.4 in.; (365 GT4 BB) 171.6 in.; (400i) 189.4 in.; (512 BB) 173.2 in. Height: (Dino 308 GT4) 47.6 in.; (308 GTB/GTS) 44.1 in.; (365 GT4 BB) 44.1 in.; (400i) 51.6 in.; (512 BB) 44.1 in.

Width: (Dino 308 GT4) 70.5 in.; (308 GTB/GTS) 67.7 in.; (365 GT4 BB) 70.9 in.; (400i) 70.9 in.; (512 BB) 72 in. Front Tread: (Dino 308 GT4) 57.8 in.; (308 GTB/GTS) 57.9 in.; (365 GT4 BB) 59.1 in.; (400i) 57.9 in.; (512 BB) 59.1 in. Rear Tread: (Dino 308 GT4) 57.8 in.; (308 GTB/GTS) 57.9 in.; (365 GT4 BB) 59.8 in.; (400i) 59.1 in.; (512 BB) 61.5 in. Standard Tires: (Dino 308 GT4) 205/70VR14; (308 GTB/GTS) 205/70VR14; (365 GT4 BB) 215/70VR15; (400i) 215/70VR15; (512 BB) 215/70VR15 front, 225/70VR15 rear.

TECHNICAL: Layout: (Dino, 308 GTB/GTS, 365 GT4 BB, 512 BB) mid-engine, rear-drive; (400i) front-engine, rear-drive. Transmission: (Dino, 365 GT4 BB, 308 GTB/GTS, 512 BB) five-speed manual in rear transaxle; (400i) five-speed manual or three-speed automatic. Standard Final Drive Ratio: (308) 3.70:1. Steering: (308) rack and pinion; (400i) recirculating ball; (512) worm and roller. Suspension (front): unequal-length Λ-arms with coil springs and anti-roll bar. Suspension (rear): (308 Dino, 308 GTB/GTS) unequal-length Λ-arms with coil springs and anti-roll bar; (365 GT4 BB, 512 BB)

1977 Ferrari 308 GTS. (FSpA/WG)

unequal-length A-arms with twin coil springs and anti-roll bar; (400i) unequal-length A-arms with coil springs, anti-roll bar and hydraulic self-leveling. Brakes: front/rear disc. Body Construction: separate body on tubular steel frame. Fuel Tank: (308 GTB) 18.5 gallon.

MAJOR OPTIONS: Leather upholstery: Dino 308 GT4 ($640). Leather/velour upholstery: GT4 ($540). Metallic paint ($320). Special colors ($140). Front spoiler: GT4 ($200). 7.5-inch star wheels: GT4 ($650).

Note: Option prices shown above were valid in 1977.

PERFORMANCE: Top Speed: (European Dino 308 GT4) 150+ mph; (308 GTB) 147 mph claimed; (365 GT4 BB) 175 mph; (512 BB) 188 mph (est). Acceleration (0-60 mph): (European Dino 308 GT4) 6.4 sec.; (308 GTB) 8.2 sec.; (308 GTS) 7.3 sec.; (365 GT4 BB) 7.2 sec.; (512 BB) 5.5 sec. Acceleration (quarter-mile): (308 GTB) 14.6 sec. claimed; (365 GT4 BB) 15.5 sec. (102.5 mph); (512 BB) 14.2 sec. (103.5 mph).

PRODUCTION/SALES: Approximately 617 Ferraris were sold in the U.S. during 1978, and at least 656 in 1979.

Manufacturer: Ferrari S.p.A. SEFAC, Maranello (Modena), Italy.

Distributor: Chinetti-Garthwaite Imports, Paoli, Pennsylvania.

HISTORY: *Road & Track* called the 512 BB "the best all-round sports and GT car we've tested." Their test car had been privately "Federalized," since none were officially certified for sale in the U.S. "If you are fond of admiring stares," said *Car and Driver* in their 1976 Buyers Guide, "the Dino 308 GT4 coupe will suit you nicely."

"There is no alternative," said Ferrari ads in 1977 Auto Show programs that featured the 308 GTS and its fiberglass body. "It's a forgiving car," they added, "so you don't have to be a racing driver to drive one." Readers were advised to consult their dealers to discuss "the Ferrari mystique."

1977 Ferrari 308 GTS. (FSpA/WG)

1977 Ferrari 308 GTB. (FSpA/WG)

1978 Ferrari 308 GT/4 interior. (FSpA/WG)

1978 Ferrari 308 GT/4. (FSpA/WG)

1978 Ferrari 308 GT/4. (FSpA/WG)

1980 Ferrari Mondial 8. Body by Pininfarina. (FSpA/WG)

MONDIAL 8 — V-8 — Although production did not start until 1981, the Mondial 8 debuted at the Geneva Auto Show in March 1980. Mondial (which means "world") was named to honor Ferrari's four-cylinder sports racers of the early 1950s. Pininfarina did the styling of this replacement for the Bertone-styled Dino 308 GT4. Despite the wheelbase's growth of four inches, the Mondial could be called a 2+2 by only the most generous definition. It carried the same transverse four-cam mid-mounted 2927-cc (179-cid) engine as the 308 series. The luxurious interior was fitted with British Connolly leather; and a first for Ferrari was the leather-rimmed steering wheel that was adjustable for reach and rake. Standard equipment included air conditioning, central door locking, remote-control mirrors, and a power antenna. An optional power sunroof was fitted to all cars bound for the U.S. market. Styling features included hidden headlamps, a rather short nose, and a long rear section—a combination that some observers thought lacking in proportion. Full-width grooves went across the hood area. A low horizontal-bar grille contained a prancing horse emblem in its center and wide amber-over-clear park/signal lights alongside. Grilled air intakes stood to the rear of the doors. At the rear were round tail lamps.

TYPE 308 GTBi/GTSi — V-8 — Fuel injection was substituted for the Weber carburetors in the hopes of keeping pace with tightening U. S. emission standards; hence the model designations received a small "i." In Italy a 2.0-liter version of the GTB/GTS was made available. The 170-hp model was taxed at a lower rate, and became more affordable to the Italian *tifosi*.

TYPE 400i — V-12 — Production of Ferrari's four-seater, not certified for U.S. sale, continued with little change.

TYPE 512 BB — FLAT-12 — Tightening U.S. emissions made the 1980 carburetor-equipped Boxer even more difficult to convert to U.S. specs.

Note: Although production of the Dino 308 GT4 had ceased, thanks to unsold units, it was still listed in some U.S. directories in 1980-81 (including 1980 Auto Show advertisements), selling for $39,998.

I.D. DATA: Ferrari's Vehicle Identification Number is embossed on a metal plate attached to the steering column, and stamped in right frame member to rear of engine (under the hood). A prefix identifying the model is followed by a five-digit sequential production number.

Model	Body Type & Seating	Engine Type/CID	P.O.E. Price	Weight (lbs.)	Prod. Total
MONDIAL 8					
Mondial 8	2-dr Coupe-2+2P	V8/179	N/A	3186	Note 1
308 GTBi/GTSi					
308 GTB	2-dr Coupe-2P	V8/179	40576	3160	Note 2
308 GTS	2-dr Targa Cpe-2P	V8/179	44912	3225	Note 2
400i					
400i	2-dr Coupe-2+2P	V12/294	N/A	3748	Note 3
512 BB					
512 BB	2-dr Coupe-2P	H12/302	N/A	N/A	Note 4

Note 1: About 703 Mondial 8 coupes were produced from 1980-82.
Note 2: About 494 Type 308 GTBi coupes were produced from 1980-82. About 1,743 Type 308 GTSi coupes were produced from 1980-82.
Note 3: About 1,306 Type 400i coupes were produced in 1979-84.
Note 4: About 929 Type 512 BB coupes were produced from 1976-81
Production Note: Approximately 2,381 Ferraris were built in 1980 (455 Type 400/512, and 1,926 Type 308).

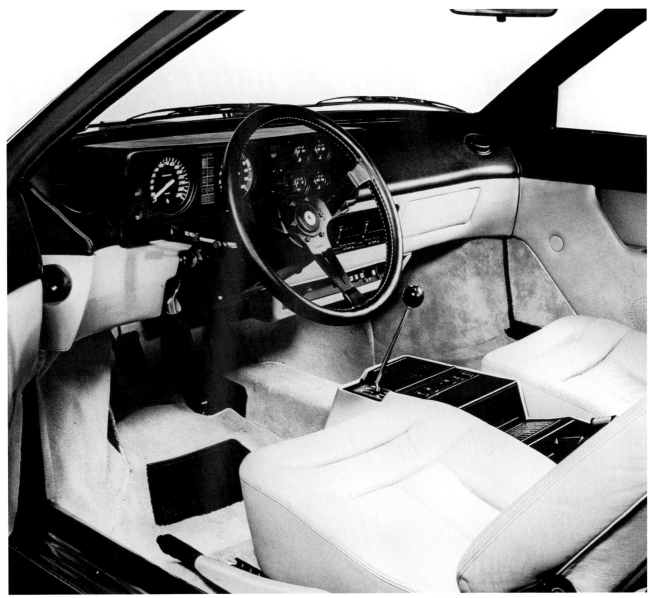

1980 Ferrari Mondial 8 interior. (FSpA/WG)

ENGINE [Base V-8 (Mondial, 308 GTBi/GTSi)]: 90-degree, dual-overhead-cam, "vee" type eight-cylinder. Light alloy block and heads. Displacement: 178.6 cid (2927 cc). Bore & stroke: 3.19 x 2.795 in. (81 x 71 mm). Compression ratio: 8.8:1. Brake horsepower: 205 at 6600 rpm. Torque: 181 lbs.-ft. at 5000 rpm. Five main bearings. Bosch K-Jetronic F.I.

ENGINE [Base V-12 (400i)]: 60-degree, dual-overhead-cam "vee" type 12-cylinder. Aluminum alloy block and heads. Displacement: 294.2 cid (4823 cc). Bore & stroke: 3.19 x 3.07 in. (81 x 78 mm). Compression ratio: 8.8:1. Brake horsepower: 325-340 at 6500 rpm. Torque: 347 lbs.-ft. at 3600 rpm. Seven main bearings. Bosch fuel injection.

ENGINE [Base Flat-12 (512 BB)]: Horizontally-opposed, dual-overhead-cam 12-cylinder. Aluminum alloy block and heads. Displacement: 302 cid (4942 cc). Bore & stroke: 3.23 x 3.07 in. (82 x 78 mm). Compression ratio: 9.2:1. Brake horsepower: 360 (DIN) at 6200 rpm. Torque: 333 lbs.-ft. at 4600 rpm. Seven main bearings. Four Weber triple-barrel carburetors.

CHASSIS: Wheelbase: (Mondial) 104.2 in.; (308 GTBi/GTSi) 92.1 in.; (400i) 106.3 in.; (512 BB) 98.4 in. Overall Length: (Mondial) 182.7 in.; (308 GTBi/GTSi) 172.4 in.; (400i) 189.4 in.; (512 BB) 173.2 in. Height: (Mondial) 49.6 in.; (308 GTBi/GTSi) 44.1 in.; (400i) 51.6 in.; (512 BB) 44.1 in. Width: (Mondial) 70.5 in.; (308 GTBi/GTSi) 67.7 in.; (400i) 70.9 in.; (512 BB) 72 in. Front Tread: (Mondial) 58.9 in.; (308 GTBi/GTSi) 57.9 in.; (400i) 57.9 in.; (512 BB) 59.1 in. Rear Tread: (Mondial) 59.8 in.; (308 GTBi/GTSi) 57.9 in.; (400i) 59.1 in.; (512 BB) 61.4 in. Standard Tires: (Mondial) 240/55VR390; (308 GTBi/GTSi) 205/70VR14; (400i) 215/70VR15; (512 BB) 215/70VR15 front, 225/70VR15 rear.

TECHNICAL: Layout: (Mondial, 308 GTB/GTS, 512 BB) mid-engine, rear-drive; (400i) front-engine, rear-drive. Transmission: (Mondial, 308 GTBi/GTSi, 512 BB) five-speed manual in rear transaxle; (400i) five-speed manual or three-speed automatic. Type 308 gear ratios: (1st) 3.23:1; (2nd) 2.18:1; (3rd) 1.52:1; (4th) 1.12:1; (5th) 0.86:1; (rev) 2.92:1. Steering: (Mondial/308) rack and pinion; (400i) recirculating ball; (512) worm and roller. Suspension (front): unequal-length A-arms with coil springs and anti-roll bar. Suspension (rear): (Mondial, 308 GTBi/GTSi) unequal-length A-arms with coil springs and anti-roll bar; (512 BB) unequal-length A-arms with twin coil springs and anti-roll bar; (400i) unequal-length A-arms with coil springs, anti-roll bar and hydraulic self-leveling. Brakes: front/rear disc. Body Construction: separate body on tubular steel frame. Fuel Tank: (308 GTBi/GTSi) 18.5 gal.

PERFORMANCE: Top Speed: (Mondial) near 150 mph; (308 GTBi) 147 mph claimed; (512 BB) 188 mph (est). Acceleration (0-60 mph): (308 GTBi) 8.2 sec.; (308 GTS) 7.3 sec.; (512 BB) 5.5 sec. Acceleration (quarter-mile): (308 GTBi) 14.6 sec. claimed; (512 BB) 14.2 sec. (103.5 mph).

PRODUCTION/SALES: Ferrari North America replaced Chinetti-Garthwaite Imports and Modern Classic Motors Approximately 779 Ferraris were sold in the U.S. during 1980.

Manufacturer: Ferrari S.p.A. SEFAC, Maranello (Modena), Italy.

Distributor: Ferrari North America (Division of Fiat Motors of North America Inc.), Montvale, New Jersey.

HISTORY: Ferrari North America and its dealers were very much aware of the fantastic increases that were taking place in the used Ferrari markets. Due to the small supply, and the wait for new cars, used Ferraris were frequently selling for 10-25% more than the dealers were charging for new. Retail prices jumped up almost 25% from the previous year. Was there a big change in the product? While the substitution of fuel injection for Webers produced some improvement in drivability, the price increase mainly reflected Ferrari's awareness of market conditions. "What can be conceived can be created" was the headline of Ferrari's ads in Auto Show programs for 1980, which spotlighted the 308 series. Sales of the new Mondial never reached impressive levels, partly due to the car's relatively tame (for Ferrari) appearance.

What can be conceived can be created

Ferrari

1980 Ferrari 308 GTSi color sheet. (FSpA/WG)

1981 Ferrari 512 BBi. (FSpA/WG)

1981

MONDIAL 8 — V-8 — Bosch K-Jetronic fuel injection replaced the former quartet of carburetors on the V-8 Mondial, introduced in 1980. Horsepower and torque were unchanged.

TYPE 308i GTB/GTS — V-8 — Like the Mondial, the 308 series switched from carburetion to Bosch K-Jetronic fuel injection, adding the letter "i" to its nameplate.

TYPE 400i — V-12 — Production of the "family" Ferrari continued with little change.

TYPE 512 BB/BBi — FLAT-12 — Late in 1981, the "Boxer" engine switched from carburetion to Bosch K-Jetronic fuel injection. Horsepower dropped to 340 (DIN), torque to 333 lbs.-ft.

I.D. DATA: Ferrari's 17-symbol Vehicle Identification Number is embossed on a metal plate attached to the steering column, and stamped in right frame member to rear of engine (under the hood). Symbol one ('Z') indicates Italy. The next two symbols identify the make ('FF' = Ferrari; 'FD' or 'DF' = Dino). Symbol four indicates engine type; symbol five is restraint system; symbols six and seven denote model ('01' = 308 GTBi; '02' = 308 GTSi; '03' = 308 GTB; '04' = 308 GTS). Next is a market designator ('Λ' = North America), followed by a check digit. Symbol 10 indicates model year ('B' = 1981). Symbol 11 ('0') is the assembly plant. Last comes the six-digit sequential production number.

Model	Body Type & Seating	Engine Type/CID	P.O.E. Price	Weight (lbs.)	Prod. Total
MONDIAL 8					
Mondial 8	2-dr Coupe-2+2P	V8/179	64684	3186	Note 1
308 GTBi/GTSi					
308 GTBi	2-dr Coupe-2P	V8/179	49845	3085	Note 2
308 GTSi	2-dr Targa Cpe-2P	V8/179	56120	3225	Note 2
400i					
400i	2-dr Coupe-2+2P	V12/294	N/A	3748	Note 3
512 BB					
512 BB	2-dr Coupe-2P	H12/302	N/A	3305	Note 4

Note 1: About 703 Mondials were produced from 1980-82.
Note 2: About 494 Type 308 GTBi coupes were produced from 1980-82. About 1,743 Type 308 GTSi coupes were produced from 1980-82.
Note 3: About 1,306 Type 400i coupes were produced in 1979-84.
Note 4: About 929 Type 512 BB coupes were produced from 1976-81.
Production Note: A total of 2,566 Ferraris (all models) were built in 1981.
Price Note: Figures shown were for 1980 models sold in 1981.

ENGINE [Base V-8 (Mondial, 308i GTB/GTS)]: 90-degree, dual-overhead-cam, "vee" type eight-cylinder. Light alloy block and heads. Displacement: 178.6 cid (2927 cc). Bore & stroke: 3.19 x 2.795 in. (81 x 71 mm). Compression ratio: 8.8:1. Brake horsepower: 205 at 6600 rpm. Torque: 181 lbs.-ft. at 5000 rpm. Five main bearings. Bosch K-Jetronic fuel injection.

ENGINE [Base V-12 (400i)]: 60-degree, dual-overhead-cam "vee" type 12-cylinder. Aluminum alloy block and heads. Displacement: 294.2 cid (4823 cc). Bore & stroke: 3.19 x 3.07 in. (81 x 78 mm). Compression ratio: 8.8:1. Brake horsepower: 310-340 at 6500 rpm. Torque: 347 lbs.-ft. at 3600 rpm. Seven main bearings. Bosch fuel injection.

ENGINE [Base Flat-12 (512 BB)]: Horizontally-opposed, dual-overhead-cam 12-cylinder. Aluminum alloy block and heads. Displacement: 302 cid (4942 cc). Bore & stroke: 3.23 x 3.07 in. (82 x 78 mm). Compression ratio: 9.2:1. Brake horsepower: 360 (DIN) at 6200 rpm. Torque: 333 lbs.-ft. at 4600 rpm. Seven main bearings. Four Weber triple-barrel carburetors.

Note: Late in the year, the 512 BB switched to Bosch K-Jetronic fuel injection to become the 512 BBi. Horsepower dropped to 340 at 6000 rpm, torque to 333 lbs.-ft.at 4200 rpm.

CHASSIS: Wheelbase: (Mondial) 104.2 in.; (308i GTB/GTS) 92.1 in.; (400i) 106.3 in.; (512 BB) 98.4 in. Overall Length: (Mondial) 182.7 in.; (308i GTB/GTS)

1981 Ferrari 512 BBi rear view. (FSpA/WG)

174.2 in.; (400i) 189.4 in.; (512 BB) 173.2 in. Height: (Mondial) 49.6 in.; (308i GTB) 44.1 in.; (400i) 51.6 in.; (512 BB) 44.1 in. Width: (Mondial) 70.5 in.; (308i GTB/GTS) 67.7 in.; (400i) 70.9 in.; (512 BB) 72 in. Front Tread: (Mondial) 58.9 in.; (308i GTB/GTS) 57.8 in.; (400i) 57.9 in.; (512 BB) 59.1 in. Rear Tread: (Mondial) 59.8 in.; (308i GTB/GTS) 57.8 in.; (400i) 59.1 in.; (512 BB) 61.9 in. Standard Tires: (Mondial) 240/55VR390; (308i GTB/GTS) 220/55VR390.

TECHNICAL: Layout: (Mondial, 308i GTB/GTS, 512 BB) mid-engine, rear-drive; (400i) front-engine, rear-drive. Transmission: (Mondial, 308i GTB/GTS, 512 BB) five-speed manual in rear transaxle; (400i) five-speed manual or three-speed automatic. Standard Final Drive Ratio: (308i) 3.71:1. Steering: (Mondial/308i) rack and pinion; (400i) recirculating ball; (512) worm and roller. Suspension (front): unequal-length A-arms with coil springs and anti-roll bar. Suspension (rear): (Mondial, 308i GTB/GTS) unequal-length A-arms with coil springs and anti-roll bar; (512 BB) unequal-length A-arms with twin coil springs and anti-roll bar; (400i) unequal-length A-arms with coil springs, anti-roll bar and hydraulic self-leveling. Brakes: front/rear disc. Body Construction: separate body on tubular steel frame. Fuel Tank: (308i) 18.5 gal.

PERFORMANCE: Top Speed: (Mondial) 137 mph; (400i) 149 mph; (512 BB) 174-188 mph (est). Acceleration (quarter-mile): (308i GTB) 15.4 sec.; (512 BB) 14.2 sec. (103.5 mph).

PRODUCTION/SALES: Approximately 904 Ferraris were sold in the U.S. during 1981.

Manufacturer: Ferrari S.p.A. SEFAC, Maranello (Modena), Italy.

Distributor: Fiat Motors of North America Inc., Montvale, New Jersey.

HISTORY: Adding a KKK turbocharger to the Italian-only Ferrari 208 boosted power to 211 hp at 7000 rpms.

1981 Ferrari 512 BBi interior. (FSpA/WG)

1981 Ferrari 512 BBi. (FSpA/WG)

1983 Ferrari Type 400i. (DA)

1982-83

MONDIAL Qv — V-8 — Who says that racing doesn't improve the breed? In 1982, the 308 and Mondial received a new engine and model designation, "Quattrovalvole," or "Qv." Horsepower jumped from 205 to 230 thanks to the substitution of four-valve-per cylinder heads for the engines former two-valve valve train. Equally important was the introduction of the Mondial cabriolet in 1983. The first true convertible since the Daytona Spyder, this model quickly

1979-84 Ferrari 400i engine. (MC)

overshadowed the coupe in popularity. It's a marvel of engineering when you consider that a convertible top, 2+2 seating, and a mid-engine drivetrain all fit within a compact 183 inches.

TYPE 308i GTB/GTS — V-8 — Production was phased out in favor of the 308 Quattrovalvole.

TYPE 308 GTB/GTS Qv — V-8 — Like the Mondial (above), the 308 series switched to a 32-valve version of the 179-cid (2927-cc) engine in 1982. At the same time, a small spoiler was added at the rear of the roof, and body-color bumpers (formerly matte black) were integrated into lower-body fairings. Transverse louvers also were inserted between the headlamps.

TYPE 400i — V-12 — Production of the four-seat Ferrari continued with little change, powered by the front-mounted 4823-cc V-12 engine.

TYPE 512 BBi — FLAT-12 — Since the advent of fuel injection in 1981, the Boxer became easier to convert to U.S. specs. This made the growing flow of gray market Boxers an even larger irritant to Ferrari's North American dealers. So, 1983 brought about a program where American customers could order a European car through their local dealer, take delivery in Europe, and then bring it into the states for legalization.

I.D. DATA: Ferrari's 17-symbol Vehicle Identification Number is embossed on a metal plate attached to the steering column, and stamped in right frame member to rear of engine (under the hood). Symbol one ('Z') indicates Italy. The next two symbols identify the make ('FF' = Ferrari; 'FD' or 'DF' = Dino). Symbol four indicates engine type; symbol five is restraint system; symbols six and seven denote model ('01' = 308 GTBi; '02' = 308 GTSi; '03' = 308 GTB; '04' = 308 GTS; '08' = Mondial). Next is a market designator ('A' = North America), followed by a check digit. Symbol 10 indicates model year ('C' = 1982; 'D' = 1983). Symbol 11 ('0') is the assembly plant. Last comes the six-digit sequential production number.

Model	Body Type & Seating	Engine Type/CID	P.O.E. Price	Weight (lbs.)	Prod. Total
MONDIAL Qv					
Mondial 8	2-dr Coupe-2+2P	V8/179	63939	3186	Note 1
Mondial 8	2-dr Cabr-2+2P	V8/179	65845	3253	Note 2
308i GTB/GTS					
308i GTB	2-dr Coupe-2P	V8/179	53745	3085	Note 3
308i GTS	2-dr Targa Cpe-2P	V8/179	60345	3225	Note 4
308 QUATTROVALVOLE					
308 GTB	2-dr Coupe-2P	V8/179	55145	2811	Note 5
308 GTS	2-dr Targa Cpe-2P	V8/179	60345	2835	Note 6
400i					
400i	2-dr Coupe-2+2P	V12/294	N/A	3748	Note 7
512 BBi					
512 BBi	2-dr Coupe-2P	H12/302	N/A	3305	Note 8

Note 1: About 1,145 Mondial Qv Coupes were produced from 1982-85.
Note 2: About 629 Mondial Qv Cabriolets were produced from 1983-85.
Note 3: About 494 Type 308 GTBi coupes were produced from 1980-82.
Note 4: About 1,743 Type 308 GTSi coupes were produced from 1980-82.
Note 5: About 748 Type 308 GTB Qv coupes were produced from 1982-85.
Note 6: About 3,042 Type 308 GTS Qv coupes were produced from 1982-85.
Note 7: About 1,306 Type 400i coupes were produced in 1979-84.

1983 Ferrari Type 400i. (DA)

1983 Ferrari 308 Turbo. (FSpA/WG)

Note 8: About 1007 Type 512 BBi coupes were produced from 1981-84.
Production Note: A total of 2,223 Ferraris (553 Type 400/512 and 1,670 Type 208/308/Mondial) were produced in 1982; followed by 2,366 (650 Type 400/512, 1,267 Type 208/308 and 449 Mondials) in 1983.

ENGINE [Base V-8 (early Mondial, 308i GTB/GTS)]: 90-degree, dual-overhead-cam, "vee" type eight-cylinder. Light alloy block and heads. Displacement: 178.6 cid (2927 cc). Bore & stroke: 3.19 x 2.80 in. (81 x 71 mm). Compression ratio: 8.8:1. Brake horsepower: 205 (SAE) at 6600 rpm. Torque: 181 (SAE) lbs.-ft. at 5000 rpm. Five main bearings. Bosch K-Jetronic fuel injection.

ENGINE [Base V-8 (late Mondial, 308 GTB/GTS Quattrovalvole)]: 90-degree, dual-overhead-cam, "vee" type eight-cylinder (32-valve). Light alloy block and heads. Displacement: 178.6 cid (2927 cc). Bore & stroke: 3.19 x 2.80 in. (81 x 71 mm). Compression ratio: 8.6:1. Brake horsepower: 230 at 6800 rpm. Torque: 188 lbs.-ft. at 5500 rpm. Five main bearings. Bosch K-Jetronic fuel injection.

ENGINE [Base V-12 (400i)]: 60-degree, dual-overhead-cam, "vee" type 12-cylinder. Aluminum alloy block and heads. Displacement: 294.2 cid (4823 cc). Bore & stroke: 3.19 x 3.07 in. (81 x 78 mm). Compression ratio: 8.8:1. Brake horsepower: 310 at 6400 rpm. Torque: 347 lbs.-ft. at 3600 rpm. Seven main bearings. Bosch K-Jetronic fuel injection.

ENGINE [Base Flat-12 (512 BBi)]: Horizontally-opposed, dual-overhead-cam 12-cylinder. Aluminum alloy block and heads. Displacement: 302 cid (4942 cc). Bore & stroke: 3.23 x 3.07 in. (82 x 78 mm). Compression ratio: 9.2:1. Brake horsepower: 340 (DIN) at 6000 rpm. Torque: 333 lbs.-ft. at 4200 rpm. Seven main bearings. Bosch K-Jetronic fuel injection.

CHASSIS: Wheelbase: (Mondial) 104.3 in.; (308 GTB/GTS) 92.1 in.; (400i) 106.3 in.; (512 BBi) 98.4 in. Overall Length: (Mondial) 182.7 in.; (308 GTB/GTS) 174.2 in.; (400i) 189.4 in.; (512 BBi) 173.2 in. Height: (Mondial) 49.6 in.; (308 GTB) 44.1 in.; (400i) 51.6 in.; (512 BBi) 44.1 in. Width: (Mondial) 70.5 in.; (308 GTB/GTS) 67.7 in.; (400i) 70.9 in.; (512 BBi) 72 in. Front Tread: (Mondial) 58.9 in.; (308 GTB/GTS) 57.8 in.; (400i) 57.9 in.; (512 BBi) 59.1 in. Rear Tread: (Mondial) 59.8 in.; (308 GTB/GTS) 57.8 in.; (400i) 59.1 in.; (512 BBi) 61.9 in. Standard Tires: (Mondial) 240/55VR390; (308 GTB/GTS) 205/70VR14; (400i) 240/55VR415; (512 BBi) 180/TR415 front, 210/TR415 rear.

TECHNICAL: Layout: (Mondial, 308 GTB/GTS, 512 BBi) mid-engine, rear-drive; (400i) front-engine, rear-drive. Transmission: (Mondial, 308 GTB/GTS, 512 BBi) five-speed manual in rear transaxle; (400i) five-speed manual or three-speed automatic. Standard Final Drive Ratio: (Mondial/308i) 3.71:1; (400i w/manual) 4.30:1; (400i A) 3.25:1; (512) 3.21:1. Steering:

1983 Ferrari 308 Quattrovalvole. (FSpA/WG)

1983 Ferrari Mondial Quattrovalvole. (FSpA/WG)

(Mondial/308/512) rack and pinion; (400i) recirculating ball. Suspension (front): unequal-length A-arms with coil springs and anti-roll bar. Suspension (rear): (Mondial, 308 GTB/GTS) unequal-length A-arms with coil springs and anti-roll bar; (512 BBi) unequal-length A-arms with twin coil springs and anti-roll bar; (400i) unequal-length A-arms with coil springs, anti-roll bar and hydraulic self-leveling. Brakes: front/rear disc. Body Construction: separate body on tubular steel frame.

PERFORMANCE: Top Speed: (Mondial) 137 mph in U.S. trim; (308 GTB) 147 mph in U.S.; (400i w/manual) 152 mph; (400i A) 149 mph; (512 BBi) 174 mph. Acceleration (quarter-mile): (Mondial) 16.5 sec. in U.S. trim; (308) 15.4 sec. in U.S. trim; (400i w/manual) 15.8 sec.; (400i A) 16.4 sec.; (512 BBi) 14.2 sec. (103.5 mph).

PRODUCTION/SALES: Approximately 686 Ferraris were sold in the U.S. during 1982.

ADDITIONAL MODELS: A 208 GTB coupe and GTS Spider also remained in production for the home market, with a 1991-cc V-8 rated 155 bhp (DIN).

Manufacturer: Ferrari S.p.A. SEFAC, Maranello (Modena), Italy.

Distributor: Fiat Motors of North America Inc., Montvale, New Jersey.

1983 Ferrari Mondial Quattrovalvole. (FSpA/WG)

1984 Ferrari Testarossa. (DG)

1984

MONDIAL QUATTROVALVOLE — V-8 —

Mondial coupe and cabriolet production with the 32-valve engine continued with little change into 1985; see previous listing for details. Standard equipment included leather upholstery, power windows, reclining bucket seats, metallic paint, heated rear window, tinted glass, central door locking, air conditioning, and light alloy wheels.

GTO — V-8 — The 1984-86 288 GTO is a perfect example of why Ferrari is at the top of desirable marques. While sales of the regular production models were doing just fine, Ferrari still took the step of developing a "halo" car. Sharing the GTO (*Gran Turismo Omologato*) nameplate with the famous mid-sixties street/track car, this new GTO promised very special pleasures for its few fortunate owners. While the appearance was similar to the 308/328 coupe, the wheelbase was 4.3-inches longer. This was necessitated by the longitudinal mounting of the four-cam, 2855-cc (174-cid) V-8 engine. Fitted with twin IHI intercooled turbochargers, and four valves-per-cylinder heads, the new engine produced 400 hp at 7000 rpm and made an impressive 366 lbs.-ft. of torque at 3800 rpm. Despite the high output, the engine was quite tractable at low speeds and provided true racecar acceleration when driven in anger. This engine actually had been developed for Lancia rally cars, as both Ferrari and Lancia were part of the Fiat Empire at this time. A twin-disc clutch sent power to the five-speed manual gearbox in the rear transaxle, which used a 2.90:1 final drive ratio.

The uninitiated would be forgiven for mistaking a GTO to be a mere 308 at first glance, since the signs of power are well integrated. Closer examination would reveal flared fenders, aggressive front and rear spoilers, and the addition of many louvers to help keep things cool. Claimed top speed was 190 mph. A GTO could accelerate to 60 mph in five seconds, and run the quarter-mile in 14.1, hitting 113 mph. Like some other Ferrari models of the 1970s and 1980s, the GTO was never certified for sale in the U.S., though a handful arrived in America via the "grey market." A road equipment package included power windows, air conditioning, and an AM/FM radio with cassette player.

TYPE 308 QUATTROVALVOLE GTB/GTS
— V-8 — Production of the 32-valve version of the 308 closed and Targa-roof coupes continued with little change. Standard equipment included leather upholstery, power windows, tinted glass, light alloy wheels, and a heated rear window.

1984 Ferrari Testarossa. (FSpA/WG)

TYPE 400i — V-12 — Production of Ferrari's four-seater continued with little change. As before, it was available with either manual or automatic transmission. Standard equipment included central door locking, power windows, and air conditioning.

TYPE 512 BBi — FLAT-12 — Ferrari's "boxer" coupe continued into 1985 without change, but soon would be replaced by the new Testarossa. Standard equipment included air conditioning, central door locking, and power windows.

I.D. DATA: Ferrari's 17-symbol Vehicle Identification Number is embossed on a metal plate attached to the steering column. Symbol one ('Z') indicates Italy. The next two symbols identify the make ('FF' = Ferrari). Symbol four indicates engine type; symbol five is restraint system; symbols six and seven denote model ('08' = Mondial; '12' = 308 GTB Quattrovalvole; '13' = 308 GTS Quattrovalvole; '14' = Mondial Quattrovalvole;

'15' = Mondial cabriolet). Next is a market designator ('A' = North America), followed by a check digit. Symbol 10 indicates model year ('E' = 1984). Symbol 11 ('0') is the assembly plant. Last comes the six-digit sequential production number.

Model	Body Type & Seating	Engine Type/CID	P.O.E. Price	Weight (lbs.)	Prod. Total
MONDIAL QUATTROVALVOLE					
Mondial	2-dr Coupe-2+2P	V8/179	59500	3285	Note 1
Mondial	2-dr Cabr-2+2P	V8/179	65000	3440	Note 2
GTO					
GTO	2-dr Coupe-2P	V8/174	83400	2555	Note 3
308 QUATTROVALVOLE					
GTB Berl	2-dr Coupe-2P	V8/179	54300	3190	Note 4
GTS Spider	2-dr Targa Cpe-2P	V8/179	59500	3230	Note 5
400i					
400i	2-dr Coupe-2+2P	V12/294	N/A	3748	Note 6
512 BBi					
512 BBi	2-dr Coupe-2P	H12/302	N/A	3305	Note 7

Note 1: About 1,145 Mondial Qv Coupes were produced from 1982-85.
Note 2: About 629 Mondial Qv Cabriolets were produced from 1983-85.
Note 3: About 41 Type 288 GTOs coupes were produced in 1984.
Note 4: About 748 Type 308 GTB Qv coupes were produced from 1982-85.
Note 5: About 3,042 Type 308 GTS Qv coupes were produced from 1982-85.
Note 6: About 1,306 Type 400i coupes were produced in 1979-84.
Note 7: About 1,007 Type 512 BBi coupes were produced from 1981-84.
Price Note: U.S. prices included $1,450 gas guzzler tax.

ENGINE [Base V-8 (Mondial, 308 GTB/GTS Quattrovalvole)]:

90-degree, dual-overhead-cam "vee" type eight-cylinder (32-valve). Light alloy block and heads. Displacement: 178.6 cid (2927 cc). Bore & stroke: 3.19 x 2.79 in. (81 x 71 mm). Compression ratio: 8.6:1. Brake horsepower: 235 (SAE) at 6800 rpm. Torque: 188 lbs.-ft. at 5500 rpm. Five main bearings. Bosch K-Jetronic fuel injection with Lambda control.

Note: European Mondial/308 engine was rated 240 bhp (DIN) with 9.2:1 compression.

ENGINE [Base V-8 (GTO)]:

90-degree, dual-overhead-cam "vee" type eight cylinder. Twin IHI turbochargers with separate intercoolers. Displacement: 174 cid (2855 cc). Bore & stroke: 3.15 x 2.79 in. (80 x 71 mm). Compression ratio: 7.6:1. Brake horsepower: 400 at 7000 rpm. Torque: 366 lbs.-ft. at 3800 rpm. Weber-Marelli electronic fuel injection.

ENGINE [Base V-12 (400i)]:

60-degree, dual-overhead-cam "vee" type 12 cylinder. Light alloy block and heads. Displacement: 294.2 cid (4823 cc). Bore & stroke: 3.19 x 3.07 in. (81 x 78 mm). Compression ratio: 8.8:1. Brake horsepower: 310-315 at 6400 rpm. Torque: 304 lbs.-ft. at 4200 rpm. Seven main bearings. Bosch K-Jetronic fuel injection.

ENGINE [Base Flat-12 (512 BBi)]:

Horizontally-opposed, dual-overhead cam 12-cylinder. Light alloy block and heads. Displacement: 302 cid (4942 cc). Bore & stroke: 3.23 x 3.07 in. (82 x 78 mm). Compression ratio: 9.2:1. Brake horsepower: 340 (DIN) at 6000 rpm. Torque: 333 lbs.-ft. at 4200 rpm. Seven main bearings. Bosch K-Jetronic fuel injection.

CHASSIS: Wheelbase: (Mondial) 104.3 in.; (GTO) 96.5 in.; (308 GTB/GTS) 92.1 in.; (400i) 106.3 in.; (512 BBi) 98.4 in. Overall Length: (Mondial) 182.7 in.; (GTO) 168.9 in.; (308 GTB/GTS) 174.2 in.; (400i) 189.4 in.; (512 BBi) 173.2 in. Height: (Mondial) 49.6 in.; (GTO) 44.1 in.; (308 GTB) 44.1 in.; (400i) 51.6 in.; (512 BBi) 44.1 in. Width: (Mondial) 70.5 in.; (GTO) 75.2 in.; (308 GTB/GTS) 67.7 in.; (400i) 70.9 in.; (512 BBi) 72 in. Front Tread: (Mondial) 58.9 in.; (GTO) 61.4 in.; (308 GTB/GTS) 57.9 in.; (400i) 57.9 in.; (512 BBi) 59.1 in. Rear Tread: (Mondial) 59.8 in.; (GTO) 61.5 in.; (308 GTB/GTS) 57.9 in.; (400i) 59.1 in.; (512 BBi) 61.9 in. Standard Tires: (Mondial) 240/55VR390; (GTO) 225/50VR16 front, 265/50VR16 rear; (308 GTB/GTS) Goodyear NCT 205/55VR16 front, 225/50VR16 rear; (400i) 240/55VR415; (512 BBi) 180/TR415 front, 210/TR415 rear.

TECHNICAL: Layout: (Mondial, GTO, 308 GTB/GTS, 512 BBi) mid-engine, rear-drive; (400i) front-engine, rear-drive. Transmission: (Mondial, GTO, 308 GTB/GTS, 512 BBi) five-speed manual in rear transaxle; (400i) five-speed manual or three-speed automatic. Type 308 gear ratios: (1st) 3.419:1; (2nd) 2.353:1; (3rd) 1.693:1; (4th) 1.244:1; (5th) 0.919:1. Steering: rack and pinion except (400i) recirculating ball. Suspension (front): unequal-length A-arms with coil springs and anti-roll bar. Suspension (rear): (Mondial, GTO, 308 GTB/GTS) unequal-length A-arms with coil springs and anti roll bar; (512 BBi) unequal-length A-arms with twin coil springs and anti-roll bar; (400i) unequal-length A-arms with coil springs, anti-roll bar and hydraulic self-leveling. Brakes: front/rear disc. Body Construction: separate body on tubular steel frame.

PERFORMANCE: Top Speed: (European Mondial) 139 mph; (GTO) 189.5 mph; (European 308 GTB) 158 mph; (400i w/manual) 152 mph; (400i A) 146 mph; (512 BBi) 174 mph. Acceleration (quarter-mile): (308) about 15.4 sec.; (Mondial) about 16.5 sec.; (GTO) 14.1 sec. (113 mph) but 12.7 sec. claimed; (400i w/manual) 14.8 sec.; (400i w/auto.) 15.6 sec.; (512 BBi) 14.2 sec. (103.5 mph).

1984 Ferrari Testarossa. (FSpA/WG)

MAJOR OPTIONS: Front spoiler (308). Metallic paint (308). Dual air conditioning (400i). Power sunroof (Mondial).

ADDITIONAL MODELS: The 1991-cc V-8 engine in the 208 GTB/GTS turbo, available in Europe, produced 220 hp.

Manufacturer: Ferrari S.p.A. SEFAC, Maranello (Modena), Italy.

Distributor: Fiat Motors of North America, Montvale, New Jersey.

HISTORY: The GTO designation reached back to the late 1950s, when Ferrari dominated GT racing with its 250 berlinetta coupes and California Spyder roadsters; and to the more potent (and quicker) 250 GTO that had debuted in 1962, with only 39 copies built. Ferrari's Testarossa debuted late in 1984 at the Paris show; see next listing for details.

1984 Ferrari Testarossa. (FSpA/WG)

1985 Ferrari 288 GTO. (DA)

1985-86

MONDIAL QUATTROVALVOLE — V-8 —

The 32-valve (four-valve per cylinder) engine improved the Mondial, but the Qv was a short-lived model and ceased production in 1985. For 1986, bore and stroke were increased to yield a new 3185 cc engine and a new model name, 3.2 Mondial (see below), debuted.

MONDIAL 3.2 — V-8 —

In their quest for ever-increasing performance, all 308 engines had a 2.0 mm increase in the bore, and a 2.6 mm longer stroke. Now displacing 3185 cc, the new engine brought increased driving fun and a new model name, Mondial 3.2. A better spark was provided by Marelli Multiplex electronic ignition to replace the prior Digiplex system. Otherwise, appearance and mechanical details were similar to the former Mondial coupe and cabriolet. Mondial styling features included hidden headlamps, horizontal hood vents, five side louvers, round tail lamps (red and amber), and four round exhaust pipes set in a black lower rear panel.

GTO — V-8 —

Continuing in limited-production for 1985, the GTO sports-racer was a fabulous market

1984-1985 Ferrari 288 GTO engine. (MC)

success for Ferrari and an even better investment for those folks that ordered early and then sold their cars to waiting buyers. Used GTOs were going for as much as two to three times the price of new models!

TESTAROSSA — FLAT-12 —

While the television show, *Magnum P.I.*, made the 308 one of the best-known Ferraris in America, the Testarossa gained its notoriety in a different way. Almost 7,200 were sold between 1985 and 1990, making it one of the most popular models ever offered in the U.S. Since the Boxer was never certified for U.S. sales, Americans could not legally buy a Ferrari flagship model from 1974 (the end of Daytona production) until this Pininfarina-designed beauty made its way into U.S. showrooms in 1985. Once again, Ferrari chose the Paris Auto Show to debut the dramatic two-seater coupe. It was the red cam covers that gave a late-1950s Ferrari sports/racer the legendary Testa Rossa ("redhead") appellation. The name was condensed to one word, Testarossa, and applied to this Eighties wonder. It was aimed squarely at the U.S. market and engineered to meet U.S. safety and emissions standards. Pininfarina designed and built the dramatically sensuous body, whose shape was honed in a wind tunnel, focusing mainly on front/rear downforce. Though it was constructed primarily of aluminum, steel was used for the roof and doors. Perhaps the most controversial styling feature were large horizontal strakes (ribs) on each bodyside, which led from just behind the door fronts into air scoops just ahead of the rear wheels. The air intakes were a necessity to feed air into the twin radiators, now located on the sides of the car, behind the cockpit. Some countries required such large openings to be covered—perhaps to protect small children and pets from being sucked in by the car's veracious appetite for air? A practical benefit of the rear-mounted radiators was to allow more luggage space up front. With a rear tread dimension nearly six inches wider than the front, the Testarossa displayed a broad and brawny back end, highlighted by monstrous rear tires. Horizontal rear slats and four round exhaust pipes completed the view from the back.

While the Testarossa shared the Boxer's horizontally-opposed 12-cylinder engine configuration, it sported new 24-valve heads, with four valves per cylinder. Despite a small drop in compression, to 8.7:1, the 4942-cc (302-cid) engine produced 380 horsepower (SAE) and 354 lbs.-ft. of torque. Bosch K-Jetronic fuel injection and Marelli Multiplex ignition continued from the prior BB model. Power was sent to a five-speed transaxle via an enlarged twin-disc clutch. Suspension details were similar to the 512 BBi: unequal-length A-arms, coil springs, and anti-roll bar up front, with twin coil springs at the rear. Thanks to a 100.4-inch wheelbase (two inches longer than the 512 BBi), the Testarossa offered a roomy, comfortable place for two people to explore the upper limits of performance. A Testarossa not only could approach 180 mph, it also was capable of accelerating to 60 mph in 5.3 seconds, and blasting through the quarter-mile in 13.6 seconds or less, hitting 105 mph at the end. Driver and passenger did not lack for comfort, either, with fine leather upholstery inside. In addition to luggage space in the nose, special fitted luggage was available, at additional cost, for the area behind the seats.

TYPE 328 GTB/GTS — V-8 — A slightly larger engine was introduced to the 3 series Ferrari, changing its name from 308 to 328. This engine was also used in the modified Mondial; the 3185-cc V-8 produced 260 hp and 213 lbs.-ft. of torque. As before, Bosch K-Jetronic fuel injection and Marelli electronic ignition were used,

1985 Ferrari 288 GTO. (DA)

1986 Ferrari Type 328 GTB and GTS. (DA)

but the latter adopted a new Multiplex system. While you would be hard pressed to detect the change, wheelbase grew fractionally, to 92.5 inches. Appearance of the 328 improved as the bumpers were now body-colored, and were smoothly integrated into the underfairing. At the rear, the four tailpipes and twin rear fog lamps also had a more integrated look. Revised, smoother-surfaced wheels retained their five-pointed star pattern.

TYPE 400i — V-12 — A few of these four-seat Ferraris were sold in 1985, but the model was replaced by the 412i (below) with a larger engine.

TYPE 412i — V-12 — It seems strange that the largest market for the "family Ferrari" went untapped. Despite the inability to sell the four-seat Ferrari in America, development continued for this continental cruiser. The 412i debuted at the Geneva Motor Show in early 1985. The bore was increased by one millimeter, enlarging the engine to 4942 cc (302 cid), and changing the name from 400i to 412i. Thanks to new Bosch K-

Jetronic fuel injection and an increase in compression to a 9.6:1 ratio, the engine produced 340 hp. Marelli Microplex electronic ignition was used, and a twin-disc clutch replaced the single-disc unit. Rarely an innovator in this area, Ferrari introduced anti-lock braking by Bosch. Large loads of luggage were handled by a self-leveling rear suspension, and a limited-slip differential helped to put the power to the ground. Styling features included sharply tapered rear side windows with black edging, long horizontal bodyside creases, and black accents on the rocker-panel bottoms and enlarged, twin-slotted front spoiler. Bumpers changed to body-color, and the back end was slightly taller. Above the low horizontal grille was Ferrari's prancing horse emblem. A gently-sloped hood wore horizontal vents, and concealed (pop up) headlamps continued from the prior model. Four round tail lamps were used (two red, two amber), along with a "412" badge and another prancing horse. Inside, flush-mounted controls replaced the original toggle switches.

TYPE 512 BBi — FLAT-12 — Production of the original 'BB' ended in 1985, replaced by the Testarossa (above).

I.D. DATA: Ferrari's 17-symbol Vehicle Identification Number is embossed on a metal plate attached to the steering column. Symbol one ('Z') indicates Italy. The next two symbols identify the make ('FF' = Ferrari). Symbol four indicates engine type; symbol five is restraint system. Symbols six and seven denote model ('08' = Mondial; '12' = 308 GTB Quattrovalvole; '13' = 308 GTS Quattrovalvole; '14' = Mondial Quattrovalvole; '15' = Mondial cabriolet; '17' = Testarossa; '18' = 308 conv; '19' = 328 GTB; '20' = 328 GTS; '21' = 3.2 Mondial; '26' = 3.2 Mondial cabriolet; '29' = 328 conv). Next is a market designator ('A' = North America), followed by a check digit. Symbol 10 indicates model year ('F' = 1984; 'G' = 1986). Symbol 11 ('0') is the assembly plant. Last comes the six-digit sequential production number.

Model	Body Type & Seating	Engine Type/CID	P.O.E. Price	Weight (lbs.)	Prod. Total
MONDIAL QUATTROVALVOLE					
Mondial	2-dr Coupe-2+2P	V8/179	59500	3285	Note 1
Mondial	2-dr Cabr-2+2P	V8/179	65000	3440	Note 2
3.2 MONDIAL					
3.2	2-dr Coupe-2+2P	V8/194	62770	3109	Note 3
3.2	2-dr Cabr-2+2P	V8/194	68070	3086	Note 4
GTO					
GTO	2-dr Coupe-2P	V8/174	76000	2555	Note 5
TESTAROSSA					
	2-dr Coupe-2P	H12/302	90170	3660	Note 6
328					
GTB	2-dr Coupe-2P	V8/194	59170	2784	Note 7
GTS	2-dr Targa Cpe-2P	V8/194	63370	2806	Note 8
400i					
400i	2-dr Coupe-2+2P	V12/294	N/A	3748	Note 9
412i					
412i	2-dr Coupe-2+2P	V12/302	65000	4009	Note 10
512 BBi					
512 BBi	2-dr Coupe-2P	H12/302	N/A	3305	Note 11

Note 1: About 1,145 Mondial Qv Coupes were produced from 1982-85.
Note 2: About 629 Mondial Qv Cabriolets were produced from 1983-85.
Note 3: About 987 3.2 Mondial Qv Coupes were produced from 1985-88.
Note 4: About 810 3.2 Mondial Qv Cabriolets were produced from 1985-88.
Note 5: About 230 Type 288 GTOs coupes were produced in 1985, 7 in 1986.
Note 6: About 7,177 Testarossas were produced from 1984-90.
Note 7: About 1,344 Type 328 GTB coupes were produced from 1985-89.
Note 8: About 6,068 Type 328 GTS Targas were produced from 1985-89.
Note 9: About 1,306 Type 400i coupes were produced in 1979-84.
Note 10: About 576 Type 412i coupes were produced in 1985-89.
Note 11: About 1,007 Type 512 BBi coupes were produced from 1981-84.

ENGINE [Base V-8 (Mondial Quattrovalvole)]: 90-degree, dual-overhead cam "vee" type eight-cylinder (32-valve). Light alloy block and heads. Displacement: 178.6 cid (2927 cc). Bore & stroke: 3.19 x 2.79 in. (81 x 71 mm). Compression ratio: 8.6:1. Brake horsepower: 230 (SAE) at 6800 rpm. Torque: 188 lbs.-ft. at 5500 rpm. Five main bearings. Bosch K-Jetronic fuel injection.

ENGINE [Base V-8 (3.2 Mondial, 328)]: 90-degree, dual-overhead-cam "vee" type eight-cylinder (32-valve). Light alloy block and heads. Displacement: 194.4 cid (3185 cc). Bore & stroke: 3.27 x 2.90 in. (83 x 73.6 mm). Compression ratio: 9.2:1. Brake horsepower: 260 at 7000 rpm. Torque: 213 lbs.-ft. at 5500 rpm. Five main bearings. Bosch K-Jetronic fuel injection.

ENGINE [Base V-8 (GTO)]: 90-degree, dual-overhead-cam "vee" type eight cylinder. Twin IHI turbochargers with separate intercoolers. Light alloy block and heads. Displacement: 174 cid (2855 cc). Bore & stroke: 3.15 x 2.79 in. (80 x 71 mm). Compression ratio: 7.6:1. Brake horsepower: 400 at 7000 rpm. Torque: 366 lbs.-ft. at 3800 rpm. Five main bearings. Weber-Marelli electronic fuel injection.

ENGINE [Base Flat-12 (Testarossa)]: Horizontally-opposed, dual overhead-cam 12-cylinder (48-valve). Light alloy block and heads. Displacement: 302 cid (4942 cc). Bore & stroke: 3.23 x 3.07 in. (82 x 78 mm). Compression ratio: 8.7:1. Brake horsepower: 380 (SAE) at 5750 rpm. Torque: 354 lbs.-ft. at 4500 rpm. Seven main bearings. Bosch K-Jetronic fuel injection.

ENGINE [Base V-12 (400i)]: 60-degree, dual-overhead-cam, "vee" type 12 cylinder. Light alloy block and heads. Displacement: 294.2 cid (4823 cc). Bore & stroke: 3.19 x 3.07 in. (81 x 78 mm). Compression ratio: 8.8:1. Brake horsepower: 340 at 6500 rpm. Torque: 347 lbs.-ft. at 3600 rpm. Seven main bearings. Bosch K-Jetronic fuel injection.

ENGINE [Base V-12 (412i)]: 60-degree, dual-overhead-cam, "vee" type 12 cylinder. Light alloy block and heads. Displacement: 302 cid (4942 cc). Bore & stroke: 3.23 x 3.07 in. (82 x 78 mm). Compression ratio: 9.6:1. Brake horsepower: 340 at 6000 rpm. Torque: 333 lbs.-ft. at 4200 rpm. Seven main bearings. Bosch K-Jetronic fuel injection.

ENGINE [Base Flat-12 (512 BBi)]: Horizontally-opposed, dual-overhead cam 12-cylinder. Light alloy block and heads. Displacement: 302 cid (4942 cc). Bore & stroke: 3.23 x 3.07 in. (82 x 78 mm). Compression ratio: 9.2:1. Brake horsepower: 340 (DIN) at 6000 rpm. Torque: 333 lbs.-ft. at 4200 rpm. Seven main bearings. Bosch K-Jetronic fuel injection.

CHASSIS: Wheelbase: (Mondial) 104.2 in.; (GTO) 96.5 in.; (Testarossa) 100.4 in.; (328) 92.5 in.; (400i/412i) 106.3 in.; (512 BBi) 98.4 in. Overall Length: (Mondial) 178.5 in.; (GTO) 168.9 in.; (Testa) 176.6 in.; (328) 168.7 in.; (400i/412i) 189.4 in.; (512 BBi) 173.2 in. Height: (Mondial) 49.6 in.; (GTO) 44.1 in.; (Testa) 44.5 in.; (328) 40.1 in.; (400i/412i) 51.6 in.; (512 BBi) 44.1 in. Width: (Mondial) 70.5 in.; (GTO) 75.2 in.; (Testa) 77.8 in.; (328) 68.1 in.; (400i/412i) 70.9 in.; (512 BBi) 72 in. Front Tread: (Mondial) 58.9 in.; (GTO) 61.4 in.; (Testa) 59.8 in.; (328) 58.0 in.; (400i/412i) 57.9 in.; (512 BBi) 59.1 in. Rear Tread: (Mondial) 59.7 in.; (GTO) 61.5 in.; (Testa) 65.4 in.; (328) 57.8 in.; (400i/412i) 59.1 in.; (512 BBi) 61.9 in. Standard Tires: (Mondial) 240/55VR390; (GTO) 225/50VR16 front, 265/50VR16 rear; (Testa) 225/50VR16 front, 255/50VR16 rear; (400i) 240/55VR415; (412i) 240/55VR16; (512 BBi) 180/TR415 front, 210TR415 rear.

1985-1988 Ferrari Mondial Cabriolet. (MC)

TECHNICAL: Layout: (Mondial, GTO, Testarossa, 328, 512 BBi) mid-engine, rear-drive; (400i/412i) front-engine, rear-drive. Transmission: (Mondial, GTO, Testarossa, 328, 512 BBi) five speed manual in rear transaxle; (400i/412i) five-speed manual or three-speed automatic. Steering: rack and pinion except (400i/412i) recirculating ball. Suspension (front): unequal length A-arms with coil springs and anti-roll bar. Suspension (rear): (Mondial, GTO, 328) unequal-length A-arms with coil springs and anti-roll bar; (Testarossa, 512 BBi) unequal length A-arms with twin coil springs and anti-roll bar; (400i/412i) unequal-length A-arms with coil springs, anti roll bar and hydraulic self-leveling. Brakes: front/rear disc; anti-lock on 412i. Body Construction: separate body on tubular steel frame; (Testarossa) aluminum body with steel roof and doors.

PERFORMANCE: Top Speed: (3.2 Mondial Cabr) 145 mph; (GTO) near 190 mph; (Testarossa) 180+ mph; (412i) 147-155+ mph. Acceleration (0-60 mph): (3.2 Mondial) 7.4 sec.; (3.2 Mondial Cabr) 7.1 sec.; (GTO) 5.0 sec.; (Testarossa) 5.3 sec.; (412i w/manual) 6.7 sec. Acceleration (quarter-mile): (Mondial) 15.0 sec.; (Mondial Cabr) 15.3 sec. (94 mph); (GTO) 12.7-14.1 sec. (up to 113 mph); (Testarossa) 13.3-13.6 sec. (105-107 mph); (412i) 15.0 sec. (96.5 mph).

PRODUCTION/SALES: Approximately 771 Ferraris were sold in the U.S. during 1986.

Manufacturer: Ferrari S.p.A. SEFAC, Maranello (Modena), Italy.

Distributor: Ferrari of North America, Hasbrouck Heights, New Jersey.

Ferrari Testarossa:
Holding the Standard High for Over a Decade

1985 Ferrari Testarossa. (DA)

"Why would anyone buy a Ferrari Testarossa, when a Volvo station wagon is more economical, practical and costs a fraction of that Italian red thing?" If you have ever uttered any statement like this, then you've probably picked up the wrong publication.

We are lucky enough to live in a world where the folks looking for basic transportation have a wide variety of automotive appliances from which to choose. It leaves all the good cars for enthusiasts like us. No one *needs* to drive a Ferrari Testarossa. I can't think of anyone that has to have a 44.5-inch, low-slung missile that can rocket you to 60 mph in only 5.3 seconds. And certainly the 182-mph maximum speed is an asset that goes wanting for most of a car's life. But the Testarossa is not a car for those with ordinary tastes.

Ferrari has always catered to those individuals who fancy themselves a bit of a racecar driver. There was a day when you could buy a street-legal Ferrari, drive it to the track, compete with a fairly good chance of victory, and then drive it home. As the laws for vehicles became more stringent, these dual-purpose cars have almost completely disappeared (Let's hear it for the Enzo Ferrari!) to be replaced by more civilized conveyances. But, the performance and styling of Ferraris continues to tell people that each vehicle is something extraordinary.

Ferrari unveiled the Testarossa to its dealers and selected customers in September 1984 in the heartland of Ferrari, Modena. The public had to stand by a couple of weeks longer until the Paris Auto Salon, and the shape that greeted the assembled throngs proved well worth the wait. Everyone had a strong opinion on this latest Ferrari.

By moving the water radiators from the nose to the sides of the car, just behind the cockpit, Ferrari was answering the complaints of the Berlinetta Boxer owners who didn't like the heat build-up from the plumbing that ran fore to aft. In order to accommodate the engine, transmission, suspension, tires, and these radiators, the Testarossa's flanks had to be stretched to a width of almost 78 inches. This produced one of the most prominent features of the car: the wide rear end.

An even more outstanding feature was the large troughs in the sides covered by a row of strakes that earned the nickname, "cheese graters." Extensive wind tunnel tests not only shaped the Testarossa for maximum downforce, they also showed that scoops this long were necessary for enough air to be sucked past the radiators to generate the proper heat exchange. Some folks accepted these as just part of the Testarossa's style, while others never grew used to this radical departure. The Ferrari 348 used a similar style for the doors.

The inside of the Testarossa provoked no such controversy. Everyone agreed that the interior struck just the right note between luxury and sport. All the traditional Ferrari elements were featured prominently. The large speedometer and tachometer were centrally placed for quick reference. From the center console, the chrome shift lever grew up through the external shift gate. A leather Momo steering wheel was just the right diameter with the prancing horse displayed proudly on the yellow horn button.

As always, the heart of a Ferrari is the engine. The Testarossa inherited the Berlinetta Boxer's flat-twelve, mid-engine layout. The 4942-cc engine received four-valves per cylinder head that helped boost the output of the engine to 380 hp at 5750 rpms. This engine reached a new height in dual-purpose driving. When heavy traffic forced its owner to trundle around town, the Testarossa was a model of civility. Fouled plugs and sputtering carburetors were just a distant memory for owners of this thoroughbred. Yet, when the open road beckoned, the Testarossa offered thrilling performance accessible to drivers of all skill levels. The wide rear end and the engine's high output still required some care when the Testarossa was pressed to the limits. The 255/50x16-inch rear tires put a lot of contact patch on the road, which contributed to a breathtaking level of acceleration, handling, and braking.

By 1992, the Testarossa was ready for a makeover and a new name, the 512TR. While the old name honored the Ferrari racecar of the 1950s, the Testa Rossa (Red Head), the 512 referred to the five-liter displacement of the engine and the twelve cylinders. There was a slight increase in the compression ratio, but the biggest change was from the Testarossa's Marelli Multiplex ignition and Bosch K-Jetronic fuel injection to Bosch's new Motronic 2.7 integrated electronic ignition/injection system. This allowed the 512TR to be sold in all 50 states. California had nixed 1991 Testarossa sales due to the lack of on-board diagnostics.

In 1995, Ferrari revised their flagship

for the final time. Now called the 512M (for modificato or modified) the biggest change to be seen was the nose of the car. Fixed units replaced the pop-up headlights, and the grille opening was smaller. The road wheels were a variation on the traditional Ferrari five-spoke star. These spokes curved out from the center, and the rim was decorated with Allen head screws. Best of all, the horsepower was boosted to 421 at 6750 rpms. As a result, 512M owners could look forward to a top speed of 192 mph, if they found the right stretch of road.

The Testarossa and its descendents proved to be very popular vehicles. From 1984 to 1991, 7,177 Testarossas were sold. The middle model, the 512TR made 2,280 buyers very happy folks between 1992 and 1994, and just 500 examples of the final version were produced between 1994 and 1996. Because so many of these cars are still around, prices have been dropping. *The Ferrari Market Letter* (770-381-1993) reports average asking prices of the 1985-87 Testarossa as $60,244, and $73,053 for the later editions. Expect to pay $113,207 for a 512TR or $161,547 if your heart's desire is the ultimate Testarossa, the 512M.

All represent a good value, and a potent symbol of all the Ferrari marque represents, despite what those Volvo owners might tell you.

1987 Ferrari F40. (DA)

3.2 MONDIAL — V-8 — The Mondial continued to be a technically wonderful car that did not find the full audience here in the U.S. that Ferrari may have hoped for.

TESTAROSSA — FLAT-12 — The Testarossa was literally the poster child for the Eighties. You would find a glorious color rendition in most every adolescent's bedroom, and many of the "grownups" spent blissful hours dreaming of owning, or at least driving this Ferrari supercar.

F40 — V-8 — Enzo Ferrari decided to celebrate 40 years of auto production in grand style. On July 21,

1987, the cover of the F40 was unveiled to a select group of journalists in Maranello. He wanted to produce "a car reminiscent of the original 250 LM," to mark this anniversary, and perhaps his 90th birthday. Pininfarina general manager Leonardo Fioravanti said the forthcoming F40 would "recover the spirit of some of the Ferrari cars of the past" and "give our customers the possibility of driving objects that are very similar to the racing cars." From some companies, this may have sounded like marketing hyperbole, but not from Ferrari. Many technological features perfected in Formula One racing were brought into the F40. The handsomely aggressive body was made from composite materials reinforced with carbon fiber and Kevlar sitting atop a steel-tube space-frame chassis. The hood, trunk lid, and doors were all made from these lightweight materials. The doors weighed a mere 3.5 lbs. apiece. Composites also were used in outer body panels.

Power for the F40 came from an improved version of the 288 GTO V-8. Fitted with twin IHI turbos that had air-to-air Behr intercoolers, the 2936-cc (179-cid) powerplant produced 478 hp (European trim) at 7000 rpm, and 425 lbs.-ft. of torque. A Weber-Marelli IAW engine management system controlled the turbo wastegate, ignition, and port fuel injection. Since the turbos delivered boost up to 16 psi, compression was held to only 7.8:1 to keep detonation under control. Claimed top speed was 201 mph, and estimates of 0-60 mph acceleration reached as low as 3.0 seconds. A F40 was expected to accelerate to 124 mph in just 12.4 seconds.

The F40's shape was crammed full of air scoops, vents, and louvers. Pininfarina's main goal in the F40's design was to achieve maximum downforce; hence the drag coefficient was an unremarkable 0.34. Up front was a deep spoiler, and the wing on the back was the largest appendage seen on American roads since the days of the Plymouth Superbird. Apart from that, the F40 displayed some resemblance to the Evoluzione, GTO, and 308/328, but with a host of unique differences in its wide body. Wheels and tires (245/40ZR 17 front and 335/35ZR 17 rear) were nearly Indy-car size. Wheelbase, at 94.5 inches, was identical to the GTO, while the F40 measured two inches shorter overall than a Testarossa. Nose and tail sections were both hinged.

Inside the F40, the atmosphere was that of a racing car, with only a few items giving away its road-going intent. Air conditioning was an option that appeared in most every F40, since only sliding Plexiglas panes were installed. They were more useful for passing through tollbooths than providing any ventilation. The stark cockpit contained no carpeting, no door panels, and no radio. The form-fitting Kevlar bucket seats were upholstered in day-glo-orange Nomex, came in three sizes, and had cut outs for the four-point safety harnesses. A sponge-like safety fuel bladder held 31.7 gallons. Suspension layout was conventional, with unequal-length A-arms and coil springs (concentric with shocks) and anti-roll bar. Three-position ride-height control, included in early models, automatically dropped the car by 20 mm at speed, but it could be raised to 20 mm above the normal position by touching a switch. The five-speed gearbox was in the rear transaxle, with 2.73:1 final drive ratio. Rack-and-pinion steering had no power assist. Vented, cross-drilled disc brakes used aluminum centers and cast-iron outer segments.

Apart from its significance as a road-going racing car, the F40 arrived just as the prices of Ferrari were rocketing to unimaginable pinnacles. When the car was first shown to the public at the Frankfurt show in September of 1987, the intended price was $280,000. By the time production started, $400,000 was the common amount needed to take delivery of an early model. With 288 GTOs trading for nearly twice that amount, it's not too surprising to hear that some F40 owners were making a substantial profit by reselling their cars for $1,000,000 and up.

TYPE 328 GTB/GTS — V-8 — Production of the successor to the 308 series, introduced in 1985, continued with little change.

TYPE 412i — V-12 — Production of the "family" Ferrari four seater, with enlarged engine as introduced in 1985, continued with little change.

I.D. DATA: Ferrari's 17-symbol Vehicle Identification Number is embossed on a metal plate attached to the steering column. Breakdown is similar to 1985-86.

Model	Body Type & Seating	Engine Type/CID	P.O.E. Price	Weight (lbs.)	Prod. Total
3.2 MONDIAL					
3.2	2-dr Coupe-2+2P	V8/194	72850	3109	Note 1
3.2	2-dr Cabr-2+2P	V8/194	78850	3086	Note 2
TESTAROSSA					
	2-dr Coupe-2P	H12/302	135050	3660	Note 3
F40					
	2-dr Coupe-2P	V8/179	280000	2425	Note 4
328					
GTB	2-dr Coupe-2P	V8/194	68000	2784	Note 5
GTS	2-dr Targa Cpe-2P	V8/194	73800	2806	Note 6
412i					
412i	2-dr Coupe-2+2P	V12/302	65000	4009	Note 7

Note 1: About 987 3.2 Mondial Qv Coupes were produced from 1985-88.
Note 2: About 810 3.2 Mondial Qv Cabriolets were produced from 1985-88.
Note 3: About 7,177 Testarossas were produced from 1984-90.
Note 4: About 1,315 Type F40 coupes were produced in 1987-82.
Note 5: About 1,344 Type 328 GTB coupes were produced from 1985-89.
Note 6: About 6,068 Type 328 GTS Targas were produced from 1985-89.
Note 7: About 576 Type 412i coupes were produced in 1985-89.
Price Note: Prices were as of 4/1/88, except for the 412 price from 1985.

ENGINE [Base V-8 (3.2 Mondial, 328)]:
90-degree, dual-overhead-cam "vee" type eight-cylinder (32-valve). Light alloy block and heads. Displacement: 194.4 cid (3185 cc). Bore & stroke: 3.27 x 2.90 in. (83 x 73.6 mm). Compression ratio: 9.2:1. Brake horsepower: 260 at 7000 rpm. Torque: 213 lbs.-ft. at 5500 rpm. Five main bearings. Bosch K-Jetronic fuel injection.

ENGINE [Base Flat-12 (Testarossa)]:
Horizontally-opposed, dual overhead-cam 12-cylinder (48-valve). Light alloy block and heads. Displacement: 302 cid (4942 cc). Bore & stroke: 3.23 x 3.07 in. (82 x 78 mm). Compression ratio: 8.7:1. Brake horsepower: 380 (SAE) at 5750 rpm. Torque: 354 lbs.-ft. at 4500 rpm. Seven main bearings. Bosch K-Jetronic fuel injection.

ENGINE [Base V-8 (F40)]: 90-degree, dual-overhead-cam, "vee" type eight-cylinder (32-valve). Two IHI turbochargers with Behr intercoolers. Displacement: 179 cid (2936 cc). Bore & stroke: 3.23 x 2.74 in. (82 x 69.5 mm). Compression ratio: 7.8:1. Brake horsepower: 471 (SAE) at 7000 rpm. Torque: 426 lbs.-ft. at 4000 rpm. Five main bearings. Weber-Marelli engine management.

ENGINE [Base V-12 (412i)]: 60-degree, dual-overhead-cam, "vee" type 12 cylinder. Light alloy block and heads. Displacement: 302 cid (4942 cc). Bore & stroke: 3.23 x 3.07 in. (82 x 78 mm). Compression ratio: 9.6:1. Brake horsepower: 340 at 6000 rpm. Torque: 333 lbs.-ft. at 4200 rpm. Seven main bearings. Bosch K-Jetronic fuel injection.

CHASSIS: Wheelbase: (Mondial) 104.2 in.; (Testarossa) 100.4 in.; (F40) 96.5 in.; (328) 92.5 in.; (412i) 106.3 in. Overall Length: (Mondial) 178.5 in.;

(Testa) 176.6-in.; (F40) 174.4 in.; (328) 168.7 in.; (412i) 189.4 in. Height: (Mondial) 48.6 in.; (Testa) 44.5 in.; (F40) 44.5 in.; (328) 40.1 in.; (412i) 51.7 in. Width: (Mondial) 70.6 in.; (Testa) 77.8 in.; (F40) 78.0 in.; (328) 68.1 in.; (412i) 70.8 in. Front Tread: (Mondial) 58.8 in.; (Testa) 59.8 in.; (F40) 62.8 in.; (328) 58.0 in.; (412i) 58.1 in. Rear Tread: (Mondial) 59.4 in.; (Testa) 65.4 in.; (F40) 63.4 in.; (328) 57.8 in.; (412i) 59.4 in. Standard Tires: (Mondial) 240/55VR390; (Testa) 225/50VR16 front, 255/50VR16 rear; (F40) Pirelli "P Zero" 245/40ZR17 front, 335/35ZR17 rear; (412i) 240/55VR16.

TECHNICAL: Layout: (Mondial, Testarossa, F40, 328) mid-engine, rear-drive; (412i) front-engine, rear-drive. Transmission: (Mondial, Testarossa, F40, 328) five-speed manual in rear transaxle; (412i) five-speed manual or three-speed automatic. Steering: rack and pinion except (412i) recirculating ball. Suspension (front): unequal-length A-arms with coil springs and anti-roll bar. Suspension (rear): (Mondial, F40, 328) unequal-length A-arms with coil springs and anti-roll bar; (Testarossa) unequal-length A-arms with twin coil springs and anti-roll bar; (412i) unequal length A-arms with coil springs, anti-roll bar and hydraulic self-leveling.

Brakes: front/rear disc; anti-lock on 412i. Body Construction: separate body on tubular steel frame; (Testarossa) aluminum body with steel roof and doors; (F40) composite body on steel-tube space frame.

PERFORMANCE: Top Speed: (Mondial Cabr) 145 mph; (Testarossa) 180+ mph; (F40) 201 mph claimed; (412i) 147-155+ mph. Acceleration (0-60 mph): (Mondial) 7.4 sec.; (Mondial Cabr) 7.1 sec.; (Testarossa) 5.3 sec.; (F40) 3.0 sec.; (412i w/manual) 6.7 sec. Acceleration (quarter-mile): (Mondial) 15.0 sec.; (Mondial Cabr) 15.3 sec. (94 mph); (Testarossa) 13.3-13.6 sec. (105-107 mph); (412i) 15.0 sec. (96.5 mph).

PRODUCTION/SALES: Approximately 1,054 Ferraris were sold in the U.S. during 1987, and 805 in 1989.

Manufacturer: Ferrari S.p.A. SEFAC, Maranello (Modena), Italy.

Distributor: Ferrari North America, Hasbrouck Heights, New Jersey.

1987 Ferrari F40. (DA)

1989 Ferrari 348 TB & TS. (FSpA/WG)

MONDIAL t — V-8 — Ferrari introduced further evidence that racing improves the breed at the 1989 Geneva Auto Show. The Mondial t had a larger, 3405-cc V-8 engine, but of greater technical interest was the transmission. Ferrari engineers devised a transverse (trasversale) mounted transmission for the 1975 Formula One car. They adapted this same technology to the Mondial t to great effect. The revised engine/gearbox layout lowered the driveline by five inches, which not only improved handling but also eased servicing since the twin-disc clutch was now mounted at the end of the car. The 3405-cc engine produced up to 300 hp and was also used in the new 348 series. The new powerplant permitted the Mondial t a 0-60 mph sprint in about 6.5 seconds, and the car would reportedly continue on to a top speed of 158 mph. New Bosch Motronic 2.5 fuel injection took advantage of the 10.4:1 engine compression and 95-octane no-lead fuel. This "update" also featured the addition of standard anti-lock brakes, and for the first time on a Ferrari, a three-position switch that offered a soft, medium, or hard ride. This was the first Ferrari with power rack-and-pinion steering. As for appearance, the fenders were no longer flared, and the bodyside air intakes had a less diagonal shape at the rear. Flush-type, body-colored door handles were installed. The sloping nose still held horizontal vents and pop-up rectangular headlamps. At the rear were the familiar four round tail lamps and four exhaust pipe outlets. Inside,

automatic air conditioning could be adjusted separately for the driver and passenger. A restyled instrument panel contained five round gauges ahead of the driver. As before, the Cabriolet was a "true" convertible, not a Targa-topped coupe.

TESTAROSSA — FLAT-12 — Production of the dramatic Testarossa continued with little change.

F40 — V-8 — By the time the F40 supercar was certified for U.S. sale, it had grown into a major legend, and was drawing prices in the legendary league, well above its official selling price.

348 — V-8 — Introduced at the Frankfurt show in September 1989, the 348 drew both applause and controversy. The applause was for the extra performance above and beyond the 328 models. The controversy was over the inclusion of the Testarossa-inspired strakes along the sides. The 348 carried the same 3.4-liter engine as the new Mondial t, introduced a few months earlier. The new powerplant delivered some 40 more horsepower than its predecessor, and was mounted longitudinally rather than crosswise (as in the 328). Dropping the engine by five inches lowered the 348's center of gravity, greatly improving the car's handling. It's wheelbase grew by four inches over the 328. With its back wheels mounted well to the rear, this Ferrari displayed minimal rear overhang. Width grew considerably. Taken together, these changes represented a larger step up in performance than either the 308qv or the 328 had. As before, styling was by Pininfarina. Testarossa sales were probably not inhibited by the inclusion of the "cheese grater" side slats, and it is doubtful that anyone bought a Porsche 911 instead of a

Ferrari 348 because of this similar feature. Perhaps the fact that these side strakes did not continue into future models speaks best of their acceptance, or lack there of. The sharply sloped nose contained hidden headlamps utilizing compound lenses and halogen bulbs. The "flying buttress" fastback roofline continued from the 308/328. Both the closed coupe and Targa-roofed version were offered.

412i Note: Only a handful of final 412i models were produced during 1989, as that model disappeared from the Ferrari lineup; see previous listings for details.

I.D. DATA: Ferrari's 17-symbol Vehicle Identification Number is embossed on a metal plate attached to the steering column. Breakdown is similar to 1985-86.

Model	Body Type & Seating	Engine Type/CID	P.O.E. Price	Weight (lbs.)	Prod. Total
MONDIAL t					
tb	2-dr Coupe-2+2P	V8/208	84080	3144	Note 1
ts	2-dr Cabr-2+2P	V8/208	92380	3236	Note 2
TESTAROSSA					
	2-dr Coupe-2P	H12/302	168050	3660	Note 3
F40					
	2-dr Coupe-2P	V8/179	423250	2425	Note 4
348					
TB	2-dr Coupe-2P	V8/208	103400	3071	Note 5
TS	2-dr Targa Cpe-2P	V8/208	109550	3071	Note 6

Note 1: About 840 Mondial t Coupes were produced from 1989-93.
Note 2: About 1,010 Mondial t Cabriolets were produced from 1989-93.
Note 3: About 7,177 Testarossas were produced from 1984-90.
Note 4: About 1,315 Type F40 coupes were produced in 1987-82.
Note 5: About 2,895 Type 348 TB coupes were produced from 1989-93.
Note 6: About 4,230 Type 328 TS Targas were produced from 1989-93.
Price Note: Prices were as of 1/1/90.

ENGINE [Base V-8 (Mondial t, 348)]: Dual-overhead-cam, "vee" type eight-cylinder (32-valve). Displacement: 208 cid (3405 cc). Bore & stroke: 3.35 x 2.95 in. (85 x 75 mm). Compression ratio: 10.4:1. Brake horsepower: 296-300 at 7200 rpm. Torque: 238 lbs.-ft. at 4200 rpm. Five main bearings. Bosch Motronic 2.5 port fuel injection.

ENGINE [Base Flat-12 (Testarossa)]: Horizontally-opposed, dual-overhead-cam 12-cylinder (48-valve). Light alloy block and heads. Displacement: 302 cid (4942 cc). Bore & stroke: 3.23 x 3.07 in. (82 x 78 mm). Compression ratio: 8.7:1. Brake horsepower: 380 (SAE) at 5750 rpm. Torque: 354 lbs.-ft. at 4500 rpm. Seven main bearings. Bosch K-Jetronic fuel injection.

ENGINE [Base V-8 (F40)]: 90-degree, dual-overhead-cam, "vee" type eight-cylinder (32-valve). Two IHI turbochargers with Behr intercoolers. Displacement: 179 cid (2936 cc). Bore & stroke: 3.23 x 2.74 in. (82 x 69.5 mm). Compression ratio: 7.8:1. Brake horsepower: 471 (SAE) at 7000 rpm. Torque: 426 lbs.-ft. at 4000 rpm. Five main bearings. Weber-Marelli engine management.

CHASSIS: Wheelbase: (Mondial) 104.3 in.; (Testarossa) 100.4 in.; (F40) 94.5 in.; (348) 96.5 in. Overall Length: (Mondial) 178.5 in.; (Testa) 176.6in.; (F40) 174.4 in.; (348) 166.7 in. Height: (Mondial cpe) 48.6 in.; (Testa) 44.5 in.; (F40) 44.5 in.; (348) 46.1 in. Width: (Mondial) 70.6 in.; (Testa) 77.8 in.; (F40) 78.0 in.; (348) 74.6 in. Front Tread: (Mondial) 59.9 in.; (Testa) 59.8 in.; (F40) 62.8 in.; (348) 59.2 in. Rear Tread: (Mondial) 61.4 in.; (Testa) 65.4 in.; (F40) 63.4 in.; (348) 62.2 in. Standard Tires: (Testa) 225/50VR16 front, 255/50VR16 rear, (F40) Pirelli "P Zero" 245/40ZR17 front, 335/35ZR17 rear.

1989 Ferrari 348 TB. (FSpA/WG)

TECHNICAL: Layout: mid-engine, rear-drive. Transmission: five-speed manual in rear transaxle. Steering: rack and pinion. Suspension (front): unequal-length A-arms with coil springs and anti-roll bar. Suspension (rear): (Mondial, F40, 348) unequal-length A-arms with coil springs and anti-roll bar; (Testarossa) unequal-length A-arms with twin coil springs and anti-roll bar. Brakes: front/rear disc; anti-locking on 348 and Mondial. Body Construction: separate body on tubular steel frame except (348) unibody; (Testarossa) aluminum body with steel roof and doors; (F40) composite body on steel-tube space frame.

PERFORMANCE: Top Speed: (Mondial) 158 mph; (Testarossa) 180 mph; (F40) 201 mph claimed. Acceleration (0-60 mph): (Mondial) 6.5 sec.; (Testarossa) 5.3 sec.; (F40) 3.0 sec. estimated. Acceleration (quarter-mile): (Testarossa) 13.6 sec. (105 mph).

Manufacturer: Ferrari S.p.A. SEFAC, Maranello (Modena), Italy.

Distributor: Ferrari North America, Hasbrouck Heights, New Jersey.

HISTORY: The Mondial t became available in the U.S. late in 1989; the 348 entered production late in 1989 and was on sale in 1990. The F40 became available in the U.S. during 1990. All models shown in this listing continued in production into the early 1990s.

1990 Ferrari F40. (WG)

1990 Ferrari F40. (WG)

1989 Ferrari 348 TS. (WG)

Most Ferraris are instant hits from the moment they are unveiled at an international auto show, until the time they quietly step aside for their replacement. The Ferrari 348 has at least 8,312 fans (total production), who will champion the 348's rightful place in the long, illustrious line of steeds from Maranello. There are others who will complain of the styling, initial build quality, and at-the-limit twitchiness as reasons not to buy. Both sides will agree, however, that any car wearing the "Ferrari" badge is worthy of a certain measure of respect.

The Ferrari lineup was initially divided between those cars designed purely for competition and those with street capabilities. Some cars, such as the GTO and 250LM, were capable of being driven on the street as well as winning races. With the advent of the Dino 206 and 246 GT, Ferrari introduced us to the idea of a "junior" line of automobiles. For a time in the mid-1970s, the Dino 308GT4 was the only Ferrari certified for sale in the USA.

The 308, 308 Quattrovalvole, and 328 were a remarkably successful series of cars. Some credit must be given to Tom Selleck's *Magnum P.I.* television show for popularizing the angular Pininfarina design. Despite an engine whose initial output was less than rip-snorting, enough of these cars were sold to keep Ferrari's finances afloat, and they even brought some prosperity. The world eagerly waited to see what the next evolution of this mid-engined V-8 line would look like.

First shown at the 1989 Frankfurt show, the 348 was immediately a source of controversy. While the overall shape was pleasing, many critics objected to the side strakes that ran along the lower half of the 348's doors. Sure, the 348 resembled the Testarossa, but these same folks didn't care for the big flat twelve's styling either. The situation grew worse when initial road tests complained of heavy steering, gearboxes that were difficult to operate, and even cases of poor build quality. Perhaps the worst gripes were that the 348 was a difficult car to drive at the limit. *Car and Driver* complained, "Above 150 mph, the wandering on the high speed oval verged on scary. (While) few people drive on public roads at this clip, Corvettes, (Porsche) 928 GTSs, NSXs and Vipers can tackle their similar top speeds with nary a misstep."

This also brings up another sore point. Shortly after the 348 hit the road, Acura introduced their high water mark, the NSX. Here was a car that equaled or exceeded the 348's performance numbers, yet cost 40% less than the Ferrari. Where the 348 demanded that the driver accept the car on its terms, the NSX placed few more demands than a contemporary Honda Accord.

Just as cars don't compete in a vacuum, automobile sales are very much tied into the world's economy. As the recession smacked the exotic car market upside the head in the early 1990s, the blow could even be felt in Maranello. Sales dropped precipitously from 4,000-plus in 1990 and 1991, to a paltry 2,200 in 1993.

Clearly Ferrari needed to do something.

They responded to the handling criticisms by numerous changes to the shocks, springs, rear suspension geometry, and alignment settings. The 348 Series Specials was introduced as a marketing exercise. A freer-flowing exhaust increased the horsepower from 300 to 312, a new front spoiler was added with paint matched to the body color, and the rear end treatment offered different lights. Perhaps the best move was the introduction of the 348 Challenge Race Series. Each of the 27 North American dealerships were required to help at least one of their clients participate in a series of regional races that offered the provocative prize of a world championship in Mugello, Italy. This idea was so successful that a Ferrari 355 and 360 Challenge Series followed. Several other manufacturers, most notably Porsche, emulated Ferrari and offered similar chances for deep-pocket owners of these sporting machines the opportunity to stretch the legs of their mounts in an environment that offered both safety and bleachers for their adoring fans.

Perhaps the best thing Ferrari did to simulate the 348 sales, was the addition of a third body style. Initially, the 348 was offered in both TB and TS bodies. The T stood for transverse (the five-speed transmission alignment in relationship to the engine). The B was for the fixed roof Berlinetta, and the S designated a lift-off roof Targa. When the 348 Spider debuted,

it was the first time you could buy a "ragtop" two seat Ferrari since the mid-Seventies Daytona Spyder. Sales were so good, that the 348 Spider continued to be produced along side its replacement, the F355.

The 348 did offer some substantial improvements over its predecessor. Instead of a tubular steel chassis, the 348 utilized a monoque with a steel tube subframe for the engine. This resulted in a much stiffer chassis, which allowed the engineers to tune the 348's suspension to offer a more compliant ride, and the opportunity to wear 215/50x17-inch front rubber and 255/45x17-inch rears. These wide tires also came in handy when it was time to stop the 348. Besides larger rotors than the 328, the 348 was the first U.S. Ferrari to offer ABS brakes.

Despite complaints of a chrome-gated shifter that was difficult to operate, *Car and Driver* did record a 0-60 time of only 5.5 seconds; 100 mph was reached in 14.1 seconds, and they saw a top speed of 165 mph.

The element that won over every magazine that tested the 348 was its engine. Displacement was bumped up from the 328's 3185 ccs to a more robust 3.405 liters. With the compression ratio experiencing a similar jump from 9.8 to 10.4:1, it's no wonder the horsepower went up by 30 to 300 eager ponies. While the 348 engine was tractable enough at low speeds, it was the frantic urge as the fluorescent orange tach needle swept up to its 7500 crescendo that seduced these scribes one by one.

It's nice that the 348's interior offers a substantial improvement in both luxurious leather trim and easier-to-use ergonomics. Some could even label the inclusion of Ferrari's first height adjustable wheel as cause for rejoicing. But, it all comes right down to the Ferrari mystique. The brand's heritage is built on racing victories, and the dedicated engineers who continually manage to exceed everyone's expectation with new engines that offer clearer, and closer views of automotive nirvana.

MONDIAL t — V-8 — While four-seat Ferraris never gained the popularity of their two-seat sibling, the Mondial offered a unique opportunity for a man to share his Ferrari fantasies (and realties) with his family. The rear seats could not hold full-size adults, but young children would be reasonably comfortable. By 1991, sales of the coupe were so slow, only the Mondial t Spyder form was available.

TESTAROSSA — FLAT-12 — There were no Testarossas certified for sale in California in 1991. Due to separate fuel and ignition management systems, Ferrari was unable to install the required onboard diagnosis system and they were not granted an exemption.

F40 — V-8 — With a sticker price of $431,250 and dealers asking for $700,000, the F40 could well be the poster child for the excess of the 1980s. From its Kevlar and carbon-fiber reinforced plastic body panels to its 478-hp V-12 engine, the F40 was a thinly disguised racecar for the street ... very thinly disguised.

348 — V-8 — Many publications called the 348 a significant step up from its 328 predecessors. A much-stiffer chassis enabled Ferrari engineers to tune the suspension for substantially better handling, and the 3.4-liter engine provided 300 very eager horsepower.

I.D. DATA: Ferrari's 17-symbol Vehicle Identification Number is embossed on a metal plate attached to the steering column. Breakdown is similar to 1985-86.

Model	Body Type & Seating	Engine Type/CID	P.O.E. Price	Weight (lbs.)	Prod. Total
MONDIAL t					
ts	2-dr Cabr-2+2P	V8/208	113300	3236	Note 1
TESTAROSSA					
	2-dr Coupe-2P	H12/302	170150	3660	Note 2
F40					
	2-dr Coupe-2P	V8/179	399150	2425	Note 3
348					
GTB	2-dr Coupe-2P	V8/208	111400	3071	Note 3
GTS	2-dr Targa Cpe-2P	V8/208	117300	3071	Note 5

Note 1: About 1,010 Mondial t Cabriolets were produced from 1989-93.
Note 2: About 7,177 Testarossas were produced from 1984-90.
Note 3: About 1,315 Type F40 coupes were produced in 1987-82.
Note 4: About 2,895 Type 348 TB coupes were produced from 1989-93.
Note 5: About 4,230 Type 328 TS Targas were produced from 1989-93.

ENGINE [Base V-8 (Mondial t, 348)]: Dual-overhead-cam, "vee" type eight-cylinder (32-valve). Displacement: 208 cid (3405 cc). Bore & stroke: 3.35 x 2.95 in. (85 x 75 mm). Compression ratio: 10.4:1. Brake horsepower: 300 at 7200 rpm. Torque: 238 lbs.-ft. at 4200 rpm. Five main bearings. Bosch Motronic 2.5 port fuel injection.

ENGINE [Base Flat-12 (Testarossa)]: Horizontally-opposed, dual-overhead-cam 12-cylinder (48-valve). Light alloy block and heads. Displacement: 302 cid (4942 cc). Bore & stroke: 3.23 x 3.07 in. (82 x 78 mm). Compression ratio: 8.7:1. Brake horsepower: 380 (SAE) at 5750 rpm. Torque: 354 lbs.-ft. at 4500 rpm. Seven main bearings. Bosch K-Jetronic fuel injection.

ENGINE [Base V-8 (F40)]: 90-degree, dual-overhead-cam, "vee" type eight-cylinder (32-valve). Two IHI turbochargers with Behr intercoolers. Displacement: 179 cid (2936 cc). Bore & stroke: 3.23 x 2.74 in. (82 x 69.5 mm). Compression ratio: 7.8:1. Brake horsepower: 471 (SAE) at 7000 rpm. Torque: 426 lbs.-ft. at 4000 rpm. Five main bearings. Weber-Marelli engine management.

CHASSIS: Wheelbase: (Mondial) 104.3 in.; (Testarossa) 100.4 in.; (F40) 94.5 in.; (348) 96.5 in. Overall Length: (Mondial) 178.5 in.; (Testa) 176.6 in.; (F40) 174.4 in.; (348) 166.7 in. Height: (Mondial) 48.6 in.; (Testa) 44.5 in.; (F40) 44.5 in.; (348) 46.1 in. Width: (Mondial) 70.6 in.; (Testa) 77.8 in.; (F40) 78.0 in.; (348) 74.6 in. Front Tread: (Mondial) 59.9 in.; (Testa) 59.8 in.; (F40) 62.8 in.; (348) 59.2 in. Rear Tread: (Mondial) 61.4 in.; (Testa) 65.4 in.; (F40) 63.4 in.; (348) 62.2 in.

TECHNICAL: Layout: mid-engine, rear-drive. Transmission: five-speed manual in rear transaxle. Steering: rack and pinion. Brakes: front/rear disc; anti-locking on 348 and Mondial. Body Construction: separate body on tubular steel frame except (348) unibody; (Testarossa) aluminum body with steel roof and doors; (F40) composite body on steel-tube space frame.

PERFORMANCE: Acceleration (0-60 mph): (348 ts) 5.6 sec.; (F40) 4.2 sec.; (Testarossa) 6.3 sec. Acceleration (quarter mile): (348 ts) 14.6 sec.; (F40) 12.8 sec.; (Testarossa) 14.5 sec. EPA Fuel Economy City/Highway miles per gallon: (348 ts) 13/18; (F40) 12/17; (Testarossa) 10/15. Top Speed: (Factory figures) (Mondial) 158 mph; (Testarossa) 180 mph; (F40) 201 mph claimed.

Performance Figures by *Motor Trend*.

Manufacturer: Ferrari S.p.A. SEFAC, Maranello (Modena), Italy.

Distributor: Ferrari North America, Hasbrouck Heights, New Jersey.

1992 Ferrari 512 TR. (FSpA/WG)

F40 production ceased in the summer of 92.

MONDIAL t — V-8 — While the Mondial t remained unchanged for 1992, a small number of "Valeo" Mondials were produced. Foreshadowing the F1 transmissions to be introduced in the F355, these cars were equipped without a clutch pedal. Instead, the clutch was engaged and disengaged by an electromechanical actuator. Fewer than 30 cars carried this option.

512 TR — FLAT-12 — The Testarossa was replaced by an updated version known as the 512 TR, which was sold in all 50 states. Harkening back to the early 1970s Le-Mans competitor, the 512M, the 5 stood for 5 liters of displacement and the 12 for 12 cylinders. Horsepower was boosted from 380 to 421.

348 — V-8 — Ferrari 348 ts and tb were sold as "serie speciale" for 1992. Production was limited to 115 cars, each receiving a numbered plaque. The changes consisted of F-40 style racing seats with matching leather covers, stickier tires, a two-inch wider rear track, different taillights, a larger front spoiler, and a monochromatic finish (the bottom was no longer painted black). A lighter, and less restrictive exhaust helped to bump horsepower from 300 to 312.

I.D. DATA: Ferrari's 17-symbol Vehicle Identification Number is embossed on a metal plate attached to the steering column. Breakdown is similar to 1985-86.

Model	Body Type & Seating	Engine Type/CID	P.O.E. Price	Weight (lbs.)	Prod. Total
MONDIAL t					
	2-dr Conv-2+2	V8/208	114000	3236	Note 1
512 TR					
	2-dr Coupe-2P	H12/302	195750	3247	Note 2
348 Serie Speciale					
TB	2-dr Coupe-2P	V8/208	111800	3071	Note 3
TS	2-dr Targa Cpe-2P	V8/208	117700	3071	Note 4

Note 1: About 1,010 Mondial t Cabriolets were produced from 1989-93.
Note 2: About 2,280 512 TR coupes were produced from 1992-94.

Note 3: About 2,895 Type 348 TB coupes were produced from 1989-93.
Note 4: About 4,230 Type 348 TS Targas were produced from 1989-93.
Note 5: A total of approximately 500 Ferraris were sold in the U.S. in 1992.

ENGINE [Base V-8 (348, Mondial t)]: Dual-overhead-cam, "vee" type eight-cylinder (32-valve). Displacement: 208 cid (3405 cc). Bore & stroke: 3.35 x 2.95 in. (85 x 75 mm). Compression ratio: 10.4:1. Brake horsepower: 312 at 7200 rpm. Torque: 238 lbs.-ft. at 4200 rpm. Five main bearings. Bosch Motronic 2.5 port fuel injection.

ENGINE [Base Flat-12 (512 TR)]: Horizontally-opposed, dual overhead-cam 12-cylinder (48-valve). Light alloy block and heads. Displacement: 302 cid (4942 cc). Bore & stroke: 3.23 x 3.07 in. (82 x 78 mm). Compression ratio: 10.0:1. Brake horsepower: 428 (SAE) at 6750 rpm. Torque: 360 lbs.-ft. at 5500 rpm. Seven main bearings. Bosch Motronic 2.7 fuel injection.

CHASSIS: Wheelbase: (Mondial) 104.3 in.; (512 TR) 100.4 in.; (F40) 94.5 in.; (348) 96.5 in. Overall Length: (Mondial) 178.5 in.; (512 TR) 176.4 in. (348) 166.7 in. Height: (Mondial) 148.6 in.; (512 TR) 44.7 in.; (348) 46.1 in. Width: (Mondial) 170.6 in.; (512 TR) 77.8 in.; (348) 74.6 in. Front Tread: (Mondial) 59.9 in.; (512 TR) 60.31 in.; (348) 59.2 in. Rear Tread: (Mondial) 61.4 in.; (512 TR) 64.7 in.; (348) 64.2 in.

TECHNICAL: Layout: mid-engine, rear-drive. Transmission: five-speed manual in rear transaxle. Steering: rack and pinion. Brakes: front/rear disc; anti-locking on 348 and Mondial. Body Construction: separate body on tubular steel frame except (348) unibody; (512 TR) aluminum body with steel roof and doors.

PERFORMANCE: Acceleration (0-60 mph): (348 ts) 5.6 sec.; (512 TR) 4.7 sec. Acceleration (quarter mile): (348 ts) 14.6 sec.; (512 TR) 12.9 sec. EPA Fuel Economy City/Highway miles per gallon: (348 ts) 13/18; (512 TR) 10/15. Top Speed: (Factory figures) (Mondial) 158 mph; (512 TR) 180 mph; (F40) 201 mph claimed.

Performance Figures by *Motor Trend.*

Manufacturer: Ferrari S.p.A. SEFAC, Maranello (Modena), Italy.

Distributor: Ferrari North America, Hasbrouck Heights, New Jersey.

1993 Ferrari 512 TR. (FSpA/WG)

1993 Ferrari 512 TR. (FSpA/WG)

1993 Ferrari 512 TR interior. (FSpA/WG)

1993 Ferrari 512 TR dash. (FSpA/WG)

1994 Ferrari 348 Spider. (WG)

Note 1: About 2,280 512 TR coupes were produced from 1992-94.
Note 2: About 252 Type 348 GTB coupes were produced from 1993-94.
Note 3: About 137 Type 348 GTS Targas were produced from 1993-94.
Note 4: About 1,090 Type 348 Spiders were produced from 193-95.
Note 5: About 50 Type 348 GT Competizione were produced in 1994.
Note 6: Approximately 420 Ferraris were sold in the U.S. in 1994.

512TR — FLAT-12 — ABS brakes were added, thereby increasing the desirability for this exotic two-seater. It was the final year for this nameplate.

348 — V-8 — Two new models were added to the 348 lineup for 1994. A Spider was available in addition to the 348 GTB closed coupe and the 348 GTS Targa roof coupe. Complete with a folding manual top, this was the first time that Ferrari had offered a convertible for its "junior" two-seat line. The other model was the 348 Challenge car (coupes only). This was available either as a converted car from the factory, or as a kit to be installed by the dealer consisting primarily of a roll cage, competition seats, and safety harness.

I.D. DATA: Ferrari's 17-symbol Vehicle Identification Number is embossed on a metal plate attached to the steering column. Breakdown is similar to 1985-86.

Model	Body Type & Seating	Engine Type/CID	P.O.E. Price	Weight (lbs.)	Prod. Total
512 TR					
	2-dr Coupe-2P	H12/302	195750	3247	Note 1
348					
GTB	2-dr Coupe-2P	V8/208	111800	3170	Note 2
GTS	2-dr Targa Cpe-2P	V8/208	122180	3300	Note 3
Spider	2-dr Conv.-2P	V8/208	131090	3290	Note 4

ENGINE [Base Flat-12 (512 TR)]: Horizontally-opposed, dual-overhead-cam 12-cylinder (48-valve). Light alloy block and heads. Displacement: 302 cid (4942 cc). Bore & stroke: 3.23 x 3.07 in. (82 x 78 mm). Compression ratio: 8.7:1. Brake horsepower: 421 (SAE) at 6750 rpm. Torque: 360 lbs.-ft. at 5500 rpm. Seven main bearings. Bosch K-Jetronic fuel injection.

ENGINE [Base V-8 (348)]: Dual-overhead-cam, "vee" type eight-cylinder (32-valve). Displacement: 208 cid (3405 cc). Bore & stroke: 3.35 x 2.95 in. (85 x 75 mm). Compression ratio: 10.4:1. Brake horsepower: 312 at 7200 rpm. Torque: 238 lbs.-ft. at 4200 rpm. Five main bearings. Bosch Motronic 2.5 port fuel injection.

CHASSIS: Wheelbase :(512 TR) 100.4 in.; (348) 96.5 in. Overall Length: (512 TR) 176.4 in.; (348) 166.7 in. Height: (512 TR) 44.7 in.; (348) 46.1 in. Width: (512 TR) 77.8 in.; (348) 74.6 in. Front Tread: (512 TR) 60.31 in.; (348) 59.2 in. Rear Tread: (512 TR) 64.7 in.; (348) 64.2 in.

TECHNICAL: Layout: mid-engine, rear-drive. Transmission: five-speed manual in rear transaxle. Steering: rack and pinion. Brakes: front/rear disc; anti-locking on 348. Body Construction: separate body on tubular steel frame except (348) unibody; (512 TR) aluminum body with steel roof and doors.

PERFORMANCE: Acceleration (0-60 mph): (348 ts) 5.6 sec.; (512 TR) 4.7 sec. Acceleration (quarter mile): (348 ts) 14.6 sec.; (512 TR) 12.9 sec. City/Highway miles per gallon: (348 ts) 13/18; (512 TR) 10/15. Top Speed: (Factory figures) (512 TR) 180 mph.

Performance Figures by *Motor Trend*.

Manufacturer: Ferrari S.p.A. SEFAC, Maranello (Modena), Italy.

Distributor: Ferrari North America, Hasbrouck Heights, New Jersey.

1994 Ferrari 348 Spider. (MC)

1995 Ferrari 512M. (DA)

512M — H12 — For its final year, 1995, the 512TR, nee Testarossa, became the 512M (Modified). The headlights were placed under clear covers instead of the previous popup design, which necessitated a change to the hood. The grille was a bit smaller, and the taillights were round instead of horizontal. An aluminum shift knob and drilled aluminum pedals helped to dress up the interior. NASA ducts were added to the hood, the wheels were a three-piece design, complete with unsightly Allen head bolts around the rim, and the connecting rods were titanium. Horsepower and torque both received a slight boost.

F348 — V8 — The 348 Spyder continued to be sold throughout the first half of 1995, when it was replaced by the F355.

F355 — V-8 — Here was a Ferrari that needed no excuses. Yes, it "only" had a V-8, but this car continued to win comparison tests right up to its demise in 1999. As part of the Ferrari celebration in Monterey, California, the coupe was first shown in August of 1994. Introduced first as a coupe, then a Targa, the Spyder model followed in a surprisingly short time. All of the

excessive styling elements of the 348 series had disappeared. In its place was a clean, aerodynamically effective design that controlled the flow of air both above and below the car. The 3495-cc engine is a model of efficiency to this day. Thanks to three intake and two exhaust valves per cylinder, 375 horsepower can be wrung out, with a full 8500 rpm available for driving pleasure. A first for Ferrari was the electrically operated cloth top on the Spyder. The electric seats even scooted forward enough to allow the top to drop down into a neat stack. The 355 Challenge cars were only available as complete cars from the factory (no dealer conversions). This time around, the modifications were quite a bit more extensive than those made to the 348 Challenge cars. These include F40 LM brakes, a carbon fiber front bumper with much larger brake cooling ducts, racing springs, shocks, and oil cooler.

456 GT — V-12 — In a long-standing tradition, Ferrari introduced a 2+2 passenger GT car. While the 2+2 models never achieved the popularity of the two-seaters, the 456 GT is truly a magnificent touring automobile. Great care was taken with the sensuous shape of the car. The only aero-appendage is a discrete flap below the rear bumper. At speeds above 75 mph it deploys in order to insure maximum stability. Powered by a 5.5-liter engine that produced 436 hp this relatively heavy car could propel its occupants to a genuine 190 mph. Both a five-speed manual and a four-speed automatic were available from the factory.

F50 — V-12 — As incredible as the F40 was, the F50 was a generation ahead in performance. Available with a removable hardtop, the car could be used as an open roadster or a closed coupe. Curiously, all U.S. cars were officially 1995 models although the F50 was sold in the U.S. in 1995, 1996, and 1997. In 1996, On-Board Diagnostics II became mandatory and in 1997, airbags were required. This was one time that the American market was at the head of the line.

I.D. DATA: Ferrari's 17-symbol Vehicle Identification Number is embossed on a metal plate attached to the steering column. Breakdown is similar to 1985-86.

Model	Body Type & Seating	Engine Type/CID	P.O.E. Price	Weight (lbs.)	Prod. Total
512M					
	2-dr Coupe-2P	H12/302	189500	3208	Note 1
F355					
	2-dr Coupe-2P	V8/213	127185	2976	Note 2
	2-dr Targa-2P	V8/213	133725	2976	Note 3
	2-dr Cabr-2P	V8/213	137075	2967	Note 4
456 GT					
	2-dr Coupe-2+2P	V12/334	224800	3726	Note 5
F50					
	2-dr Targa Cpe-2P	V12/287	487000	2712	Note 6

Note 1: About 500 512M coupes were produced from 1994-96.
Note 2: About 4,915 Type 355 Berlinetta coupes were produced from 1994-99.
Note 3: About 2,577 Type 355 GTS Targas were produced from 1994-99.
Note 4: About 3,714 Type 355 Spyders were produced from 1994-99.
Note 5: About 1,936 Type 456 GT Coupes were produced from 1992-1997.
Note 6: About 349 Type F50s were produced from 1995-97.
Note 7: Approximately 700 Ferraris were sold in the U.S. in 1995.
Note 8: Approximately 750 Ferraris were sold in the U.S. in 1996.

ENGINE [Base V-8 (F355)]: Dual-overhead-cam, "vee" type eight-cylinder (32-valve). Displacement: 213 cid (3500 cc). Bore & stroke: 3.55 x 3.03 in. Compression ratio: 11.1:1. Brake horsepower: 375 at 8250 rpm. Torque: 268 lbs.-ft. at 6000 rpm. Bosch Motronic 5.2 fuel injection.

ENGINE [Base V-12 (456 GT)]: Dual-overhead-cam "vee" type (48-valve). Light alloy block and heads. Displacement: 334 cid (5500 cc). Bore & stroke: 3.46 x 2.95 in. Compression ratio: 10.6:1. Brake horsepower: 436 at 6250 rpm. Torque: 398 lbs.-ft. at 4500 rpm. Seven main bearings. Bosch Motronic 5.2 fuel injection.

ENGINE [Base Flat-12 (512 M)]: Horizontally-opposed, dual-overhead-cam 12-cylinder (48-valve). Light alloy block and heads. Displacement: 302 cid (4942 cc). Bore & stroke: 3.23 x 3.07 in. (82 x 78 mm). Compression ratio: 10.4:1. Brake horsepower: 432 (SAE) at 6750 rpm. Torque: 367 lbs.-ft. at 5500 rpm. Seven main bearings. Bosch K-Jetronic fuel injection.

1996 Ferrari F355. (MC)

1995 Ferrari 456GT 2+2. (DA)

ENGINE [Base V-12 (F50)]: Dual-overhead-cam "vee" type (48-valve). Light alloy block and heads. Displacement: 287 cid (4600 cc). Bore & stroke: 3.35 x 2.72 in. Compression ratio: 11.3:1. Brake horsepower: 513 at 7000 rpm. Torque: 347 lbs.-ft. at 6500 rpm. Seven main bearings. Bosch Motronic 5.2 fuel injection.

CHASSIS: Wheelbase: (F355) 96.5 in.; (512M) 100.4 in.; (456 GT) 102.4 in.; (F50) 101.6 in. Overall Length: (F355) 167.3 in.; (512 M) 176.4 in.; (456 GT) 186.2 in.; (F50) 176.1 in. Height: (F355) 46.1 in.; (512 M) 44.7 in.; (456 GT) 51.2 in.; (F50) 44.1 in. Width: (F355) 74.8 in.; (512 M) 77.8 in.; (456 GT) 75.6 in.; (F50) 78.2 in. Front Tread: (F355) 59.6 in.; (512 M) 60.3 in.; (456 GT) 62.4 in.; (F50) 63.8 in. Rear Tread: (F355) 63.6 in.; (512 M) 64.7 in.; (456 GT) 63.2 in.; (F50) 63.1 in.

TECHNICAL: Layout: Front engine/rear drive, except F355, F50 mid-engine, rear-drive. Transmission: (F355) six-speed manual; five-speed manual in rear transaxle. Steering: rack and pinion. Body Construction: separate body on tubular steel frame, aluminum body with steel roof and doors; (F50) composite body on steel-tube space frame.

PERFORMANCE: Acceleration (0-60 mph): (F355B) 4.7 sec.; (F355S) 4.9 sec.; (F50) 3.7 sec. Acceleration (quarter mile): (F355B) 12.8 sec.; (F355S) 13.4 sec. Top Speed (Factory figures): (F355) 183 mph; (512 M) 196 mph; (F50) 202 mph claimed.

Performance Figures by *Motor Trend*.

Manufacturer: Ferrari S.p.A. SEFAC, Maranello (Modena), Italy.

Distributor: Ferrari North America, Englewood Cliffs, New Jersey.

1995 Ferrari 355 Spyder. (DG)

Ferrari F355: Who Says You Can't Go Home Again?

1995 Ferrari F355 Berlinetta. (WG)

Everyone has those special moments that leave such an indelible imprint that the memories are cherished and re-lived forever.

I had the good fortune to work as the parts department manager at Luigi Chinetti Motors in Greenwich, Connecticut, in the mid-1970s. This experience left me filled with many magical memories of time spent driving the magnificent stallions that bear the fabled prancing horse logo. I've spent nearly 30 years trying to recapture that magic, and not succeeding until my recent drive in a yellow F355 F1 Coupe.

Thanks to the generosity of Werner Pfister, Sales Manager at Miller Motorcars, Inc., (342 West Putnam Avenue, Greenwich, CT 06830, 203-629-3890) I had the opportunity to wring out the Ferrari that holds the distinction of being the best-selling car in Ferrari's proud 51-year history.

While it was four-cylinder racers and V-12 street cars that earned Ferrari such a strong reputation in the 1950s, it was the 1975 introduction of the 308 GTB that truly launched the immensely popular, mid-engine V-8 line. Dashing Tom Selleck's *Magnum P.I.* was responsible for introducing many folks to the glamour of Ferrari. For all its popularity, the 308 was replaced by the similar, but improved 328 and 348.

The 355 was first shown to the world in the spring of 1994. Introduced as a Berlinetta closed coupe, it was supplemented by the lift-off-roof GTS model within a matter of months. In 1995, Beverly Hills' Rodeo Drive saw the unveiling of the handsome F355 Spyder. Later that year the 355 Challenge cars were launched as replacements for the successful 348 Challenge cars. But, lovers of Ferraris who use them to commute got a greater boon in 1997, when the 355 F1 model was shown.

Unlike many "manu-matic" cars that merely allow you to manually shift an automatic transmission, the 355 F1 utilizes a six-speed manual box with hydraulic actuators that allow an average driver to equal the speed (0.2 seconds) of a Formula One driver's shifts. While many Tifosi still prefer the gated shifter and purity of the manual, nearly 80% of the 1998-99 F355s came equipped with the F1 transmission and its steering column mounted shift "paddles."

My return to West Putnam Avenue stirred many memories of Luigi Chinetti and his legendary dealership. Once located down the road at 600 West Putnam, the final years of Chinetti's business were spent in the same historic stone building that Miller Motorcars now occupies.

I was stunned by the beauty of the yellow 355 F1 Berlinetta that greeted me at Miller Motors. Pictures do not do justice to the form that the geniuses at Pininfarina have wrought. Seen in three dimensions, one is impressed by both the low height, and the generous width of the F355. No matter which angle the car is viewed from, it's a knockout.

The outside door handles are hidden in the upper part of the side fresh air intake. The door opens wide, and entry is surprisingly easy for this six-footer into

1995 Ferrari 355 Berlinetta. (WG)

1996 Ferrari F355 Berlinetta. (DA)

such a low car. The seats offer a wide range of adjustments and hold you firmly in place without feeling too confining. A 200-mph speedometer and a 10,000-rpm tachometer dominate the instrument panel.

The fuel-injected, 3496-cc aluminum V-8 fires instantly and immediately smoothes into a steady idle that belies its lofty 11:1 compression ratio. For the first time in a Ferrari, five-valves-per-cylinder heads promote such free breathing that 375 horsepower is reached at a heady 8250 rpm. A torque figure of 268 lbs.-ft. at 6000 rpm means that this engine is much happier as the tach needle climbs towards its 8500-rpm redline.

Since my car had been fitted with the F1 transmission, starting off was as simple as pulling the right hand paddle back to you, and stepping on the gas. Superb visibility in all directions makes driving the low-slung F355 less of a challenge than you might think. Sure, there's a significant gawk factor, but in toney Greenwich most glances don't evolve into encounters.

I was impressed with how comfortable this slinky sportscar is to drive. The front magnesium wheels are shod with 225/40x18-inch tires, and the

1996 Ferrari F355 Spyder. (DA)

rears wear 265/40x18-inch rubber. Despite the low profile of the tires, the electronically adjustable aluminum shocks do a great job of soaking up the pavement imperfections.

Moving up the entrance ramp to I-95, I wound the engine out to redline. As advertised, shifts come blindingly fast with just a tug of the F1 paddle. While we come nowhere near the 183-mph top speed, a quick blast down the highway provides a glimpse of the high-speed stability that is bred in to this product of racing heritage.

Departing the Interstate gave me the opportunity to test the four-wheel ventilated disc brakes. Under eye-popping deceleration, the yellow car merely yawns. Normal driving leaves so much capacity in reserve that the car barely seems to wake up, as if it's saying, "Can't you do better than this?"

A secluded back road provided the opportunity to dip into the deep reservoir that is the F355's handling surplus. There is no evidence of oversteer or understeer. The car just flat goes around the corner. I suggest you use a racetrack if you wish to seek the car's ultimate level of adhesion, because the F355's capabilities are so Olympian.

Even with 11,273 cars produced from 1994 to 1999, the F355 still qualifies as a rare car, if not a rare Ferrari. Thirty years ago the idea of using a Ferrari as an everyday driver may have seemed absurd, but the F355 offers comfort, refinement, and a level of civility unavailable in even the finest luxury cars from three decades ago. Plus, you have the world's greatest amusement park ride available whenever you choose to exercise your right ankle.

Thanks, Werner, the Ferrari magic is alive and well, and the F355 is a powerful way to bring home those peak experiences that made the supercars from Maranello legendary.

1996 Ferrari F355 Berlinetta. (DA)

1996 Ferrari F50. (FSpA/WG)

1995-1997 Ferrari F50 engine. (MC)

1996 Ferrari F50. (FSpA/WG)

1996 Ferrari F50. (FSpA/WG)

1997 Ferrari F50. (DA)

F355 — V-8 — Regarded by many as the best production V-8 Ferrari, the F355 had it all. A sleek, sexy shape was backed up by mechanicals that could deliver on the promise of the gorgeous bodywork. Available as a Berlinetta (Coupe), GTS (Targa), or Spyder (Convertible), the F355 was the pinnacle of many enthusiasts' aspirations throughout the late 1990s.

550 MARANELLO — V-12 — With its front V-12 engine and rear-mounted six-speed transaxle, the Maranello was a long-awaited successor to the beloved 365 GTB4-Daytona. With 436 horsepower emanating from a silky-smooth V-12 engine, the Maranello provides classic Ferrari front-engine/rear-wheel drive sensations with the added benefit of modern reliability and a hundred extra horsepower.

456 GT — V-12 — While four-seat Ferraris never have enjoyed the popularity that the true two-seat sportscars have, most any enthusiast would be thrilled to have the opportunity to drive a 456 GT. An automatic transmission car, known as the 456 GT A was available for the first time.

1997 Ferrari F50. (DA)

F50 — V-12 — If you designed a pure racing car that could be driven legally on the street, it may very well wind up looking like the F50. From its composite body built on a steel tube frame to its exotic 512-hp V-12, the F50 represented the ultimate in performance for Ferrari in the 1990s. Never before had so much Formula One technology been directly transferred to a street car. With this model, one no longer had to choose between an open Barchetta or a closed Berlinetta; the removable hardtop gave you two cars for the price of one. Oh yes, the price of $491,000 meant that F50s were available only to those with the desire to own the best, and the pocketbook to match.

I.D. DATA: Ferrari's 17-symbol Vehicle Identification Number is embossed on a metal plate attached to the steering column. Breakdown is similar to 1985-86.

Model	Body Type & Seating	Engine Type/CID	P.O.E. Price	Weight (lbs.)	Prod. Total
F355					
	2-dr Coupe-2P	V8/213	127185	2976	Note 1
	2-dr Targa-2P	V8/213	133725	2976	Note 2
	2-dr Cabr-2P	V8/213	137075	2967	Note 3
550 MARANELLO					
	2-dr Coupe-2P	V12/334	204000	3726	N/A
456 GT					
	2-dr Coupe-2+2P	V12/334	224800	3726	Note 4
F50					
	2-dr Targa Cpe-2P	V12/287	487000	2712	Note 5

Note 1: About 4,915 Type 355 Berlinetta coupes were produced from 1994-99.
Note 2: About 2,577 Type 355 GTS Targas were produced from 1994-99.
Note 3: About 3,714 Type 355 Spiders were produced from 1994-99.
Note 4: About 1,936 Type 456 GT Coupes were produced from 1992-1997.
Note 5: About 349 Type F50s were produced from 1995-97.
Note 6: A total of 798 Ferraris were sold in the U.S. in 1997.

ENGINE [Base V-8 (F355)]: Dual-overhead-cam, "vee" type eight-cylinder (32-valve). Displacement: 213 cid (3500 cc). Bore & stroke: 3.55 x 3.03 in. Compression ratio: 11.1:1. Brake horsepower: 375 at 8250 rpm. Torque: 268 lbs.-ft. at 6000 rpm. Bosch Motronic 5.2 fuel injection.

ENGINE [Base V-12 (550 Maranello)]: Dual-overhead-cam "vee" type (48-valve). Light alloy block and heads. Displacement: 334 cid (5500 cc). Bore & stroke: 3.46 x 2.95 in. Compression ratio: 10.8:1. Brake horsepower: 485 at 7000 rpm. Torque: 568 lbs.-ft. at 5000 rpm. Seven main bearings. Bosch Motronic 5.2 fuel injection. (456 GT) same as V-12 above except Compression ratio: 10.6:1. Brake horsepower: 436 at 6250 rpm. Torque: 398 lbs.-ft. at 4500 rpm.

ENGINE [Base V-12 (F50)]: Dual-overhead-cam "vee" type (48-valve). Light alloy block and heads. Displacement: 287 cid (4600 cc). Bore & stroke: 3.35 x 2.72 in. Compression ratio: 11.3:1. Brake horsepower: 513 at 7000 rpm. Torque: 347 lbs.-ft. at 6500 rpm. Seven main bearings. Bosch Motronic 5.2 fuel injection.

1997 Ferrari 550 Maranello. (DA)

CHASSIS: Wheelbase: (F355) 96.5 in.; (550 Maranello) 98.4 in.; (456 GT) 102.4 in.; (F50) 101.6 in. Overall Length: (F355) 167.3 in.; (550 Maranello) 179.1 in.; (456 GT) 186.2 in.; (F50) 176.1 in. Height: (F355) 46.1 in.; (550 Maranello) 50.3 in.; (456 GT) 51.2 in.; (F50 44.1 in. Width: (F355) 74.8 in.; (550 Maranello) 76.2 in.; (456 GT) 75.6 in.; (F50) 78.2 in. Front Tread: (F355) 59.6 in.; (550 Maranello) 64.3 in.; (456 GT) 62.4 in.; (F50) 63.8 in. Rear Tread: (F355) 63.6 in.; (550 Maranello) 62.4 in.; (456 GT) 63.2 in.; (F50) 63.1 in.

TECHNICAL: Layout: Front engine/rear drive, except F355, F50 mid-engine, rear-drive. Transmission: (F355) six-speed manual, five-speed manual in rear transaxle; 456 GT also available with an automatic transmission. Steering: rack and pinion. Body Construction: separate body on tubular steel frame; aluminum body with steel roof and doors; (F50) composite body on steel-tube space frame.

PERFORMANCE: Acceleration (0-60 mph): (F355B) 4.7 sec.; (F355S) 4.9 sec.; (550 Maranello) 4.2 sec.; (F50) 3.7 sec. Acceleration (quarter mile): (F355B) 12.8 sec.; (F355S) 13.4 sec.; (550 Maranello) 12.5 sec. Top Speed (Factory figures): (F355) 183 mph; (550 Maranello) 199 mph; (F50) 202 mph claimed.

Performance Figures by *Motor Trend*.

Manufacturer: Ferrari S.p.A. SEFAC, Maranello (Modena), Italy.

Distributor: Ferrari North America, Englewood Cliffs, New Jersey.

1997 Ferrari 550 Maranello. (DA)

1998 Ferrari M456 GT/GTA. (WG)

The F50 was no longer available for 1998.

F355 — V-8 — Ferrari made an F-1 style shifting mechanism available for the F355 in 1998. For a $9,500 premium over the manual transmission model, the shift lever was replaced by a small toggle switch on the console used to engage reverse gear, and two paddles extending from either side of the steering column. Pull the right one and the manual gearbox was shifted up electronically faster than most mere humans could accomplish the feat. Pull the left paddle and a downshift was over so fast you had to listen closely to hear the engine being blipped for the perfect match of the synchromesh. Pull both paddles towards you and neutral was selected. This proved to be a very popular option with as high as 90% of F355s being ordered this way in traffic-congested cities.

550 MARANELLO — V-12 — Unchanged for 1998.

456GT — V-12 — Unchanged for 1998.

I.D. DATA: Ferrari's 17-symbol Vehicle Identification Number is embossed on a metal plate attached to the steering column. Breakdown is similar to 1985-86.

Model	Body Type & Seating	Engine Type/CID	P.O.E. Price	Weight (lbs.)	Prod. Total
F355					
	2-dr Coupe-2P	V8/213	128225	2976	Note 1
	2-dr Targa-2P	V8/213	137725	2976	Note 2
	2-dr Cabr-2P	V8/213	138115	2967	Note 3
550 MARANELLO					
	2-dr Coupe-2P	V12/334	204000	3726	N/A
456 GT					
	2-dr Coupe-2+2P	V12/334	2248003726	Note 4	

Note 1: About 4,915 Type 355 Berlinetta coupes were produced from 1994-99.
Note 2: About 2,577 Type 355 GTS Targas were produced from 1994-99.
Note 3: About 3,714 Type 355 Spiders were produced from 1994-99.
Note 4: About 1,936 Type 456 GT Coupes were produced from 1992-1997.
Note 5: A total of 854 Ferraris were sold in the U.S. in 1998.

ENGINE [Base V-8 (F355)]: Dual-overhead-cam, "vee" type eight-cylinder (32-valve). Displacement: 213 cid (3500 cc). Bore & stroke: 3.55 x 3.03 in. Compression ratio: 11.1:1. Brake horsepower: 375 at 8250 rpm. Torque: 268 lbs.-ft. at 6000 rpm. Bosch Motronic 5.2 fuel injection.

ENGINE [Base V-12 (550 Maranello)]:
Dual-overhead-cam "vee" type (48-valve). Light alloy
block and heads. Displacement: 334 cid (5500 cc). Bore
& stroke: 3.46 x 2.95 in. Compression ratio: 10.8:1.
Brake horsepower: 485 at 7000 rpm. Torque: 568 lbs.-ft.
at 5000 rpm. Seven main bearings. Bosch Motronic 5.2
fuel injection.

ENGINE [456 GT]: Dual-overhead-cam "vee" type
(48-valve). Light alloy block and heads. Displacement:
334 cid (5500 cc). Bore & stroke: 3.46 x 2.95 in.
Compression ratio: 10.6:1. Brake horsepower: 436 at
6250 rpm. Torque: 398 lbs.-ft. at 4500 rpm. Seven main
bearings. Bosch Motronic 5.2 fuel injection.

CHASSIS: Wheelbase: (F355) 96.5 in.; (550
Maranello) 98.4 in.; (456 GT) 102.4 in. Overall Length:
(F355) 167.3 in.; (550 Maranello) 179.1 in.; (456 GT)
186.2 in. Height: (F355) 46.1 in.; (550 Maranello) 50.3
in.; (456 GT) 51.2 in. Width: (F355) 74.8 in.; (550
Maranello) 76.2 in.; (456 GT) 75.6 in. Front Tread:
(F355) 59.6 in.; (550 Maranello) 64.3 in.; (456 GT) 62.4
in. Rear Tread: (F355) 63.6 in.; (550 Maranello) 62.4 in.;
(456 GT) 63.2 in.

TECHNICAL: Layout: Front engine/rear drive,
except F355 mid-engine, rear-drive. Transmission:
(F355) six-speed manual, five-speed manual in rear
transaxle; 456 GT also available with a four-speed
automatic transmission; F355 available with an
electronic F1 mechanism for automatically shifting the
manual gearbox. Steering: rack and pinion. Body
Construction: separate body on tubular steel frame;
aluminum body with steel roof and doors.

PERFORMANCE: Acceleration (0-60 mph):
(F355B) 4.7 sec.; (F355S) 4.9 sec.; (F355 F1) 4.6 sec.;
(550 Maranello) 4.2 sec. Acceleration (quarter mile):
(F355B) 12.8 sec.; (F355S) 13.4 sec.; (F355 F1) 13.5
sec.; (550 Maranello) 12.5 sec. Top Speed (Factory
figures): (F355) 183 mph; (550 Maranello) 199 mph
claimed.

Performance Figures by *Motor Trend*.

Manufacturer: Ferrari S.p.A. SEFAC, Maranello
(Modena), Italy.

Distributor: Ferrari North America, Englewood Cliffs,
New Jersey.

1998 Ferrari M456 GT/GTA. (WG)

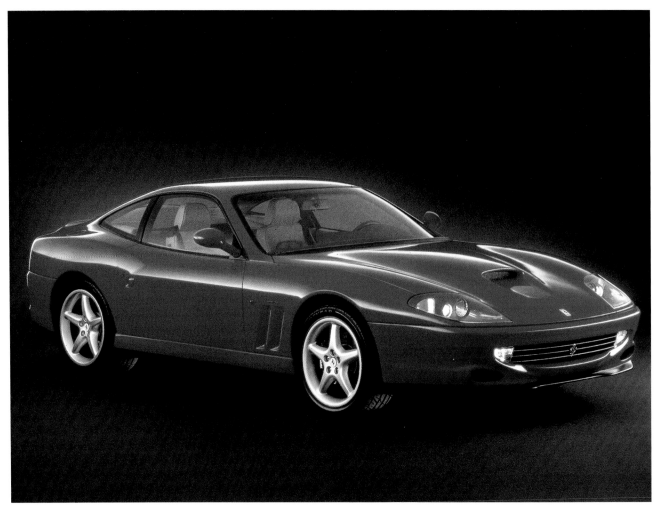

1999 Ferrari 550 Maranello. (WG)

F355 — V-8 — Unchanged for its final year of production. However, a Fiorano Spyder was available. This car made standard equipment many of the 355 Challenge parts. These included a partial carbon fiber interior, a mesh rear grille, the Ferrari shield on the front fenders, drilled brake rotors, and a heavy-duty (but not racing) suspension.

550 MARANELLO — V-12 — Unchanged for 1999.

456 M GT — V-12 — The luxurious 456 received a number of subtle improvements. The hood, headlights, and front bumpers were all mildly modified. The moveable rear wing was no longer moveable, instead it was now always open. (Unlike most wings that sat atop the trunk lid, this one was at the bottom of the rear valance.) The wheel centers were changed from the traditional yellow to silver.

I.D. DATA: Ferrari's 17-symbol Vehicle Identification Number is embossed on a metal plate attached to the steering column. Breakdown is similar to 1985-86.

Model	Body Type & Seating	Engine Type/CID	P.O.E. Price	Weight (lbs.)	Prod. Total
F355					
	2-dr Coupe-2P	V8/213	128225	2976	Note 1
	2-dr Targa-2P	V8/213	137725	2976	Note 2
	2-dr Cabr-2P	V8/213	138115	2967	Note 3
550 MARANELLO					
	2-dr Coupe-2P	V12/334	208000	3726	N/A
456 GT					
	2-dr Coupe-2+2P	V12/334	224800	3726	Note 4

Note 1: About 4,915 Type 355 Berlinetta coupes were produced from 1994-99.
Note 2: About 2,577 Type 355 GTS Targas were produced from 1994-99.
Note 3: About 3,714 Type 355 Spyders were produced from 1994-99.
Note 4: About 1,936 Type 456 GT Coupes were produced from 1992-1997.
Note 5: A total of 792 Ferraris were sold in the U.S. in 1999.

ENGINE [Base V-8 (F355)]: Dual-overhead-cam, "vee" type eight-cylinder (32-valve). Displacement: 213 cid (3500 cc). Bore & stroke: 3.55 x 3.03 in. Compression ratio: 11.1:1. Brake horsepower: 375 at 8250 rpm. Torque: 268 lbs.-ft. at 6000 rpm. Bosch Motronic 5.2 fuel injection.

ENGINE [Base V-12 (550 Maranello)]: Dual-overhead-cam "vee" type (48-valve). Light alloy block and heads. Displacement: 334 cid (5500 cc). Bore & stroke: 3.46 x 2.95 in. Compression ratio: 10.8:1. Brake horsepower: 485 at 7000 rpm. Torque: 568 lbs.-ft. at 5000 rpm. Seven main bearings. Bosch Motronic 5.2 fuel injection.

ENGINE [456 GT]: Dual overhead-cam "vee" type (48-valve). Light alloy block and heads. Displacement: 334 cid (5500 cc). Bore & stroke: 3.46 x 2.95 in. Compression ratio: 10.6:1. Brake horsepower: 436 at 6250 rpm. Torque: 398 lbs.-ft. at 4500 rpm.

CHASSIS: Wheelbase: (F355) 96.5 in.; (550 Maranello) 98.4 in.; (456 GT) 102.4 in. Overall Length: (F355) 167.3 in.; (550 Maranello) 179.1 in.; (456 GT) 186.2 in. Height: (F355) 46.1 in.; (550 Maranello) 50.3 in.; (456 GT) 51.2 in. Width: (F355) 74.8 in.; (550 Maranello) 76.2 in.; (456 GT) 75.6 in. Front Tread: (F355) 59.6 in.; (550 Maranello) 64.3 in.; (456 GT) 62.4 in. Rear Tread: (F355) 63.6 in.; (550 Maranello) 62.4 in.; (456 GT) 63.2 in.

TECHNICAL: Layout: Front engine/rear drive, except F355 mid-engine, rear-drive. Transmission: (F355) six-speed manual, five-speed manual in rear transaxle. 456GT also available with a four-speed automatic transmission F355 available with an electronic F1 mechanism for automatically shifting the manual gearbox. Steering: rack and pinion. Body Construction: separate body on tubular steel frame; aluminum body with steel roof and doors.

PERFORMANCE: Acceleration (0-60 mph): (F355B) 4.7 sec.; (F355S) 4.9 sec.; (F355 F1) 4.6 sec.; (550 Maranello) 4.2 sec. Acceleration (quarter mile): (F355B) 12.8 sec.; (F355S) 13.4 sec.; (F355 F1) 13.5 sec.; (550 Maranello) 12.5 sec. Top Speed (Factory figures): (F355) 183 mph; (550 Maranello) 199 mph claimed.

Performance Figures by *Motor Trend*.

Manufacturer: Ferrari S.p.A. SEFAC, Maranello (Modena), Italy.

Distributor: Ferrari North America, Englewood Cliffs, New Jersey.

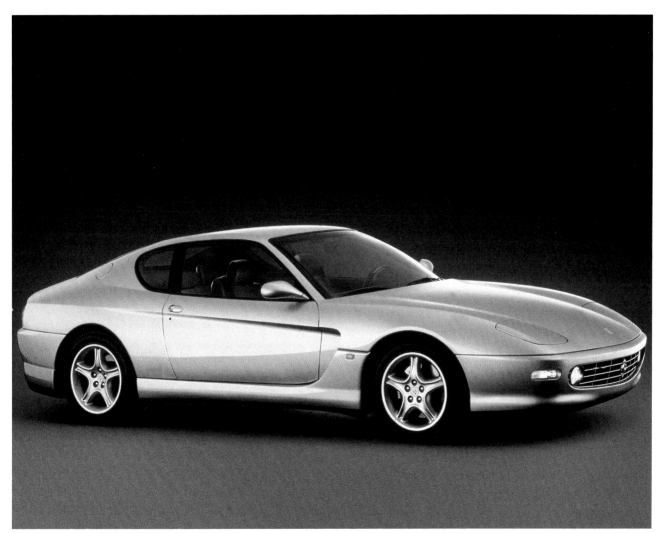

1999 Ferrari M456 GT. (WG)

1999 Ferrari 355 Spider. (FSpA/WG)

Ferrari's 360 Modena:
A Stunning Achievement in Looks and Function

1999 Ferrari 360 Modena. (MC)

Ferrari stands alone in blending racing heritage into their streetcars to create the stuff of dreams. They have achieved victories and championships in Grand Prixs, sport car races, and the classic endurance contests such as Le Mans. Names like Hill, Lauda, Scheckter, Villeneuve, and now Schumacher elicit warm memories of glorious Ferrari victories. The Ferrari 360 Modena echoes those places and these illustrious drivers as beauty, speed, and exotic engineering are combined to create a driving experience that goes beyond the sublime.

What would you do if you had to replace the most commercially successful model in your 50-year history? If you were Ferrari President Luca Cordero di Montezemolo, it might go something like

this, "I want you to make the F355's replacement faster, lighter, more economical, and of course it must be beautiful." I'm pleased to report they have succeeded in spades!

Ferrari invited their dealers, a few select customers, and the press to their July 19, 1999, launch of the 360 Modena at the Meadowlands horsetrack in New Jersey. The journalists were treated to a presentation on the development of this latest marvel from Modena, Italy. The luminaries in attendance were Sig. Montezemolo, Sig. Gian Luigi Longinotti Buitoni, president of Ferrari North America and Sig. Sergio Pininfarina, head of the firm responsible for so many landmark designs. The words of these fabled men kept the audience spellbound as the tale of the 360 Modena unfolded.

They sketched out the development of the aluminum chassis made from extruded, stamped, and cast components. (Aluminum has been the material of choice for Ferrari competition cars right from the start.) With the 360 Modena, components were designed from scratch to take advantage of the material's light weight and excellent rigidity.

Emphasis was placed on this being the first Ferrari designed from the passenger compartment out. Access and egress were given a high priority so the driver and passenger can be as comfortable getting in and out as they will be when seated. Despite the mid-engine location, there is room behind the seats for a weekend's worth of luggage, or that ubiquitous trunk-measuring tool, a pair of golf bags. Nose-mounted twin radiators allow a surprising amount of room in the front luggage compartment as well.

More than 5,000 hours were spent in the wind tunnel shaping both the top and bottom of the Modena, to achieve remarkable downforce with no add-on appendages. While the loving care for airflow management is readily apparent to anyone who studies the overall shape, ducts, and scoops, the underside hides lessons learned on the racetracks of the world. Hidden marvels, such as lower rear suspension arms shaped like airfoils, were revealed to the curious scribes. The opening in the front bumper directs air under the car, while the extractors at the rear help to create significant downforce as speed increases. The result is equal air pressure on both front and rear axles, providing a stability that is a Ferrari hallmark.

As always, the centerpiece of any Ferrari is its engine. The 3.6-liter V-8 is showcased beneath a see-through engine cover/rear window. It makes an exotic contribution to the 360's good looks. This state-of-the-art, five-valves-per-cylinder engine puts out a potent 400 horsepower at 8500 rpm, and propels the Modena to 60 mph in only 4.5 seconds.

Looking for a way to dramatize the engine's output? Well, Ferrari is known as a company that does things in a flamboyant fashion. The assembled throng was treated to the first sighting of the 360 Modena barreling down the Meadowland horse track's front straight followed by, you guessed it—400 thundering thoroughbred horses!

In person, the Modena seems wider, lower, and longer than its pictures. While some may decry the lack of Ferrari's trademark eggcrate grille, the twin nostrils do have their place in Ferrari's long line of illustrious competition cars. The side profile is unmistakably Ferrari, with classic five-spoke alloy wheels flickering through high wheel arches. The rear view bears a strong family resemblance to the 550 Maranello. A small lip on the engine cover (that cleverly incorporates the high-mounted brake light) and four chrome-tipped exhaust pipes frame the four round taillights. Of course, the prancing horse emblem is featured prominently in the center of it all.

The highlight of the day was getting to slide behind the wheel and put this thoroughbred through its paces on a parking lot course. The doors open invitingly wide, and the doorsills are low, making entry an easy feat even for this six-footer.

Facing you is a classic instrument panel with the ten-grand tachometer front and center. The speedometer is to the right, and water temperature, oil pressure, and oil temperature are to the left. Four large circular vents flank the instrument binnacle, below which you will find the radio and climate controls.

Several of the cars were equipped with Ferrari's conventional, six-speed manual with its gated gearbox, but my Modena had the F1 transmission that brings out the Michael Schumacher in everyone. On either side of the steering wheel are two large paddles used for upshifting and downshifting. This system allows the driver to keep his hands on the wheel and complete a shift faster than any human can.

A tug on the right paddle causes the

large numeral "1" to appear in the prominent gear indicator. Step on the drive-by-wire throttle and move on out. The test track started with a long straight that encourages you to bring the engine up to the 8500-rpm redline. The unique piercing wail seems worth $100,000 all by itself, eliciting memories of both vintage Ferraris and modern F1 racing cars, all in the same exhaust note. This is one area where the engineers have met and exceeded expectations.

Power is strong on the bottom end of the rev range, but seems positively omnipotent when the engine sings its lovely song the loudest. Handling is difficult to assess in the limited confines of the parking lot, but the precise steering promises excellent control. Driving a Ferrari around a parking lot is something like taking a racecar to the grocery store—sure, you can do it, but it doesn't begin to test the mettle of either the car or the driver.

The Modena delights with both civility at slow speeds and extreme competence when you press the car a bit harder. Unquestionably, the 360 Modena is a worthy successor to the F355. It might even steal some sales from its big brother, the 550 Maranello. The car is that great.

1999 Ferrari 360 Modena. (FSpA/WG)

2000 Ferrari 360 Modena. (DG)

F360 MODENA — V-8 — On July 19, 1999, the U.S. press was treated to the sight of the brand-new F360 Modena leading 400 horses down the front stretch of the Meadowlands Racetrack. This stylish introduction announced that Ferrari had developed a very worthy successor to its best-selling model ever, the F355. The Modena's 400-hp V-8 was incorporated into the design; it was lovingly displayed beneath the rear window. The outrageously exotic sound was only exceeded by the outstanding acceleration. Alco was a partner in developing one of the very first all-aluminum chassis. Rather than rely on tacked-on wings for aerodynamic efficiency, the 360's shape was carefully sculpted for maximum downforce and stability. The underside was crafted for downforce to an almost greater extent than the topside. The primarily flat bottom includes twin air tunnels that terminate in flares at the back end of the car. The lower suspension arms are shaped to take additional downforce from the air rushing through these

venturi. The F360 showed the world that Ferrari would continue to lead the world in producing the most desirable of sportscars. Winning the F-1 World Driving and Constructors' Championship was just icing on the cake. As of this writing, Modenas were changing hands for tens of thousands over the retail price.

550 MARANELLO — V-12 — Unchanged for 2000.

456 GT — V-12 — Unchanged for 2000.

I.D. DATA: Ferrari's 17-symbol Vehicle Identification Number is embossed on a metal plate attached to the steering column. Breakdown is similar to 1985-86.

Model	Body Type & Seating	Engine Type/CID	P.O.E. Price	Weight (lbs.)	Prod. Total
F360 MODENA					
	2-dr Coupe-2P	V8/219	138225	3064	Note 1
550 MARANELLO					
	2-dr Coupe-2P	V12/334	212000	3726	Note 1
456 GT					
	2-dr Coupe-2+2P	V12/334	224800	3726	Note 1

Note 1: A total of 1,023 Ferraris were sold in the U.S. in 2000.

ENGINE [Base V-8 (F360 Modena)]: Dual-overhead-cam, "vee" type eight-cylinder (32-valve). Displacement: 219 cid (3586 cc). Bore & stroke: 3.55 x 3.11 in. (65x79 mm). Compression ratio: 11.1:1. Brake horsepower: 400 at 8500 rpm. Torque: 380 lbs.-ft. at 4750 rpm. Bosch Motronic M 7.3 fuel injection.

ENGINE [Base V-12 (550 Maranello)]: Dual-overhead-cam "vee" type (48-valve). Light alloy block and heads. Displacement: 334 cid (5500 cc). Bore & stroke: 3.46 x 2.95 in. Compression ratio: 10.8:1. Brake horsepower: 485 at 7000 rpm. Torque: 568 lbs.-ft. at 5000 rpm. Seven main bearings. Bosch Motronic 5.2 fuel injection.

ENGINE [456 GT]: Dual overhead-cam "vee" type (48-valve). Light alloy block and heads. Displacement: 334 cid (5500 cc). Bore & stroke: 3.46 x 2.95 in. Compression ratio: 10.6:1. Brake horsepower: 436 at 6250 rpm. Torque: 398 lbs.-ft. at 4500 rpm.

CHASSIS: Wheelbase: (F360) 102.3 in.; (550 Maranello) 98.4 in.; (456 GT) 102.4 in. Overall Length: (F360) 176.3 in.; (550 Maranello) 179.1 in.; (456 GT) 186.2 in. Height: (F360) 47.7 in.; (550 Maranello) 50.3 in.; (456 GT) 51.2 in. Width: (F360) 75.6 in.; (550 Maranello) 76.2 in.; (456 GT) 75.6 in. Front Tread: (F360) 65.7 in.; (550 Maranello) 64.3 in.; (456 GT) 62.4 in. Rear Tread: (F360) 63.6 in.; (550 Maranello) 62.4 in.; (456 GT) 63.2 in.

TECHNICAL: Layout: Front engine/rear drive, except F360 mid-engine, rear-drive. Transmission: (F360) six-speed manual five-speed manual in rear transaxle. 456 GT also available with a four-speed automatic transmission; F360 available with an electronic F1 mechanism for automatically shifting the manual gearbox. Steering: rack and pinion. Body Construction: separate body on tubular steel frame; aluminum body with steel roof and doors. F360 Aluminum chassis, engine, suspension, and bodywork.

PERFORMANCE: Acceleration (0-60 mph): (F360) 4.0 sec.; (550 Maranello) 4.2 sec. Acceleration (quarter mile): (F360) 12.4 sec.; (550 Maranello) 12.5 sec. Top Speed (Factory figures): (F360) 183 mph; (550 Maranello) 199 mph claimed.

Performance Figures by *Motor Trend*.

Manufacturer: Ferrari S.p.A. SEFAC, Maranello (Modena), Italy.

Distributor: Ferrari North America, Englewood Cliffs, New Jersey.

2000 Ferrari 360 Modena. (WG)

2000 Ferrari 360 Modena. (WG)

2000 Ferrari 360 Modena Coupe F1. (WG)

2000 Ferrari 360 Modena Coupe F1 interior. (WG)

2000 Ferrari 360 Modena Coupe F1 engine. (WG)

2001 Ferrari 360 Modena Spider. (WG)

F360 MODENA — V-8 — Not content with the over 1-year wait for the coupe version of the highly successful Modena, Ferrari unveiled the equally stunning and powerful 360 Spyder. Although the useful shelf behind the seats disappeared, Ferrari and Pininfarina managed to produce a vehicle that was as beautiful with the top up as it was with the top down. The F-1 transmission continued to be a very popular option.

550 MARANELLO — V-12 — Ferrari is very adept at creating excitement at the end of the model line. Rather than having Maranello sales end with a whimper, a new version had them going out with a bang! A limited edition 550 Barchetta was available for a brief time in late 2001. All 500 of these no-top beauties were snatched up sight unseen by eager Ferrari aficionados.

456 GT — V-12 — Unchanged for 2001. Still offered as manual transmission GT and automatic transmission GTA.

I.D. DATA: Ferrari's 17-symbol Vehicle Identification Number is embossed on a metal plate attached to the steering column. Breakdown is similar to 1985-86.

Model	Body Type & Seating	Engine Type/CID	P.O.E. Price	Weight (lbs.)	Prod. Total
F360 MODENA					
	2-dr Coupe-2P	V8/219	144620*	3064	Note 1
	F-12-dr Coupe-2P	V8/219	117185*	3064	Note 1
	2-dr Conv.-2P	V8/219	161475*	3064	Note 1
	F-12-dr Conv.-2P	V8/219	171185*	3064	Note 1
550 MARANELLO					
	2-dr Coupe-2P	V12/334	215340*	3726	Note 1
Barch	2-dr Roadster-2P	V12/334	258000*	3726	Note 1
456GT					
	2-dr Coupe-2+2P	V12/334	226975*	3726	Note 1
	GTA2-dr Coupe-2+2P	V12/334	232170*	3726	Note 1

*Unlike most every other price in this book, these prices include the MSRP, plus transportation, dealer prep, and any applicable gas-guzzler taxes.

Note 1: A total of 1,185 Ferraris were sold in the U.S. in 2001.

ENGINE [Base V-8 (F360)]: Dual-overhead-cam, "vee" type eight-cylinder (32-valve). Displacement: 219 cid (3586 cc). Bore & stroke: 3.55 x 3.11 in. (65x79 mm). Compression ratio: 11.1:1. Brake horsepower: 400 at 8500 rpm. Torque: 380 lbs.-ft. at 4750 rpm. Bosch Motronic M 7.3 fuel injection.

ENGINE [Base V-12 (550 Maranello)]: Dual-overhead-cam "vee" type (48-valve). Light alloy block and heads. Displacement: 334 cid (5500 cc). Bore & stroke: 3.46 x 2.95 in. Compression ratio: 10.8:1. Brake horsepower: 485 at 7000 rpm. Torque: 568 lbs.-ft. at 5000 rpm. Seven main bearings. Bosch Motronic 5.2 fuel injection.

ENGINE [456 GT]: Dual-overhead-cam "vee" type (48-valve). Light alloy block and heads. Displacement: 334 cid (5500 cc). Bore & stroke: 3.46 x 2.95 in. Compression ratio: 10.6:1. Brake horsepower: 436 at 6250 rpm. Torque: 398 lbs.-ft. at 4500 rpm.

CHASSIS: Wheelbase: (F360) 102.3 in.; (550 Maranello) 98.4 in.; (456 GT) 102.4 in. Overall Length: (F360) 176.3 in.; (550 Maranello) 179.1 in.; (456 GT) 186.2 in. Height: (F360) 47.7 in.; (550 Maranello) 50.3 in.; (456 GT) 51.2 in. Width: (F360) 75.6 in.; (550 Maranello) 76.2 in.; (456 GT) 75.6 in. Front Tread: (F360) 65.7 in.; (550 Maranello) 64.3 in.; (456 GT) 62.4 in. Rear Tread: (F360) 63.6 in.; (550 Maranello) 62.4 in.; (456 GT) 63.2 in.

TECHNICAL: Layout: Front engine/rear drive, except F360 mid-engine, rear-drive. Transmission: (F360) six-speed manual five-speed manual in rear transaxle; 456 GT also available with a four-speed automatic transmission; F360 available with an electronic F1 mechanism for automatically shifting the manual gearbox. Steering: rack and pinion. Body Construction: separate body on tubular steel frame; aluminum body with steel roof and doors. (F360) Aluminum chassis, engine, suspension, and bodywork.

PERFORMANCE: Acceleration (0-60 mph): (F360) 4.0 sec.; (550 Maranello) 4.2 sec. Acceleration (quarter mile): (F360) 12.4 sec.; (550 Maranello) 12.5 sec. Top Speed (Factory figures): (F360) 183 mph; (550 Maranello) 199 mph claimed.

Performance Figures by *Motor Trend*.

Manufacturer: Ferrari S.p.A. SEFAC, Maranello (Modena), Italy.

Distributor: Ferrari North America, Englewood Cliffs, New Jersey.

2001 Ferrari 360 Modena Spider. (WG)

2002 Ferrari Enzo. (FSpA/WG)

Tifosi throughout the world rejoiced as Michael Schumacher captured the World Driving Championship with a record six races remaining in the season. When he and his teammate Rubbins Barichello captured the Formula One Manufacturer's Championship a few races later, no one was surprised.

F360 MODENA — V-8 — Demand for this remarkable mid-engine rocket ship continued at an all-time high. In order to avoid the one-year waiting list for coupes or the three-year delay for a Spider, desperate buyers were known to pay $50,000-$150,000 over list price for slightly used models. The F-1 electronically controlled, fast-acting transmission continued to be a very popular option. In addition to the street coupe and convertible models, the 360 Challenge cars provided their well-heeled owners with a vehicle ready to race. Ferrari continued to offer their Challenge Series throughout the world. National champions advanced to the world championship, held every year in Italy for the season's finale.

575M MARANELLO — V-12 — To some people, the 550 Maranello represents the classic Ferrari. Ferrari may not have invented the front-engined V-12 two-seater with the rear transaxle for improved weight distribution, but many will say they have advanced it to the pinnacle of this layout. So, while the 575 M may look very similar to its predecessor, the changes were significant enough to warrant the "M" for modified in the car's name. Displacement was increased from 5500 cc to 5750 cc with an appropriate increase in horsepower and torque. The availability of the F1 transmission was a first for a V-12 Ferrari. Unlike an automatic or the modern "manualmatics," this transmission is a true manual gearbox that is shifted faster than a mere mortal can hope to achieve. Look for the two paddles on either side of the transmission and the tiny chrome reverse lever on the console.

456 GT — V-12 — Unchanged for 2002. Still offered as manual transmission GT and automatic transmission GTA.

I.D. DATA: Ferrari's 17-symbol Vehicle Identification Number is embossed on a metal plate attached to the steering column. Breakdown is similar to 1985-86.

Model	Body Type & Seating	Engine Type/CID	P.O.E. Price	Weight (lbs.)	Prod. Total
F360 MODENA					
	2-dr Coupe-2P	V8/219	146815*	3064	Note 1
F-1	2-dr Coupe-2P	V8/219	156894*	3064	Note 1
	2-dr Conv.-2P	V8/219	167029*	3064	Note 1
F-1	2-dr Conv.-2P	V8/219	177079*	3064	Note 1
Challenge	2-dr Conv.-2P	V8/219	183920*	2580	Note 1
575 MARANELLO					
	2-dr Coupe-2P	V12/334	221870*	3726	Note 1
F-1	2-dr Roadster-2P	V12/334	231265*	3726	Note 1
456GT					
	2-dr Coupe-2+2P	V12/334	231785*	3726	Note 1
GTA	2-dr Coupe-2+2P	V12/334	235825*	3726	Note 1

*Unlike most every other price in this book, these prices include the MSRP, plus transportation, dealer prep, and any applicable gas-guzzler taxes.

Note 1: A total of 1,200 Ferraris were sold in the U.S. in 2002.

ENGINE [Base V-8 (F360)]: Dual-overhead-cam, "vee" type eight-cylinder (32-valve). Displacement: 219 cid (3586 cc). Bore & stroke: 3.55 x 3.11 in. (65 x 79 mm). Compression ratio: 11.1:1. Brake horsepower: 400 at 8500 rpm. Torque: 380 lbs.-ft. at 4750 rpm. Bosch Motronic M 7.3 fuel injection.

ENGINE [Base V-12 (575M Maranello)]: Dual-overhead-cam 65-degree "vee" type (48-valve). Light alloy block and heads. Displacement: 350.7 cid

2002 Ferrari Enzo interior. (FSpA/WG)

(5748 cc). Bore & stroke: 3.46 x 2.95 in. (89 x 77mm). Compression ratio: 11.5:1. Brake horsepower: 515 at 7000 rpm. Torque: 434 lbs.-ft. at 5000 rpm. Seven main bearings. Bosch Motronic 5.2 fuel injection

ENGINE [456 GT]: Dual-overhead-cam "vee" type (48-valve). Light alloy block and heads. Displacement: 334 cid (5500 cc). Bore & stroke: 3.46 x 2.95 in. Compression ratio: 10.6:1. Brake horsepower: 436 at 6250 rpm. Torque: 398 lbs.-ft. at 4500 rpm.

CHASSIS: Wheelbase: (F360) 102.3 in.; (575M Maranello) 98.4 in.; (456 GT) 102.4 in. Overall Length: (F360) 176.3 in.; (575M Maranello) 179.1 in.; (456 GT) 186.2 in. Height: (F360) 47.7 in.; (575M Maranello) 50.3 in.; (456 GT) 51.2 in. Width: (F360) 75.6 in.; (575M Maranello) 76.2 in.; (456 GT) 75.6 in. Front Tread: (F360) 65.7 in.; (575M Maranello) 64.3 in.; (456 GT) 62.4 in. Rear Tread: (F360) 63.6 in.; (575M Maranello) 62.4 in.; (456 GT) 63.2 in.

TECHNICAL: Layout: Front engine/rear drive, except F360 mid-engine, rear-drive. Transmission: (F360) six-speed manual five-speed manual in rear transaxle; 456 GT also available with a four-speed automatic transmission; F360 available with an electronic F1 mechanism for automatically shifting the manual gearbox. Steering: rack and pinion. Body Construction: separate body on tubular steel frame; aluminum body with steel roof and doors. (F360) Aluminum chassis, engine, suspension, and bodywork.

PERFORMANCE: Acceleration (0-60 mph): (F360) 4.0 sec.; (575M Maranello) 4.2 sec. Acceleration (quarter mile): (F360) 12.4 sec.; (575M Maranello) 12.5 sec. Top Speed (Factory figures): (F360) 183 mph; (575M Maranello) 199 mph claimed.

Performance Figures by *Motor Trend*.

Manufacturer: Ferrari S.p.A. SEFAC, Maranello (Modena), Italy.

Distributor: Ferrari North America, Englewood Cliffs, New Jersey.

2002 Ferrari Enzo. (FSpA/WG)

2002 Ferrari Enzo dash. (FSpA/WG)

2002 Ferrari 575M Maranello. (FSpA/WG)

2002 Ferrari 575M Maranello. (FSpA/WG)

2002 Ferrari 360 Spider. (FSpA/WG)

2002 Ferrari 360 Spider. (FSpA/WG)

2002 Ferrari 360 Modena. (FSpA/WG)

2002 Ferrari 360 Modena. (FSpA/WG)

2002 Ferrari 360 Challenge. (FSpA/WG)

2002 Ferrari 360 GT. (FSpA/WG)

2002 Ferrari 456M. (FSpA/WG)

2002 Ferrari 456M. (FSpA/WG)

2003

ENZO FERRARI — V12 — There was much speculation on what Ferrari would do to surpass the F50. Those who thought that brutal car could not be bettered were in for a disappointment. Many thought the model would wear an F-60 badge, but when the model was revealed in the middle of the summer of 2002, the designation was "Enzo Ferrari" or as it will probably become known as, "The Enzo." Ferrari president Luca di Montezemolo summed up their goal as follows, "In 1999 we won the manufacturers' championship; in 2000 we added the drivers' championship for the first time in 21 years. We won the last championship of the 20th century, and the first of the 21st century. I wanted to celebrate this with a car very much like a Formula One. After honoring Modena and Maranello, we felt this was the right car to honor the name of our founder." One look at the squat shape tells you this car was made for the track. Its 6.0-liter V-12 is the largest displacement Ferrari since the 712 Can-Am racecar. The interior is lavished with carbon fiber and all the touches that make a race driver proficient at his task, with very little embellishments for the street.

F360 MODENA — V-8 — As this book goes to press, demand for the 360 is finally beginning to abate. This doesn't mean that any bargains are available. Asking prices for slightly used models (under 5,000 miles) are starting to approach Ferrari North America's MSRPs.

575M MARANELLO — V-12 — Unchanged from its mid 2002 launch.

456 GT — V-12 — Unchanged for 2002. Still offered as manual transmission GT and automatic transmission GTA.

I.D. DATA: Ferrari's 17-symbol Vehicle Identification Number is embossed on a metal plate attached to the steering column. Breakdown is similar to 1985-86.

Model	Body Type & Seating	Engine Type/CID	P.O.E. Price	Weight (lbs.)	Prod. Total
ENZO					
	2-dr Coupe-2P	V12/365	650000	3009	
F360 MODENA					
		V8/219	144620*	3064	
F-1	2-dr Coupe-2P	V8/219	117185*	3064	
	2-dr Conv.-2P	V8/219	161475*	3064	
F-1	2-dr Conv.-2P	V8/219	171185*	3064	
575M MARANELLO					
	2-dr Coupe-2P	V12/334	215340*	3726	
456GT					
	2-dr Coupe-2+2P	V12/334	226975*	3726	
GTA	2-dr Coupe-2+2P	V12/334	232170*	3726	

*Unlike most every other price in this book, these prices include the MSRP, plus transportation, dealer prep, and any applicable gas-guzzler taxes.

ENGINE [V-12 (Enzo]: Dual-overhead-cam, 60 degree "vee" type twelve-cylinder (48-valve). Displacement: 365 cid (5998 cc). Bore & stroke: 3.62 x 2.96 in. (92 x 75.2 mm). Compression ratio: 11.1:1. Brake horsepower: 650 at 7800 rpm. Torque: 585 lbs.-ft. at 5500 rpm. Bosch Motronic ME 7 ignition with sequential electronic fuel injection.

ENGINE [Base V-8 (F360)]: Dual-overhead-cam, "vee" type eight-cylinder (32-valve). Displacement: 219 cid (3586 cc). Bore & stroke: 3.55 x 3.11 in. (65 x 79 mm). Compression ratio: 11.1:1. Brake horsepower: 400 at 8500 rpm. Torque: 380 lbs.-ft. at 4750 rpm. Bosch Motronic M 7.3 fuel injection.

ENGINE [Base V-12 (575M Maranello)]: Dual-overhead-cam 65-degree "vee" type (48-valve). Light alloy block and heads. Displacement: 350.7 cid (5748 cc). Bore & stroke: 3.46 x 2.95 in. (89 x 77mm). Compression ratio: 11.5:1. Brake horsepower: 515 at 7000 rpm. Torque: 434 lbs.-ft. at 5000 rpm. Seven main bearings. Bosch Motronic 5.2 fuel injection.

ENGINE [456 GT]: Dual-overhead-cam "vee" type (48-valve). Light alloy block and heads. Displacement: 334 cid (5500 cc). Bore & stroke: 3.46 x 2.95 in. Compression ratio: 10.6:1. Brake horsepower: 436 at 6250 rpm. Torque: 398 lbs.-ft. at 4500 rpm.

CHASSIS: Wheelbase: (F360) 102.3 in.; (575M Maranello) 98.4 in.; (456 GT) 102.4 in. Overall Length: (F360) 176.3 in.; (575M Maranello) 179.1 in.; (456 GT) 186.2 in. Height: (F360) 47.7 in.; (575M Maranello) 50.3 in.; (456 GT) 51.2 in. Width: (F360) 75.6 in.; (575M Maranello) 76.2 in.; (456 GT) 75.6 in. Front Tread: (F360) 65.7 in.; (575M Maranello) 64.3 in.; (456 GT) 62.4 in. Rear Tread: (F360) 63.6 in.; (575M Maranello) 62.4 in.; (456 GT) 63.2 in.

TECHNICAL: Layout: Front engine/rear drive, except F360 mid-engine, rear-drive. Transmission: (F360) six-speed manual five-speed manual in rear transaxle; 456 GT also available with a four-speed automatic transmission; F360 and 575M available with an electronic F1 mechanism for automatically shifting the manual gearbox. Steering: rack and pinion. Body Construction: separate body on tubular steel frame; aluminum body with steel roof and doors. (F360) Aluminum chassis, engine, suspension, and bodywork.

PERFORMANCE: Acceleration (0-60 mph): (Enzo) 3.5 sec.; (F360) 4.0 sec.; (575M Maranello) 4.0 sec. Acceleration (quarter mile): (F360) 12.4 sec.; (550 Maranello) 12.3 sec. Top Speed (Factory figures): (Enzo) 217 mph; (F360) 183 mph; (575M Maranello) 199 mph claimed.

Manufacturer: Ferrari S.p.A. SEFAC, Maranello (Modena), Italy.

Distributor: Ferrari North America, Englewood Cliffs, New Jersey.

The First Ferrari Deemed Worthy of the Name, Enzo

2003 Ferrari Enzo. (FSpA/MC)

There was much speculation on what Ferrari would do to surpass the F50. Some said it was the ultimate expression of Ferrari's racing technology distilled to the essence that could be used on the street. Those who thought such a brutal car could not be bettered were in for a surprise. As the spy shots were circulated, the conjecture was that this new model would wear an F-60 or FX badge. But when the car was revealed in the middle of the summer of 2002, the designation was the "Ferrari Enzo Ferrari," or as it will probably become known, "The Enzo." The timing of the introduction couldn't have been more fortuitous. Michael Schumacher had just clinched the 2002 World Championship for Drivers the day before, and who could imagine a better way for Ferrari to celebrate the victory?

Ferrari president Luca di Montezemolo summed up their goal with the Enzo as follows.

"In 1999 we won the manufacturers' championship; in 2000 we added the drivers' championship for the first time in 21 years. We won the last championship of the 20th century, and the first of the 21st century. I wanted to celebrate this with a car very much like a Formula One. After honoring Modena and Maranello, we felt this was the right car to honor the name of our founder."

One look at the squat shape tells you this car was made for the track. Unlike the F40 and F50, it wears no wing on its tail. Instead, hundreds of hours were spent in the wind tunnel tuning both the top and bottom of the car providing maximum downforce with minimal drag.

Where the F40 and F50 wore bodies that bore some resemblance to previous Ferrari street models, the latest design from Pininfarina looks more like a machine whose sole purpose is quick lap times at the racecourse. The nose comes to a point with struts angling off to either side, recalling current F1 front ends. Unlike many 2002 vehicles that push the wheels out to the corners of the car, the Enzo's front wheels are pushed back almost into the cockpit. The hood flares out from that proud nose badge and is flanked by radiator air outlets. The front fenders terminate several inches outboard of the doors, leaving additional outlets for hot air to exit from the front. By the way, those doors swing up to allow easier access to the cockpit. It is said that the inspiration was the 512 M Le Mans racer.

The rear end is wide, with bulges atop the fenders that start with large openings for the engine, and terminate in four taillights that look more like a Pagani Zonda than any previous Ferrari. The rear of the car also has a wide grille for additional hot air removal, and four tailpipes flank the diffusers that are so crucial to the underbody's generation of downforce. Just as on the 360 Modena, the engine is a styling element, and is clearly visible through the rear window.

The 5998-cc V-12 is the largest displacement Ferrari since the 712 Can-Am racecar. This engine relies on more than cubic inches to produce its 660 horsepower and 484 lbs.-ft. of torque. The aluminum heads and blocks of the 65-degree V-12 might not sound too exotic, but the Nikasil-lined cylinder walls and titanium connecting rods are features you'd be hard pressed to find in any engine not bound for the racetrack. The Enzo's continuously variable intake and exhaust valve timing is becoming more prevalent in street engines, but the telescoping intake manifold, that helps boost the torque, is a device right out of the F1 engineers' current playbook. Both the valve covers and the airbox are topped with carbon fiber for lightweight

and state-of-the-art racing appearance.

Ferraris have become well known for their chrome-gated shift levers. It was considered a badge of honor to be able to manipulate the shifter through the squared-off pattern with enough speed for quick shifts, but not so quick as to overcome the baulky-when-cold syncros. The Enzo's six-speed transmission is controlled by two carbon fiber paddles on either side of the steering wheel, just like in current Formula One cars. This system allows you to engage the next cog faster than any normal human can accomplish the task with a conventional transmission. Unlike the F360 Modena and the 575 Maranello, reverse is not selected by a tiny lever on the console. Instead, a button on the steering wheel engages reverse.

The interior is lavished with carbon fiber and all the touches that make a race driver proficient at his or her task. There are very few accommodations to street use. The flat-topped steering wheel is literally festooned with buttons to enable the Enzo's pilot to perform numerous tasks without removing his hands from the wheel. Even the turn signals are buttons in the two horizontal spokes. The top of the wheel contains seven lights to keep you informed. Red and yellow diodes at the right and left ends tell you when you need to take a closer look at the instruments. Even though there is a large 10,000-rpm tachometer in the center of the instrument cluster, five lights atop the steering wheel insure that your progress from 6000 to 8000 rpms is carefully monitored.

There are no stereo, cruise control, or satellite navigation systems available in the Enzo. The only concession to creature comforts is the optional air-conditioning. Entertainment is amply provided by the sights of the racing cockpit, the sounds of that fabulous V-12 behind your ears, and the high-g-force sensations the Enzo can produce. Britain's *Top Gear* magazine reports a scant 3.65 seconds needed to scoot to 62 mph. Keep your foot on the drilled aluminum throttle and you'll reach 124 mph in only 9.5 seconds. Remarkably, the Brembo carbon-ceramic disc brakes can then haul the Enzo back down to zero in only 5.7 additional seconds.

Typically, Ferrari has eschewed driver's aids for their top performance model; this is not so with the Enzo. Electronic traction control allows just the right amount of wheel spin to achieve maximum acceleration, but cuts back on the power when the pilot seems to be in danger of melting the enormous Bridgestone Potenza RE050 Scuderia 345/35xZR 19-inch rear tires. Antilock circuitry help the 2345/35xZR 19-inch front tires decelerate the Enzo at a rate that will leave your stomach behind.

Ultimate performance does not come cheap. The list price for this very special legend-in-the-making is $670,000. Production is supposed to be limited to only 349 units, of which a mere 70 will be allotted to the United States. Given that there are more then 220 orders placed, it is very unlikely that you will find one in your garage. But the Ferrari factory can rest assured that somewhere up there Enzo is probably smiling at the thought of his namesake sitting atop the supercar pinnacle.

2003 Ferrari Enzo. (FSpA/MC)

The Ferrari 575M: Hooligan or Electronic Wizard?

2003 Ferrari 575M. (FSpA/MC)

Does anyone ever think less of James Bond when he pulls off an amazing feat of daring, if he uses the latest electronic gizmo from Q? Variations on this question may plague the *tifosi* that test the new-for-2002 Ferrari 575M Maranello. Its predecessor, the 550 Maranello, impressed drivers with its comfortable Grand Touring nature, but was not averse to exercising its sporting capabilities. Now that Ferrari has their lower priced Maserati brand to fulfill the comfortable fast car roles, the 550 has evolved into a no-holds-bared, rip-snorting sportscar.

When the 550 was introduced for the 1997 model year, there was much surprise and rejoicing. When the Boxer replaced the Daytona in 1974 as the flagship of the Ferrari sportscars, its mid-engine design allowed a more "exotic car look." The popularity of the next model at the top of the heap of regular production Ferraris, the Testarossa, (and the 512M it eventually became) seemed to indicate that Ferrari had completely abandoned the front engine/rear transaxle classic Berlinetta layout. With the unveiling of the 550 Maranello, the Ferrari performance king had come full circle, back to this cherished design.

Mid-engine cars may look more exotic and offer a theoretical advantage of weight concentration in the center of the vehicle's mass; but the packaging problems often require their owners to suffer poor rear visibility, lots of noise and heat just behind their ears, and minimal luggage space. With the engine in front, and the transmission packaged with the final drive in a tidy transaxle, all of these problems are eliminated at the outset.

When the extent of electronic aids

woven into the 575M's fabric was revealed, there were some critics who thought the replacement for the 550 was going to be a softer, less focused car. Nothing could be further from the truth. Just as the Ferrari Formula One team utilizes the latest developments to allow their pilots to push their mounts even faster, the 575's pile of computer chips is just one of the ways the new Maranello is even a more pure thoroughbred than the original 550.

The 5474 cc V-12 engine receives an addition of 1 mm to the bore and 2 mm to the stroke, resulting in a new total displacement of 5748 cc. Horsepower is boosted by 30 to 515 hp, and the torque now plateaus at 15 more foot pounds, for a total of 426 lbs.-ft. If you are fond of Ferrari's characteristic dual distributors for their V-12s you're out of luck. A high-intensity coil now lives atop each spark plug cap. While some fans take delight in the complexity of the 365 GTC/4's 54 individual elements of the six-carburetor throttle linkage, the 575M connects the driver's right foot to the engine via a throttle by wire.

Valve timing is now variable on both the intake and exhaust valves. Once the spent gas vapors are past the valves, their journey out the tailpipe is speeded along, thanks to lowered backpressure. There is even a valve in the mufflers that varies the pressure to optimize high and low speed requirements. Where the 360 Modena's V-8 sings the soprano version of the Ferrari chorus, the 575M is now clearly a bass. The V-12's song can still be described as a wail at high rpms, but it's a wail from a barrel-chested banshee.

The conductor of all things electronic in the 575 is the Bosch Motronic ME 7.3.2 fuel injection and electronic control unit. Besides such ordinary tasks as metering fuel and providing a precise spark, the Bosch wizard also communicates with the Adaptive Suspension, Anti-Lock Brakes, Launch Control, and the F1 transmission's brain.

This is the first use of Ferrari's patented electro hydraulic manual transmission shifter coupled with a V-12.

While some purists might bemoan the emasculation of such a fine steed by the removal of the classic, chrome-gated shifter, it will only take one drive to convince them of the advantages that a 220-millisecond gear change can provide. Unlike a typical torque converter equipped automatic transmission, the 575M has a real manual transmission residing in the back end. Just like World Champion, Michael Schumacher's car, the Maranello changes gears with just a pull on the paddles located on either side of the steering wheel. There is no need to take your hands off the thick, leather steering wheel. It even blips the engine just the right amount for downshifts. Further control can be exercised by selecting low grip, sport, or automatic, instead of normal mode. Ferrari North America predicts that 80% of their customers will step up to the $250,000 price of admission from the manual transmission's $240,000 MSRP.

You would be forgiven if you couldn't tell whether the car that just whizzed by you was a 550 or a 575M. The external Modifications (M) are rather subtle. The 575M's hood wears a larger scoop that gulps 15% more air. And, the grille is also larger; the better to handle increased cooling requirements. The latest variation on the classic Ferrari five-spoke wheels is designed to pull air in to help cool the massive 330mm front/310mm Brembo brake rotors.

Perhaps the best indication of the seriousness of the 575M's supersport intention is the "Sport" button. Not only does this setting increase the speeds at which the F1 shifter selects the next gear, it also affects the suspension, throttle response, and traction control system. (The use of continual full throttle will kick the car into Supersport mode, but this is primarily for track use only.) Rather than distract the pilot with questions about settings, the Sport mode allows him to push the 575M much harder than the 550 could ever run, even with Schumacher behind the wheel. With 225 different road surfaces in its brain, the suspension takes the input from the front wheels' journey, and in 80 milliseconds evaluates the road, then adjusts the back shocks for optimal grip. Ferrari reports a twenty percent improvement in lateral grip over the 550.

The 575M can also simulate the excitement of the start of a Grand Prix with the activation of launch control. The procedure involves the selection of sport mode, turning off the ASR (Automatic Slip Regulation), applying the brake, bringing the revs up, then releasing the brake. The result is the perfect amount of wheel spin to catapult the 575M to 60 mph in only 4.2 seconds. If you keep your foot on the throttle, you'll see 202 mph on the speedometer, assuming you have the place and bravery to complete this task. You might not be up to it, but for the 575M it's just another day of being the best.

2003 Ferrari 575M. (FSpA/MC)

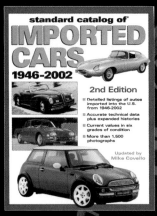

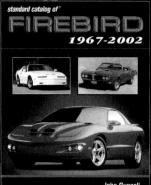